# PRAISE FOR *WE NEED YOU IN THE LOCKER ROOM*

"If you are one of those tens of millions of Americans who loves football beyond any other sport -- and who simultaneously worries if it can be played safely—then Dr. David Kaufman's book is the definition of a must-read. Like such classics as *Paper Lion* and *A Fan's Notes*, it provides a fascinating, unique, and immensely readable perspective on a game we only think we really know. For Kaufman, that perspective is his as a neurologist assigned to the Michigan State Spartans, making him an intimate witness to both the drama, teamwork, and courage of young athletes—and the toll this violent game exacts on their bodies. This book is a page-turner about a championship season and a smart, sensitive argument for how football can be preserved."
—Samuel G. Freedman, award-winning author of 10 nonfiction books who runs a renowned book-writing seminar each spring at Columbia University's Graduate School of Journalism.

"With a winning mixture of humor and heart, David Kaufman's *We Need You in the Locker Room* gives readers a play-by-play view from the sidelines—and the training room—of a legendary college football team. This is no ordinary sports story; Kaufman takes us by the hand and leads us through a narrative that is part science, part memoir, and part love letter to Spartan football. Kaufman's humanity suffuses every word."
—Matthew Van Meter, author of *Deep Delta Justice*

"This book captures some of the best years of my life, spent alongside unforgettable people. Dr. Kaufman brings a unique perspective on a program that was on the rise, achieving incredible things thanks to the efforts of people like him. I know readers will enjoy and appreciate his insight into this remarkable journey."
—Benny Fowler, former MSU Spartan wide receiver (2010-2013). Fowler played 8 years in the NFL and was an important member of the Denver team that won Super Bowl 50. He is the author of *Silver Spoon: The Imperfect Guide to Success*.

"Dr. Kaufman offers an insider's view on a remarkable season for a Division 1 football team. His perspective blends both the excitement of sport and the importance of keeping athletes healthy and performing their best."

—Sally Nogle, Head Athletic Trainer, Michigan State University, 2013 to 2023, member, National Athletic Trainers' Association Hall of Fame

"In this profoundly moving account of his time acting as the "sideline neurologist" for the Michigan State University football team, Dr. David Kaufman invites us into a journey about what we learn and gain when we celebrate the successes of others, make ourselves vulnerable in moments of need, and pursue life with a sense of service. As his colleague and friend Father Jake Foglio might have said, Dr. Kaufman reminds us that to be a good professional, we must first be a good human."

—Professor Morgan Shipley, Inaugural Foglio Endowed Chair of Spirituality at Michigan State University

"Having a neurologist on the sidelines isn't just a safety measure; it's a commitment to the well-being of every athlete, ensuring that the mind is as protected as the body."

—Jeff Monroe, Head Athletic Trainer, Michigan State University, 1985 to 2012

"A must-read for any Michigan State fan or football enthusiast. This book captures a rare and invaluable perspective—highlighting a special time, with special people, at a special place. It's an unforgettable journey through the heart of Michigan State football."

—Jack Allen: two-time All-American and Academic All-American, and 2014 Rose Bowl Champion as center for Michigan State University (2011 through 2015)

# MORE FROM THE SAGER GROUP

### The Stacks Reader Series

*The Cheerleaders: A True Story* by E. Jean Carroll
*An American Family: A True Story* by Daniel Voll
*Flesh and Blood: A True Story* by Peter Richmond
*An Accidental Martyr: A True Story* by Chip Brown
*Death of a Playmate: A True Story* by Teresa Carpenter
*The Detective: And Other True Stories* by Walt Harrington
*Soldiers in the Army of God: A True Story* by Daniel Voll
*Original Gangster: A True Story* by Paul Solotaroff
*The Dreamer Deceiver: A True Story* by Ivan Solotaroff
*Mary in the Lavender Pumps: A True Story* by Joyce Wadler

### General Interest

*The Stories We Tell: Classic True Tales*
*by America's Greatest Women Journalists*
*New Stories We Tell: True Tales by America's New Generation of Great*
*Women Journalists*
*Newswomen: Twenty-five Years of Front-Page Journalism*
*The Someone You're Not: True Stories of Sports, Celebrity, Politics &*
*Pornography* by Mike Sager
*Lifeboat No. 8: Surviving the Titanic* by Elizabeth Kaye
*Stopping the Road: The Campaign Against a Trans-Sierra Highway*
by Jack Fisher
*Notes from the Road: A Filmmaker's Journey through American Music*
by Robert Mugge
*What Makes Sammy Jr. Run?: Classic Celebrity Journalism Volume 1,*
*edited by* Alex Belth
*Secrets of Ash: A Novel of War, Brotherhood, and Going Home Again*
*by* Josh Green

# We Need You
## IN THE Locker Room

## A Neurologist's Journey Behind the Scenes of Major College Football

# DAVID KAUFMAN

## FOREWORD BY COACH MARK DANTONIO

Cover design and Interior design
by Siori Kitajima for PatternBased.com

Cataloging-in-Publication data for this book
is available from the Library of Congress.

ISBN-13:
Ebook: 978-1-958861-46-2
Paperback: 978-1-958861-47-9
Hardcover: 978-1-958861-50-9

Published by The Sager Group LLC
(TheSagerGroup.net)

# We Need You
## IN THE Locker Room

## A NEUROLOGIST'S JOURNEY BEHIND THE SCENES OF MAJOR COLLEGE FOOTBALL

## DAVID KAUFMAN

### FOREWORD BY COACH MARK DANTONIO

THE SAGER GROUP

Artifex Te Adiuva

*"By curious paradox through the very fact of their respect for the past, people came to reconstruct it as they consider it ought to have been."*

— Marc Bloch, French medievalist

# DEDICATION

I dedicate this book to the Michigan State University football teams, their coaches, and the men and women from MSU who supported them on and off the field from 2010 to 2013.

A sincere thanks to my fellow writers from the early 1970s at the University of Wisconsin's *Daily Cardinal*. Each assured me I would never make it as a sportswriter and urged me to look for some other line of employment. A very, very special thanks to Sam Freedman, who guided me through the challenges of writing this book.

I would also like to express my love and admiration for my muse, Laurie Kaufman, MD. Without her there is no book, and, truth be known, there is no neurologist. My apology to my children, Matt and Sarah, who both found a way to deal with me during the last three and a half decades. My only regret about becoming a football sideline neurologist for MSU was not being with my family in the upper deck of Spartan Stadium during MSU football's glory years.

# CONTENTS

# FOREWORD

The game of football, in so many ways, teaches us about life: the discipline, the precision, the inches won and lost, the euphoria of a big win, and the disappointment of any loss. It speaks to us about the word *team*, the creativity in schemes and techniques that are taught and needed to be successful in the three basic areas of offense, defense, and special teams. Passion, hard work, encouragement, mental and physical training, organization, confidence, endurance, excitement, adversity, and injury all leave an undeniable mark on those who have played or coached on the many levels of this great game.

In his book, Dr. David Kaufman takes us behind the scenes and into the world of major college football at the highest level. Focusing on the 2010 season and later the 100th Rose Bowl in 2014, Doc gives his readers an in-depth look at Michigan State football initially from the eyes of a spectator and later as a member of our medical staff. In a newly formed position as a neurologist, Dr. Kaufman was tasked with evaluating concussion protocol in 2010. Now in his thirteenth year, David has long since been a staple within the inner circle at MSU Football.

His accounts and experiences move from the seriousness of a life-saving evaluation and hands-on treatment of an acute game-day injury to his sometimes funny and self-deprecating sense of humor. In between, the very fabric of the program and the game itself is detailed and documented through the many trials and tribulations that occurred that season.

I have always maintained that there are five major points of emphasis that must be adhered to in order to be successful in any program, athletic or otherwise. First, you must develop sincere and meaningful relationships. They must be built on a sense of commitment, communication, and trust with one another. Entering the 2010 season as a new face, the author soon established himself as a person who truly cared about our team, staff, and coaches. He didn't push. He let us pull him into our circle and was deeply appreciated.

Second, you must strive to learn, educate, and evaluate yourself in a constant manner. Concussion protocol, CTE, and the many variances of it were new and often misunderstood traumatic injuries that were bursting onto the scene in 2009–2010. David gave us all a sense of understanding and calm, an esteemed specialist in that area of injury.

Third, you must win. Winning was all around us in 2010, as we were 11–1 and co-champions in the Big Ten Conference. Winning, however, comes to us in many forms. His work with our players—and one player in particular—was instrumental in our long-term success.

Fourth, you must look to improve each other's lives; as I say, "Be a Light." Check box number four, as Doc was kind, appreciative, generous, and oftentimes quite funny.

Finally, you must work. Few people understand the time, dedication, and pressure that our medical staff deals with daily to be a part of Michigan State football.

In conclusion, Dr. Kaufman's book brings these five elements for success to life for his readers. It will bring a smile to your face, a tear to your eye, and it will firmly set your feet in stone and demonstrate the camaraderie, focus, determination, and grit that has always been at the heart of Michigan State football. It is a must read for all Spartans.

Go Green!

—Mark Dantonio
Head Coach (2007–2020)
Michigan State University

# AUTHOR'S NOTE

This book is a chronicle based on my own experience as a "sideline neurologist," one of the sports medicine physicians and surgeons who worked with the Michigan State University football teams at a time when college and professional sports were beginning to focus on the risk of brain injury to athletes.

I have described my experience on the field, on the road and in the treatment facilities in detail, and I have provided information about various medical issues and procedures that I addressed. However, my book is not a medical guide and will not enable the reader to diagnose or treat an injury or condition. Urgent medical attention should be sought from appropriate experts in the event of any sports injury.

Members of the MSU football team from the 2010 decade, Coach Mark Dantonio and his fellow coaches, MSU's sports medicine team, and MSU's athletic trainers of that era are among the most remarkable people I have ever met. I was impressed with their discipline, their dedication to their sport and to each other. I did my best to honor them, and if I failed, allow me to apologize. There were a few incidents that occurred later in the decade that I moved into the 2010 football season to allow brevity in describing this experience.

It is clear that football and other collision sports are potentially dangerous. Sarah Kaufman, MD, PhD, a clinician scientist working in neurodegenerative diseases, reminds me that, "Football is among the most modifiable risk factors to prevent neurodegenerative diseases." I certainly agree with my daughter, but there is also risk in driving a car. Both are so engrained in the social fabric of society that people will continue to do both. The key is how to make things safer.

In explaining what it was like behind the scenes of Spartan football, I focus on MSU's iconic coach, Mark Dantonio. I am very grateful for his willingness to have a neurologist available to his players in real time on the sidelines. Neither he nor I was aware I would end up writing an account of this experience more than a decade later.

I also focus on four members of the medical team (Drs. Pearson and Shingles, and Certified Athletic Trainers Nogle and Monroe), along with the team clergy (Father Jake Foglio). I grew quite close to those five people. In this description, their actions represented a far larger group of sports medicine physicians, surgeons, and athletic trainers who practiced here at MSU. I have rarely met a finer group of people, and I consider them all family to this day.

—David Kaufman, DO
East Lansing, Michigan
Summer, 2024

# ANNOUNCEMENT

Part of my intent in writing this account is to donate all royalties after expenses to the Father John (Jake) Foglio Endowed Chair of Spirituality at Michigan State University and the George Webster Endowment for MSU Football Players (who wish to complete their degree after they are done playing football).

This link shows where to mail a check (payable to "Michigan State University") or how to give online: Givingto.MSU.edu

For the "Father John Foglio Chair of Spirituality in College of Arts and Letters" use:

- Allocation Code: Write "Father Foglio AE00107" in the memo line
- Account number: MSRT101307

For the "George Webster Scholarship Fund" use:

- Allocation Code: Write "Webster Fund AA0029" in the memo line.
- Account number: MSRN031259

Send donations to: Spartan Fund, 535 Chestnut Rd, Room 200W, Spartan Stadium, East Lansing, MI 48824.

To donate by phone, call 517-432-4610 (please make sure to indicate that it is for the Father John Foglio Chair of Spirituality in College of Arts and Letters or the George Webster Scholarship Fund).

To donate online, Michigan State's University Development, click on "Give Now" and search for the George Webster Expendable Scholarship Fund: Givingto.MSU.edu

All gifts are tax deductible and will be given Spartan Fund credit. If you have questions about the George Webster Scholarship Fund, you may contact the Spartan Fund at 517-432-4610 or by email at spartanfund@ath.msu.edu.

# CHAPTER ONE

## *Panic in a Tunnel*

The screaming. The yelling. The noise was unbearable. I took three deep breaths, but I was still shaking. My heart beat rapidly; I was scared to death. I was stuck in a narrow, two-story, stone-covered tunnel. I could barely move, and now it was getting hard to breathe. There were 150 of us jammed together, none of us able to move more than a few inches in any direction. Then the jumping started. Claustrophobia, hyperventilation, panic, and even fear were not novel for me. Jumping was. I quickly concluded jumping is never appropriate for a brain doctor. I yelled that conclusion right into the ear of my former medical student, friend, and colleague, Mike Shingles. He was an orthopedic trauma surgeon extraordinaire and twenty years my junior. No matter how playful Mike seemed, I knew that when it mattered, there was no better sports orthopedic surgeon anywhere.

I wanted to tell Mike that his new job was to make sure I was not trampled to death by this mob of humongous student-athletes, but he could not hear what I was saying. Mike was just laughing as he jumped in unison with the players. Suddenly, he leaned in to get a closer look at me and must have noticed I was, indeed, afraid. Mike delivered a quick, well-placed *whack* to my back and shouted above the noise, "Hey! Dave! Wake up!"

Hearing Mike brought me back to the moment. I gave him a high five, and I was ready to go. No more fear, no more profound nausea. I simply shook my head and then tried to jump in unison with everyone else.

Just ahead of us was Sally Nogle. Long, tall, blond, Sally was a thirty-year veteran of athletic training for MSU and the US Olympic teams. Still lithe and athletic, she was already in the National Athletic Trainers' Hall of Fame  and was the trailblazer for women in football athletic training. Sally was not only a friend to the student-athletes, but a mother figure as well. But she was fearsome when angered.

Sally turned and saw Mike and me bouncing like yo-yos along with her players. She did not laugh. Instead, she gave us her unblinking, five-second "stare of death." Chastened, Mike and I immediately stopped jumping. We turned back into chin-up, thin-lipped university physicians. That look was hard to maintain because we were both so happy. I settled in with a simple half-smile. Sally nodded her head to signal that we were forgiven. She had her game face on and expected the same of her physicians.

She understood the next four hours would be the most important her sports-medicine team—and its physicians—would face in all our years together at Michigan State University. How did I get here, I wondered, and what exactly was I doing in the middle of such chaos? Indeed, what was a slightly plump, middle-aged, tenured professor of neurology at Michigan State University doing in the middle of a college football team that was getting ready to run onto the field for the 2014 Rose Bowl Game?

I was sad Sally's fellow athletic trainer, Jeff Monroe, was not in that tunnel with us. Jeff had retired as MSU's lead athletic trainer just a month before this Rose Bowl-season started, after spending thirty years with the team. Part of me felt empty at his absence among us. It was Jeff who was responsible for me being in this tunnel, as we all faced one of the most important moments in MSU's history.

Close by, poised and ready to go, his arms folded and his poker face on, was Dr. Randy Pearson. Randy was the lead team physician, and he had held that coveted position for more than two decades; he was as good a physician as the university had. He kept everything simple—that was his gift, and a quality I admired about him.

No matter how bad the situation, Randy was able to make even the most complicated medical situation seem simple. He was always smart, down to earth, and best of all remarkably accurate in his ability to make a diagnosis. That made him prized as a colleague, especially when we shared challenging cases in the hospital. From Muskegon, at the western edge of Michigan, he also had a sense of small-town common-sense wisdom about him.

Just a little further up in the tunnel, nearly out of my sight, was eighty-four-year-old Father Jake Foglio, a Catholic priest and an ethics and humanity professor at the MSU College of Human Medicine. Father Jake was the team clergy and the fifth and final principal on the MSU football medical team. Father Jake was five foot two and 110 pounds and so was barely visible among the gigantic players. He had a neatly trimmed beard, white as winter, and was wearing his infectious, soulful smile. I knew his impact on this team was immeasurable. He may have been the tiniest person in that tunnel, but he was one of the biggest human beings I had ever encountered. His flock at MSU consisted of so many people—including most of the coaches, staff, and players in the tunnel—it would be impossible to count them all.

I called Father Jake "The Doctor of Soul," based on his uncanny ability to use his spirituality to heal. He was both respected and beloved because of his dignity, virtue, and common-sense values. Father Jake's gift was the ability to calm any player (any person, for that matter) with just a few words. That paid dividends, big time. Today, he was wearing a brand-new Spartan Green official Rose Bowl travel sweat suit along with his old, faded green baseball cap with the block letter S on the front. Because I had been his roommate on football road trips, I knew he had worn that hat since he was an undergrad at MSU six decades before. Father Jake had been a Marine deployed during the Korean War era, which had given him a passionate heart. That fact, along with his dignity and the spicy repertoire of his biting commentary, pushed his "Spartan Spirit" rating off the charts.

Right then, Father Jake was sharing a word and a smile with our punter, a three-time Academic All-American named Mike Sadler. Without question, Mike was one of the funniest human beings I had ever met and a fan favorite. Wearing a perpetual smile, even during the tightest games, Mike was the go-to guy for multiple trick plays out of punt formation. He was just a little taller and slightly thicker than Father Jake. Otherwise, I thought he might be the exact replicate of Father Jake as an undergrad sixty-five years before.

Next to Mike was Mylan Hicks, a five-foot-eleven speedster. He was from Detroit, like so many on this team. Towering over the three of them was Jack Allen, the team's 305-pound Academic All-American and All-Big Ten center. Father Jake turned from Mike and Mylan and then looked up at Big Jack to whisper some secret words of encouragement. No doubt he was predicting how well all of them would do on this day. I watched our quarterback, Connor Cook, dance by me. He stopped to give Father Jake a hug. The two of them exchanged a secret whisper and then another hug. Everyone seemed ready.

As I waited inside that painfully loud and suffocating Rose Bowl tunnel, the sports fan in me realized I was about to run onto one of college football's biggest stages, courtesy of Michigan State University, my home for the past thirty years. I was in the middle of my football family and alongside its medical team. We were all assembled and ready to do our best to win the Rose Bow, a goal twenty-six years in the making.

Then, suddenly, *Bango!*

The Spartans' head coach, Mark Dantonio, shut it all down from the front of the tunnel with a simple look over his shoulder. Everybody stopped jumping and the tunnel went silent. I could hear my own heartbeat as we all silently followed Coach D. forty feet to the tunnel's opening. We all knew Dantonio had supplied the intelligence and toughness—and just the right amount of loyalty, dignity, and spirituality—to take MSU from near the bottom of the Big Ten to the promised land: the Rose Bowl.

Silently, we all watched a man wearing a red hat at the mouth of the tunnel, apparently a Rose Bowl staffer of some kind. He finally raised his left arm and signaled it was time. When he dropped his arm, Coach D., his players, equipment personnel, and our medical staff burst out of the tunnel as if shot from a cannon. We were greeted by a roar so loud it made that unbearable noise in the tunnel just minutes ago seem like a whisper.

It was glorious—New Year's Day in Pasadena, and seventy-three degrees. All of us emerged into the sunlight as one perfect swarm. The grass was bright green and decorated at the center with a huge red, green, and yellow rose under a sun so bright it hurt my eyes. The San Gabriel Mountains and a cloudless blue sky surrounded us. I was running with athletes, coaches, and medical personnel whose secrets and life stories I knew as well as those of my own family. I felt for each one of these people as if they were my own child.

We finished the seventy-yard sprint to our sideline and eventually stood silently with the rest of the ninety-five thousand people in the stadium to get ready for the national anthem. On the opposite sideline were the Stanford Cardinal, equally at attention. Then, Kirk Cousins, quarterback of the 2009–2011 MSU teams and at that time a member of the NFL's Washington, DC football team, walked up next to me, shook my hand, and deadpanned, "Dr. Kaufman, may I stand here next to you?"

I responded, "Hey, you're Kirk Cousins, making millions of dollars a year playing quarterback in the NFL. Near as I can figure, Kirk, you can stand wherever you damn well please! What in the world are you doing here today?"

"Dr. Kaufman, I am completing my circles." We both understood exactly what that meant. He was seeing a life's ambition through to the end by being at the Rose Bowl helping a team he loved. We shook hands and then hugged.

As the national anthem started, I thought about the change and growth I had undergone in my journey from tenured university professor to this team's sports neurologist. What a brutal transition these past four years had been. But I had earned the right to be here. When the four fighter jets flew low and directly overhead at the end of the anthem, I offered up my usual silent prayer that no one would need a brain doctor on this day.

# CHAPTER TWO

# Coming Down from the Upper Deck

**W**hy was a tenured professor of neurology on the sidelines for the 2014 Rose Bowl and how did it end up being me? The short answer is that a concussion "crisis" overtook the country during the 2010s, and my good friend, Jeff Monroe, who was MSU's head athletic trainer, and others insisted I get involved with MSU football to help protect his student-athletes.

Neurology was tasked with answering two simple questions: just how serious is a sports related concussion, and how do we best protect professionals and student-athletes? My university decided to help answer these globally relevant questions by embedding an established clinical neuroscientist researcher into its football team. The next thing I knew, I was asked to transform from a stuffy clinician–researcher into a sports neurologist. That journey would prove to be quite painful.

In the twenty-first century's first decade, reports began to emerge at the American Academy of Neurology (AAN) and elsewhere about potential long-term brain damage from sports concussions. The AAN released communications strongly implying sports concussion should be recognized as a public-health issue. Initially, I thought that proposal was ridiculous. Then professional players began to talk about the emotional and mental hazards of playing football.

Significant research published in high-impact journals about an apparently new disease called chronic traumatic encephalopathy

(CTE) soon followed. Mothers were becoming afraid to allow their children to play football or other collision sports—such as hockey, rugby, and even soccer—because of the fear of CTE. As the dangers of collision sports like football emerged, people wondered if these sports should actually be banned.

Back then, according to multiple mainstream stories, CTE was a horrible and inevitable occurrence related to playing football. It would first rob you of your humanity and then cause you to become suicidal or worse. Some reports implied there would be no escaping CTE if you played football, even in high school.

As a neurologist, I understood boxing and steel-cage mixed martial arts were bad news, but banning football? It almost seemed un-American. But I began to worry as more research surfaced about CTE. In December 2009, when National Football League spokesman Greg Aiello first admitted in a *New York Times* interview there were indeed long-term issues associated with concussions, I, and many other neurologists, became riveted by this issue. Congressional hearings[1] followed, books were written, and blockbuster movies eventually got made about concussion. I really began to wonder if football would survive as a sport, and that prospect bothered me deeply.

Personally, I saw football as a family-oriented autumn ritual that served as the catalyst for friends, families, and entire communities to come together. It was an incredible outdoor spectacle, complete with huge and excited crowds mingling together against a backdrop of marching bands, all cheering on loyal sons against feared rivals.

As I knew well from my decades on the campus of MSU, the sport enriched, connected, and then galvanized people. It was uniquely American and deeply embedded in the culture of our society for more than a hundred years. I was convinced losing football, or changing it into something unrecognizable, would have more than minor social consequences.

But I also understood the power of clinical neuroscience research. The emerging data strongly suggested there could well be potential danger to the brains of people playing football. I was conflicted about

---

[1] https://www.govinfo.gov/content/pkg/CHRG-111hhrg53092/html/CHRG-111hhrg53092.htm

the social and scientific debates swirling around me, but I had little time to do anything meaningful about it.

I was having a pretty successful academic career. I was good at obtaining grants from the National Institutes of Health (NIH) and similar extramural funding. I was winning awards as a teacher and clinician, all while authoring more than a hundred scientific papers. I was lecturing extensively in the United States and Europe and teaching my beloved MSU medical students, residents, and fellows. I was also the founding chair of the Department of Neurology at a terrific Big Ten university, where I was surrounded by absolutely wonderful faculty and staff.

More than any of those academic accomplishments, I was truly happy. Laurie, who I married in 1974, was also a tenured associate professor in endocrinology at MSU. My children, Matt and Sarah, were on their way to getting postgraduate educations: Sarah was heading to medical school, and Matt was getting his masters in health administration. By 2010, I felt I had done it all, and my life was essentially complete. Everything was terrific, until a day in July 2010 when Jeff Monroe walked into my house and started talking about "we need a neurologist in the locker room and on the field."

Back in those days, when I spent game days in the upper deck of Spartan Stadium, I thought I had a good understating of what actually happened on a football field. I knew there were athletic trainers and a few doctors who helped the football team out. I really did not pay any attention to sports medicine, and no one had heard of a thing called "sports neurology."

My family had gone to football games faithfully from the day Laurie and I first arrived on campus in 1984. Three years later, under coach George Perles, MSU won a Big Ten championship, and Laurie and I went to Pasadena for the 1988 Rose Bowl. I thought every year would be just as exciting, that Rose Bowl trips would come nice and easy. Sadly, that was not the way it went. Before the start of the Mark Dantonio era in 2007, MSU was on its fourth head football coach in twenty years. The team had not returned to the Rose Bowl, and, truthfully, was just not that good.

In the spring of 2010, I read an article about Dr. Jeff Kutcher, who had testified at a hearing before the US House of Representatives Committee on the Judiciary on January 10. It was the second committee hearing titled "Legal Issues Relating to Football Head Injuries." Dr. Kutcher was from the University of Michigan—MSU's archrival in all things. The article also announced the University of Michigan had "acquired a sports neurologist." The article said: "Jeff Kutcher, M.D., will help reduce the number of concussions for Michigan football and help make the game safer." I remember thinking, "Gee, that's interesting," but I gave the subject no further thought. However, that article created a cascade of events that changed my calm, predictable life into controlled chaos.

Anyone living around the Great Lakes knows about MSU's rivalry with the U of M. Whenever U of M did something, MSU always seemed compelled to do the same. U of M had a sports neurologist, so—presto!—MSU would now need a sports neurologist. One might ask, "Okay, but how or why was it me?" A few months after the U of M announcement, Jeff Monroe, the head athletic trainer, invited himself over my lake house for a drink.

Jeff breezed into my home through the massive lakeside sliding door. Without a word, he flopped down on my green leather couch and stared out at the water for a long time while remaining silent. Jeff had this incredibly charming, almost Southern, drawl when he spoke. His utter and complete disdain for U of M was also one of the more endearing things about him. He grew up in Ohio and worked as an athletic training student at THE Ohio State University. He typically used the term "blue bellies," a reference to U of M's football jerseys, to describe anything having to do with the place. In fact, the words "University of Michigan" or Wolverine had never passed through Jeff's lips in the twenty-five years I had known him, except when he spoke about their outstanding sports medicine group, including their exceptional lead athletic trainer Paul (Schmidty) Schmidt.

Eventually, he turned and looked up at me and said, "Dave, these dang concussion issues are gettin' more and more important to the administration, alums, and all of us in athletics here at MSU. We need to be takin' point out in front of this issue. We have to. It is the right thing. It's important to us, my boys playing, and to football as a whole. Then, them blue bellies got this sideline neurology thing goin' on, so we have to get with it, too."

Jeff was an irascible, straight-talking, fiery, hardworking man. Trim and athletic even into his fifties, he had sandy brown hair and soulful eyes. Jeff was legendary at MSU and as good a friend as a man could have—if he liked you. Otherwise, look out. He was well known as the on-campus "dad" to the football players. He was absolutely dedicated to getting them the best care available, as quickly as possible. I was first introduced to him in 1985 by Ken Marton, the team optometrist. Jeff built my lake house's deck, got to know Laurie and the kids, taught me a lot about football, and occasionally would ask me to consult on a player with a nagging neurologic issue. We eventually became close and shared many a night talking football and drinking Scotch.

It was a late July afternoon, the annual dog-day cicadas droning in background, "Those blue bellies will be havin' an advantage with this neurology thing," he drawled.

Jeff walked over to my wet bar and shook his head as if he were disgusted about U of M having an advantage in anything. He found and then began to rummage around my liquor cabinet, discovering a well-hidden, unopened bottle of eighteen-year-old Glenfiddich. I frowned as he took out two very large glasses and poured us both a long drink.

He went on about the emerging public panic over concussion as he sauntered back over to me and flashed a smile. He said, "Dave, here, have a drink. You need one. You know, I think you should see what it's actually like on the sidelines during a game. Come to one of the preseason practices in August. Maybe you should eventually come down from the upper deck and get a close look during a game."

I did not tell my good friend that it would be an unbelievable dream come true for me. As he started working on about a hundred and twenty dollars' worth of Scotland's finest export, I was speechless until I choked out the word, "Fascinating."

As Jeff went on to describe how useful an on-field neurologist might be, my mind was racing elsewhere. I had already said to myself, "Oh, my God. Could something so special like that actually happen to me? That would be unbelievable. Oh, my God!"

I remained silent as Jeff tried to sell me on the concept for the next ten minutes. I went into a dreamlike state as he rambled on. I recalled watching the 1966 MSU–Notre Dame game on TV. They were the two top-ranked teams in the nation, and they fought to a 10–10 tie in the "Game of the Century." The spectacle inspired me to try out for my high-school football team. I suffered a broken arm during my first practice, and my parents let me know my football career was over.

Still, I was infatuated with football. While going to college at the University of Wisconsin, I joined the student newspaper, the *Daily Cardinal*—knowing reporters could secure great seats for football games. For my next gambit, I wormed my way into a class called Fundamentals of Football taught by the University of Wisconsin coaches. The course was only available to physical education majors, but I bypassed that requirement on the pretense that I was on assignment from the *Daily Cardinal* to cover the class.

Sadly, I did not realize that varsity players would be the "teaching assistants," and the coursework was largely physical. I thought I would be learning about downfield blocking while talking to the coaches and playing touch football. Instead, I participated in daily on-field "labs" that were in reality we students acting as tackling dummies for the varsity players.

Class members were pounded to a pulp learning how to block and tackle correctly by the "teaching assistants." After each class, I was a physical wreck. I walked home slowly, nursing an endless series of arm and leg injuries. But I fell deeply in love with football from that class.

Near semester's end, there was a formal football game complete with referees and first down markers played at Wisconsin's seventy-eight-thousand–seat Camp Randall Stadium. The class was divided into red and white teams and we practiced for two weeks as separate squads. We wore regulation Badger uniforms; I was number 68 for the white squad.

I was terrified until I was informed that the "teaching assistants" were not going to play. I realized I was now one of the bigger guys on the field. That immediately changed my "poor me" attitude to a more aggressive version of myself. At practice, I began shouting things like, "Let's get ready to rumble!"

The coaches soon anointed me starting defensive end, probably based on my girth. I also had the ability to run over the five-foot-nine, 170-pound physical education majors who were required to sign up for the class. Weighing in at 230 pounds and at six feet three, I found myself pulverizing them during the three-hour practice sessions. It was glorious!

Just prior to playing in the required "game," I could hardly contain myself. There I was, in the actual varsity locker room, about to fulfill a lifelong dream of running out onto a college football field with my brothers in combat. I ignored the reality that these folks were people I had met only eight weeks before and were simply required to get these three credits to complete their major. Unlike them, I was there solely for glory—and maybe to write a story for the college paper.

Before the game, I could not have been more excited. Sadly, when my team burst onto the stadium floor from the locker-room tunnel, I immediately recognized that something important was missing. Where was the noise? Where was the energy? There were absolutely no fans in the enormous Camp Randell stadium. Not a soul. I could hear my own voice echo when I called out for a drink of water. The total and complete emptiness of that enormous stadium took the luster off of the experience just a bit.

During the game, I got knocked around enough to feel like I was on a roller coaster. I soon understood that football was not so much a contact sport as a truly violent collision-level free-for-all. I also learned two important lessons about football: The first was how to enact revenge; the other was what a concussed player looked like up close.

While defending a running play, I was loafing. An offensive guard hit me from behind just as I was tiptoeing toward the running back. I got pounded face-first to the ground and was wondering if the pain involving my entire left side would ever stop. The more annoying thing was that my assailant stood above me, quietly laughing as I rolled around the ground whimpering.

The athletic trainer quickly came over and carefully checked me out. After he was sure I was okay, he said, "Hey, number 68, try to be less like a Girl Scout and more like a football player. Get up, get back into the game, and pretend to be a man this next quarter."

His words and the urgency in his voice, though slightly demeaning, were also compelling. So I stepped it up and played with as much intensity as an out-of-shape, nineteen-year-old human could muster. I waited for just the right moment and flattened that same offensive guard when he was not looking. Fortunately, my premeditated collision was just out of sight from the referees on the field.

The athletic trainer shook his head, and as he walked past me, gave me a quick elbow to the ribs. He bent over and quietly tended to my adversary, who was on the ground wailing at the top of his lungs. I, however, was greeted warmly by my coach and teammates as I walked, triumphant, to the sidelines.

In the second half, an offensive center did not get up after blocking on a passing play. He had gone head-to-head with our middle linebacker and went down like he'd been shot. His eyes were still open, but he did not move. I had a slightly queasy feeling as I looked him over and I struggled not to throw up. The same athletic trainer came over and said to us, "concussion." After a few minutes, three of us helped the player walk off the field, but that moment shook me deeply. I just did not notice the intensity of the pain that could be inflicted on a football player while seated in the upper deck during a real football game. After a few weeks, I no longer gave that concussion a second thought—until four decades later, when Jeff Monroe came over my house looking to recruit a team neurologist.

As Jeff poured another eighty dollars' worth of that eighteen-year-old Scotch into my glass, I came back to the present. I was absolutely hooked on the possibility of watching a game on the field. What an incredible experience that might be! Jeff implied I might need a bit of training before that opportunity and suggested I really should go to the preseason practices during August "to get a feel for what the action might be like."

"Dave," he said, "with all you have going on, could you make time to come over to practices during the afternoon?"

I tried to be coy, while thinking about what an unbelievable, once-in-a-lifetime opportunity it would be to see a college football game up close. I lowered my voice and somehow choked out, "Well, Jeff, maybe I might be able to move a few things around. I have to think about it a little."

As Jeff spoke, my mind was racing. I was a huge college football fan, and here he was telling me that I had a chance to be as close as any superfan could possibly get to a college football team without putting on pads. I thought back to the first and last time I was on the field during a real college football game. That was in 1969, at a point when the Wisconsin Badgers had gone 0–22–1 over the last three seasons. Yes, they had not won a single football game from 1967 to 1969.

Back then, I had shared with my friend Laurie how much fun football games were in Madison. I was trying hard to court her, but she never seemed to have enough time to spend with me. I suggested she come visit and see a game. I really did not know where I stood with her back then. I hoped she might see that I was a fun-loving guy, and somehow that might win her heart. The reality was she was both premed and a Pom-Pom cheerleader at Northwestern University, so any time she spent with me in Evanston was very limited.

On October 11, 1969, Laurie actually showed up in Madison with those dreamy green eyes and long blond hair. It was immediately clear to my fellow *Daily Cardinal* sportswriters that she was way out of my league, and they told her as much while we walked over as a group to Camp Randall Stadium for the game against the University of Iowa. During the mile-long trek, my fellow writer, Jim Podgers, leaned over and whispered too loudly, "Dave, it had better be a damn good football game. Otherwise, it's over for you and the blond."

I soon found myself with eight *Daily Cardinal* staffers and the green-eyed beauty, stuffed into six seats in the very upper deck of Camp Randall stadium. One of my mentors at the *Cardinal* pointed out just before kickoff how sad it was for "someone as good-looking as Laurie to be out in public with Kaufman."

Laurie assessed that comment carefully, looked around at everyone, and then shook her head *yes* in silent but polite agreement.

That's when I started consuming large quantities of the rum I had smuggled into the stands. I had to dull the realization my relationship with Laurie was about to go nowhere.

As the game dragged on, it was business as usually as the Iowa Hawkeyes pounded the Badgers and took a 17–0 lead into the fourth quarter. I knew time was running out and I needed a personal miracle. After such a dull game, I was sure Laurie would give me a handshake, say a quick goodbye, get back on the train to Evanston, and that would be that. Then, suddenly, things changed.

Hit by a lightning bolt of competence, the Badgers' passing game began to click. After two quick Wisconsin touchdowns, people started to realize there was actually a chance, for the first time in three years, for the Badgers to somehow win a game. With two minutes and eight seconds left, Neil Graff hit Randy Marks, for the go-ahead score. Then, on the following kickoff, Iowa fumbled into the end zone for a safety to make it 23–17. There was pandemonium in the stands! Even Laurie was beginning to pay attention. Not a single person I knew had ever seen a Badger football victory live. Now, no matter how unbelievable, it was possible. We all moved down to the lower deck to get a closer look.

After the safety, Wisconsin received the Iowa kick but failed to move the ball, using only ultra-conservative plays. Following the Badger punt, Iowa took over and played with urgent desperation. The Hawkeyes marched the ball right down the field and got within striking distance of the Wisconsin goal line to potentially win the game. I was so nervous I couldn't look, but I did notice Laurie was now clutching my arm out of anxiety. Then, with less than thirty seconds left, Neovia Greyer intercepted the ball for the Badgers.

As the defensive back began running with the ball, the fans could not be contained. Euphoria was followed by mayhem. Thousands and thousands of fans rushed onto the field even though Greyer was still running! This forced the refs to flee for their lives as they called the game over with twenty-four seconds left. Players were carried off the field in triumph and both goalposts quickly came down as fifty-five thousand other people, including Laurie and me, were dancing on the playing field.

Eventually, the Wisconsin marching band helped clear the field of ecstatic fans, and the tuba section led the parade out of the stadium, down University Avenue to State Street. All of us followed, filling Madison's main boulevard from the University's Bascom Hill an entire mile to the State Capital, as one of the wildest nights of my life commenced.

The police pulled half barrels of beer into the street and helped serve the beverage, apparently, to reduce the overcrowding in the bars. Elroy "Crazy Legs" Hirsch, Wisconsin's athletic director, gave an ad hoc speech atop the Flamingo bar sign in the middle of the crowd. Hippies danced with town people, undergrads hugged their professors, and even Laurie treated me very differently. We all danced the night away along with thousands and thousands of others on Madison's State Street. It was one of the most memorable moments of my life.

Eventually, Laurie, with that flowing blond hair, looked me in the eye and asked, "David, tell me the truth. Is it like this every Saturday night in Madison?"

Without hesitation I said, "Why, yes, Laurie. Of course, it is. It is exactly like this every Saturday night in Madison. Maybe you should transfer?"

Sure enough, the following year she did. Two years later, Laurie was in medical school as I pursued my major in history and continued to write sports for the *Daily Cardinal*. She seemed happy, and I loved going to the games, talking to the coaches and athletes, and hearing their stories. But I was also fascinated by Laurie's description of doctors assembled in the hospital to help patients.

Her description was surprisingly reminiscent of finely organized sports teams at work, except her stories literally described life or death. The best part was that Laurie was in the middle of it all, an integral member of a team working together to fight disease and help their patient.

After hearing her stories for a while, I reflected on my own life's course. As a sportswriter, I loved what I did, but I could only observe and then report. I could never actually help the team I was assigned to, except to point out which athlete was doing well and who might need to be encouraged a bit more.

In the end, I was envious that Laurie and her doctors made up a team that was actually allowed to directly help people. Her delicately told stories about life and death were so much better than any I could ever possibly write. I was inspired, and I decided to change the course of my life.

After some pretty tough premed coursework and much stress over the Medical College Admission Test (MCAT), I was accepted at my hometown medical school, Philadelphia College of Osteopathic Medicine. Laurie and I relocated to Philly and married. While I was going through medical school, she concluded her residency in internal medicine at Thomas Jefferson University.

Then, in an act I realized much later in life was meant to complete our circles, we went back to the University of Wisconsin. I did my neurology residency and visual electrophysiology fellowship. Laurie studied endocrinology. We both then did additional fellowships within the Harvard system, and moved from Boston to Michigan State University's medical schools as faculty in late summer 1984.

I soon fell in love with MSU and its Spartan sports teams. Laurie and I went to the Rose Bowl with fifty thousand other Spartan fans in 1987, and it was mesmerizing. The spectacle of the game itself was as special as everyone predicted it would be. Sitting at the thirty-yard line, thirty rows up, I could not believe how close everything was compared to my seats back home in Spartan Stadium's extreme upper deck. MSU triumphed over the University of Southern California and I was in absolute heaven. I could have died happy at that moment.

Meanwhile, at MSU's medical schools, work was going very well as the NIH grants started coming in for Laurie and me. Eventually, we both won tenure, and I was given the privilege of starting the MSU Department of Neurology in 2000. For the next ten years, I could not imagine anything that could make me happier. That was, until Jeff Monroe entered my home, poured some of my awfully expensive Scotch and asked me, "How do we make football safer?"

# CHAPTER THREE

# *How Fantasy Became Reality*

"Dave," said Jeff, finishing off that bottle of Scotch, "we've got to get our players more protection and get this game safer. Guys like you need to step up. People are talking about getting rid of the game. We all need to think through how to make it safer." He leaned in and asked, "Dave, what do you think? Are you in?"

Truthfully, during the twenty-five years I had sat in the upper deck at Spartan Stadium, I had daydreamed quite often about some freak event where I would be summoned down to the field, perhaps by an overhead announcement that asked for a neurologist to treat an injured Spartan football player. I would get the star diagnosed, fixed up, and back onto the field. In my fondest daydream, maybe the coach would one day actually learn my name. I might somehow become a useful part of the team as a doctor and, in the wildest part of the unreachable fantasy, be asked to travel with them, to all the Big Ten cities and beyond. Maybe one day I would even be asked to go to a Bowl Game with them.

That sort of daydream may be more common in late middle-aged men than one might think. Of course, such dreams never come true. But here was Jeff Monroe laying out a path for such a thing. I stared back at Jeff, but I resisted blurting out, "Oh, my God! Jeff! That would be a dream come true! Bless you! Where do I sign?"

Instead, I resorted to my sterile, slightly aloof, clinically detached, precise academic voice. "Jeff, realistically speaking, this may or may not be a relevant clinical research opportunity. I have to carefully weigh this. Precisely, what would be the total time commitment you would need me to structure within my current academic portfolio and responsibilities?"

Laurie, overhearing all of this, and of course fully aware of my intense love of college football, immediately recognized my "academic chair's voice." She wandered over to figure out what kind of nonsense I was trying to pull on my good friend Jeff. She gave me a Coke to sober me up and then flashed me a wide-eyed stare that silently implied, "Dave, what on earth would prevent you from doing something so glorious?"

I took the bait. I turned to her and asked with as much sincerity as I could possibly muster, "Sweetheart, would you mind if I wasn't sitting with you during the games in the upper deck so I might spend some time with Jeff on the field?"

She quickly flashed one of her full-face smiles, no doubt remembering how obnoxious I am when yelling obscenities from the upper deck at the refs from hundreds of yards away from the playing field. Laurie let me know in our secret, facial-expression code that she would be totally thrilled to get rid of me on Saturdays. However, she responded quite calmly, "David, this is a fascinating concept that you should at least consider, regarding the academic opportunity it could provide to MSU, our Colleges of Osteopathic and Human Medicine, and you."

That's how I ended up getting invited to MSU's football team summer practices in August 2010. I had no idea that sports neurology would be so different from my specific area of subspecialty, office-based neuro-ophthalmology. As a clinical neuro-ophthalmologist I am sent unusual cases that either a neurologist or an ophthalmologist or both could not diagnose. My medical team and I would usually spend an hour or more trying to understand the cause of the patient's visual issues, surrounded by a variety of technical equipment needed to examine both the eye and the brain in a very precise way.

As I came to the football practice field during MSU football's four-week summer camp, after long and tedious days in clinic, Jeff tried to prepare me for the harsh reality that sports neurology is nothing like neuro-ophthalmology. Sadly, I just didn't get it right away.

Soon enough, Jeff turned up the heat and began to deliver relentless critiques of my style. "Don't walk over and talk to the players," went a typical evaluation. "Let them come to you. If you are examining someone, keep the explanations simple. They are in the middle of doing their job with total focus on the game. Do not confuse them with a lot of technical stuff. Get them better or disqualify them. Stay out of their heads. Just do your job and then disappear back into the sidelines."

Perhaps the most chilling thing he taught me was around week three of my crash course. "Dave, most important of all, if a ball is thrown towards you on the sidelines, pay attention to the players and not the ball. The ball will not send you to the hospital. A player running you over will."

Jeff was a humble, kind, down-to-earth friend until I began my work as his team neurologist. From day one, he made it clear there was nothing more important than his players and their health. Nothing. He delivered my preseason mental beatings constantly, cramming my brain's limbic system with everything I was supposed to know in that four-week crash course in "sports neurology."

I'm a professor and chair of a Big Ten academic department, so it had been quite a while since anyone had the fortitude—otherwise known as *cojones*—to yell at me face to face. But I was wise enough to realize these scoldings were designed to change me from a stuffy academic clinician into a sports neurologist as quickly as possible. Jeff was driven to whip me into shape, so maybe, somehow, I could one day actually make a difference in the health of his players.

After four weeks of preseason practices at the Duffy Daugherty Football Building, I found myself getting ready to be on the football field for opening day of the 2010 season. It was unbelievable! I fought traffic, parked several blocks away, and walked with the enormous crowd, proudly wearing a *Home Bench Access* badge around my neck.

At Spartan Stadium, instead of heading to the upper deck with the masses, I walked over to the players' entrance by the north end zone. After Jeff appeared, three MSU security guards, still eyeing me carefully, let me pass. As Jeff and I walked toward the Spartans' locker room, he leaned over to me and whispered in my ear, "Dave, try hard not to screw up too badly today, okay?"

I was then handed a green "game day" shirt by the team's well-respected and longtime equipment manager, Bob Knickerbocker. White-haired and nearing sixty, Mr. Nick, as he was lovingly called by his staff and players, said, "Well, Doc, you're new, but you might be useful out there with these concussions and all. Good luck. Here, use this shirt so you won't look too out of place behind the bench."

He tossed me a green game-day shirt, the same as worn by the athletic trainers, team doctors and coaches. It was emblazoned with a white Spartan warrior helmet on the left and the words Michigan State on the back. Despite being honored with a bunch of awards at MSU, including being asked to give a TED Talk about my research and invited to deliver a medical school graduation speech, the simple act of putting on that XXL shirt was among the top thrills I had ever experienced.

It was September 4, 2010. I believed this warm and sunny Saturday afternoon would be among the best days of my life. That thought did not last very long.

As we were walking into the locker room, Jeff leaned in close and said: "Dave, I know you are going to be bad at this sports neurology thing in the beginning, but I think you can eventually do it. The first games will be the hardest. We all know you actually have no clue what is truly happening on a football field. You think you do, but you don't. I will help you with that because maybe you might actually help one of my guys. That will make all this pain I will endure teaching you worthwhile. Got it?"

I understood Jeff was doing his best to get me ready to change from outsider to part of his well-oiled medical team, a group that had been together for years. Jeff continued. "Dave, before you go into the locker room, I want you to know something. Please realize a neurologist may be the lowest form of life on a football team. Keep that in mind, will you? You are no longer the chair of neurology at MSU. In this locker room and on that field, you are nothing more—but nothing less—than a member of my sports medicine staff. Probably the lowest member. Got it?"

Those statements from my close friend stunned me a bit. He had changed from a very nice Dr. Jekyll into a fear-inducing Mr. Hyde. But the thought of fulfilling my lifelong ambition to help my university's football team was enough to encourage me to follow him into that ancient, foul-smelling, cave-like area masquerading as a locker room. Once inside, I suddenly realized the transition from a fan located in a safe and comfortable seat in upper-deck next to my family to an on-field doctor with enormous responsibility for my university's student-athletes brain and spine health was probably the longest distance I would ever travel in my career as a neurologist.

I found a wooden stool in the corner of the locker room and took a seat. The more I thought about all of this, the more nervous I became. Jeff had the ability and moral authority to reduce a veteran, tenured professor into a pile of whimpering humanity with just a few sentences. I started to feel panic, my old nemesis, take over my thinking in the dim light of the sweltering locker room populated by 105 football players, and dozens of coaches, support staff, and members of the medical team.

Jeff came back over for one last swipe at my self-confidence. "Dave, try not to do anything so bad you are in the newspaper or on TV. Understand? You are going to see and experience organized chaos. Anything can happen. Be ready. People will get hurt today. It's not like being in that upper deck, simply watching, nice and safe, sitting on your behind like you have done for the last two or three decades. This is not going to be like waiting for the Coke man to come by to sell you a soda.

"Some of the folks in this locker room are going to get hurt today," he continued. "Most will be players. But often enough, someone like you or a coach standing on the sidelines, not paying attention, gets rolled up, run over, and breaks a leg. Listen to me very carefully, my man. Always, and I mean always, watch the players, not the ball. That is the key. Watch the players and not the ball. Try to avoid getting whacked so hard we send you to the hospital. Fair?"

I quickly nodded *yes*, even more afraid than I had been. I started to sweat a little, then came a subtle stomach-churning light-headedness that I recognized as an emerging panic attack. The annoying knot in my stomach got worse and worse. It used to only come with final exams in medical school, but here it was again. I had not even gone out onto the field for pregame warm-ups and I was already doing my best not to throw up. I took a deep breath, looked around, and saw 105 young men taking off their suits and ties and putting on football gear.

Everyone was totally quiet. Some were putting on a black dye-like substance under their eyes to prevent glare. I never understood the purpose of that except it did enhance the menacing and evil look they projected. It reminded me of soldiers putting on camouflage or war paint prior to battle. Finally, silently, everyone gathered at the front of the tiny locker room. They all went into the tunnel and out onto the Spartan Stadium field for pregame warm-ups.

I stayed behind with the medical team as we reviewed the emergency protocols. We all eventually drifted out of the locker room, up the tunnel, and onto the field. As I was walking across the grass on the north part of the field, I was lost in thought, thinking about everything Jeff had tried to teach me. I noticed a perfectly thrown pass by quarterback Kirk Cousins and was mesmerized by the tight spiral the ball made. Just then, a 235-pound, six-foot-two freshman, getting ready for his first game as a Spartan, *whooooshed* by my chin, scaring me senseless.

Le'Veon Bell had been running down the pass from his quarterback when he noticed me and at the very last second did an acrobatic spin move to avoid clobbering me. Le'Veon ever so lightly grazed my chin but grabbed my arm so I wouldn't fall. I realized he could have run me over except he was just that gifted an athlete. "Nice move, Doc," Le'Veon said over his shoulder with an infectious, lighthearted laugh.

He seemed like a passionate athlete with a man-sized body and impossibly joyous personality. He also could have crushed my chest if he hadn't figured out a way to avoid hitting me. He shouted to me as he got ready to run another pass route, "Hey, Doc, I'll be using that spin move in the game. Look for it."

I stood there, mouth wide open, more shaken up than ever. Just then, Jeff leaned over, poked his thumb into my ribs, and whispered, directly into my ear, "Dave, watch the player, NOT THE BALL. If you watch the ball like you just did, a player will knock you into next Thursday. Remember?"

He added, "Dave, you could be the worst rookie doctor I have ever had to break in. What are you? Maybe fifty-eight, sixty? If one of these guys hits you, I am not going to be looking all over the place for the broken pieces of your body. Got me? Do me a favor and try not to die today. Okay?"

I was becoming more nervous by the second. I took a deep breath, tried to calm down, and told Jeff a lie. "Everything is fine, Jeff. Stop worrying about me so much."

Just then, a whistle blew. As we moved off the field and back into that tiny locker room for final coaching instructions prior to kick off, that knot in my stomach got worse and worse.

By the 2010 season, MSU's fourth-year coach, Mark Dantonio, had righted the ship from the tragic John L. Smith era, and Spartan Nation had sky-high hopes for a championship. They were 9–4 in 2008 and, despite a 6–7 record for 2009, their performance in the Alamo Bowl was quite good, though they lost to Texas Tech 41–31. The sports pages all asked the same question: Would this finally be the year MSU would claim a Big Ten title and go back to the Rose Bowl after two decades of mediocrity?

The experience of being inside a Division I locker room twenty minutes prior to the season's first game was a remarkable thing. The room itself looked like it had been left unchanged for the past fifty years. It was a gray L-shaped space about the size of two large living rooms. To call it crowded would be a gross understatement. It was crammed with players, coaches, and staff. Off to one side was Mr. Nick's equipment room and to the other the showers and bathrooms.

The medical staff area was incompletely separated from the team by a temporary, prefabricated partition that left the athletic trainers and physicians visible to everyone. There were three black-padded examination tables. I was surprised to see a coat-hanger from the ceiling serving as an IV pole, and three old-time X-ray view boxes on the wall. To enter the locker room, everyone walked up six steps and looked right into the medical area as they entered. There was simply no privacy for whatever pregame treatment was being given to a player.

I sat on a stool off in a corner and tried to calm my nerves. I watched some of the players getting their ankles retaped and saw pregame manipulations being performed by Jeff and co-lead athletic trainer Sally Nogle. As the knot in my stomach got worse, I started rocking back and forth on the three-legged stool, like some kindergartener. Thoughts raced through my head: How would the team do today? How would I do? Would I be needed? Would I make a jackass of myself and in front of millions on TV? How badly was I about to screw up?

The locker room itself seemed way too quiet, almost silent. I sensed everyone had at least a little of those first-game jitters, just like me. Of course, I was the only one rocking back and forth, making obnoxious squeaking noises every time I moved. No one was saying a word. I was totally oblivious to the scene I was creating. Eventually, I looked up and noticed a lot of the players and all the athletic trainers and medical staff staring at me as I rocked back and forth on that stool.

About then, strength and conditioning coach, Ken Mannie, started walking over toward me. I recognized him from his pictures in the local newspaper. "The difference maker," I remember one very flattering sports columnist saying about him. Mannie had been hired by Nick Saban, who was then the head coach, in December 1994. Mannie had a graying flat-top crewcut, a weather-beaten rugged face with a prominent chin covered by a goatee and mustache. But his most prominent feature were his cold, black, shark-like eyes. His expressionless face, his warrior-like aura, and, most of all, those eyes staring at me and the bulging muscles trying to burst out of his game-day shirt made him a very intimidating individual.

Coach Mannie also had the reputation of being the team "enforcer"; he expected everyone to have a work ethic equal to his. At summer practices, I noticed Ken let any player or even a position coach know when they were not doing their best. He did it loudly and with gusto. His deep baritone voice, chronically hoarse from yelling, was his weapon of choice. I noticed he used that weapon with great effectiveness during the pre-season practices I attended.

Ken Mannie was also once called the "scariest man alive" by my son, Matt. The two had met ten years earlier during an MSU summer football camp for fifteen-year-old boys. Matt would come home each day after camp and invariably state at dinner: "Coach Mannie is the meanest man that ever lived. He might feed one of us kids to a meat grinder someday during this summer camp. I hope it's not me."

Matt also assured Laurie and me that Coach Mannie did whatever was needed to get that last ounce of performance and even courage from the fifteen-year-olds he was coaching. One could only imagine what he did to help the performance of star collegiate players. Matt described Coach Mannie as the most effective motivator he was ever exposed to.

That was all okay, except it was this same Coach Mannie who was now walking over to where I was still rocking back and forth on that stool, squeaking up a storm. I was getting more and more nervous as he got closer. He eventually was literally looming right over me like the shadow of death. For a few seconds he said nothing. I looked around and the place seemed frozen; no one was moving. I could hear my own breathing while my heart was palpitating away at about 120 beats per minute.

I looked up at Coach Mannie, who had bent down to station himself just a couple of inches from my face. During the silence, I had time to wonder why he was now nose to nose with me. Suddenly he broke the silence by asking in a whisper, just loud enough to be heard throughout the now silent locker room, "Doc, what's wrong?"

I picked my head up, looked him in the eye and stopped rocking. I half-whispered back, "Coach, I guess I'm nervous."

Coach Mannie then stood up ramrod straight. He raised his voice from that understated whisper, all the way up to Marine drill sergeant ear-shattering volume. "DOC, YOU'RE WHAT? YOU'RE NERVOUS?"

He then bent back down and was once again nose to nose with me. I felt all the collective fear that had built up in me over the last few weeks getting ready for this first game come directly to attention. At that moment, I realized my son was right. This guy was indeed a very scary dude, and I hoped I would not die in some unknown first-game ritualized event. Coach Mannie at the top of his lungs then shouted, "LOOK, YOU'RE NOT NERVOUS! YOU'RE *EXCITED*! GOT THAT, DOC? YOU'RE EXCITED!"

With that, Coach Mannie hit me, tenured professor, and all, hard on my chest with the open palm of his right hand. It made a loud *whoomph* and startled the hell out of me. That sound also got the attention of the players who were watching all of this play out while standing motionless. After looking around at everyone in the locker room, Coach Mannie then turned back to me and leaned in. He again yelled, "DOC, WE NEED YOU AND EVERYBODY IN HERE TO BE EXCITED, NOT NERVOUS."

Looking up again at his players, he added, "YOU ALL GOT THAT?"

He pulled away from me and for about five of the longest seconds I had ever lived, nobody in that locker room moved or said a word. Mannie then turned and began to walk back toward the coaches' room. As he disappeared, the players all looked at each other wide-eyed. Slowly, they started to talk about what they had just seen and then they all started to laugh.

At first, it was a low snicker from a few of the players, but then came that louder deeper sound that starts low down in the belly and just rolls out of your face like joyous thunder. Then everyone started talking and laughing like they were in some house party. "Uh-oh," I thought. "First game and these guys are already laughing at me!"

Eventually, Sally Nogle came close, looked me over, and, after realizing I was okay, turned around and gave a group laughing it up in a corner some sort of prolonged stare. They settled right down, started nodding their heads at me to make it clear they were laughing with me, not at me. Some who just a few seconds before had been pointing were now giving me a thumbs-up or slapping high fives with their locker mates. Everyone in that room had started talking and now the place was buzzing with excitement. I suspect it was because they had seen a brain doctor pounded into shape by their own Coach Mannie and that set the mood just right.

I was now sitting up straight on that stool, totally at attention and not moving after getting smacked in the chest by the strength and conditioning coach. This was not the way I wanted to start things off on my first game-day adventure. Everyone else was whooping it up, yelling and talking. Coach Mannie had changed the mood in that locker room from nervous to excited, all with that one perfectly timed lesson delivered at the expense of the new guy, namely me.

As for my butterflies, they were gone. I started laughing along with everyone else and no longer thought about anything other than the task ahead. I will also believe for the rest of my life that the moment lifted MSU's football team just enough to help them forget about their own first-game jitters. The locker room was alive with chatter and laughter and the guys were now amped up. The mood had become electric.

I sat back and took it all in. I had just been acknowledged by a coach publicly as useful enough to pay attention to, brain doctor or not. I was now an "official" part of the team. Over the next few minutes, a few of the guys came over to give me a fist bump. Most did not say a word, but they would give me a head nod or a wink to let me know I was now a part of them.

As I collected myself, and took a deep breath, I slowly noticed things began to settle down just a bit. The pregame locker room turned toward a precise routine leading up to the one o'clock start time. There was even a large numerical countdown clock that ticked off the minutes and seconds prior to kickoff.

The expected routine was listed on a white board and was followed to the second regarding who should be where, when, and what they should be doing. This carefully orchestrated pregame efficiency surprised me, but I suspected it was a way to get everybody into an organized ritual, so they would be mentally ready for what was to come.

With thirteen minutes and thirty seconds left prior to kickoff, the players gathered around their specialty coaches. Each group was made up of six to fifteen players, and they listened intensely to what their position coach had to say. Some players offered gentle head-nodding, others quiet encouragement, and one or two were overly exuberant. They might shout, "Yeah, let's get this going. Let's do this!" With eight minutes and thirty seconds left, they combined into larger groups made up of the offensive, defensive, and special teams. Each group was again reviewing the expected plays and game plan they had studied all week.

I could not help but watch the quiet efficiency of quarterback Kirk Cousins. Even before this first game of the season, he had impressed me when I was sitting in the upper deck in 2009 and then even more at the 2010 summer practices. Although Cousins was an exceptional athletic talent, what was most impressive according to the sportswriters were his insights, intellect, and, above all, his leadership. With seven minutes and thirty seconds before the team was to go out to start the game, there was a short break. Cousins walked over and told me matter-of-factly, "Dr. Kaufman, good to have a neurologist within the team. We all appreciate you trying to make the game a little safer. That means a lot to us."

With that five-second exchange, even before he walked away, I realized that he was articulate and intelligent, a born leader. He had somehow figured out my name, did not address me as "Doc," but rather Doctor, and understood my ultimate role on the team. In that instant, I became a Kirk Cousins fan for life.

He showed respect even toward a newbie like me. I began to more fully understand the sportswriters' statements that his true gift was leadership, and that it would eventually allow him to earn millions of dollars playing in the NFL. Those five seconds also drew me even closer to considering that one day I might actual be acknowledged as a true part of the team.

The pregame count down continued. At five minutes and thirty seconds prior to kickoff, the locker-room lights went down and a two-minute video was shown of spectacular plays that the current team's starters had made in the previous year. Finally, Coach

Dantonio quietly called the players together for this first game of the 2010 season. They all listened intently to what he described. In a methodical, measured tone, he pointed out what was needed to defeat today's opponent, Western Michigan University. I was impressed with how riveted the players were in listening to their head coach. No more chatter, no more useless movements. They were laser-focused as he spoke, each looking him right in the eye.

I also found myself listening carefully to what Coach D. had to say. Here was a man who had essentially single-handedly changed the culture within this team. It was palpable and appreciated campuswide. He was considered a true Spartan who genuinely cared about our university and the community. In the four years since he had taken over as head football coach at MSU, the team had risen from doormat to title contender, according to the newspapers. What allowed Coach D. to do that? What was it about him that was so special that he was accomplishing what so many thought impossible? It was unclear to me and to so many of us on campus. I guessed that enigma would have to wait a bit longer than one pregame speech to figure out.

# CHAPTER FOUR

# *"We Need You in the Locker Room!"*

**W**e all left the locker room and headed straight up the hundred-foot tunnel leading to the field. Sally Nogle came over to me again, this time to actually walk alongside me and talk. I knew of her already; I distinctly remembered being in the stands for my first Spartan football game back in 1984. Laurie and I had watched a woman athletic trainer run onto the field to help an injured football player. We said nothing at the time but later noted that was an amazing thing. It struck both of us that she must be exceptional to be able to lead the way in this area of inclusion. By 2010, women in athletic training were more widely accepted, but Sally had been there at the start of it all. I had followed her career enough over the years to realize Sally was nationally relevant; on our campus, she was an iconic figure. Now I was actually walking alongside her as we got closer to the front of the tunnel.

Sally let me know, in her maternal voice, that it was going to be okay. She said, "Dave, I know you are all excited and everything, but try not to do anything foolish. Stick close to me and just do your best when we need you. Also, listen to what Jeff says, but maybe not the way he says it. That will also help you a lot."

The Western Michigan Broncos were already on the field when the MSU players, coaches, and medical staff were lined up in the tunnel precisely two minutes before the scheduled kickoff time. After some final words from Coach D., who stood at the front of the tunnel, everyone started hollering as they got ready to run onto the field. As was the opening-day tradition, all the other MSU varsity athletes from every sport lined up on the field to make a "human tunnel" for the football team members to run through. The weather was beautiful—bright and sunny at seventy degrees.

As the team poured out of the tunnel, I found myself running as fast as I possibly could trying to keep up with Sally and not be trampled by the players around us. Just as I exited, I heard the wall of noise and it made me freeze up just a little. A wall of noise is the best way I can explain the sudden roar of seventy-five thousand people, all on their feet, yelling and cheering. It was unique and inspiring. I had goose bumps everywhere, never having realized how loud it actually got at ground level.

In the upper deck it is all nice and polite, almost quiet. Yet down here on the field it was painfully loud. We all ran toward the west sideline and lined up for the national anthem. Across the way, dressed in brown and yellow uniforms, were the Broncos, complete with their support people and medical team. In all my years as a fan, I'd never really noticed the folks who were not playing or coaching, but today it was easy to see them and understand they, too, were there to contribute, big time.

The game was close and hard-fought throughout the first quarter as both teams traded touchdowns. I just followed Sally everywhere while doing my best to not get in the way. I immediately noticed how fast players were moving and how hard they hit each other. Hearing a loud *thwack* when two players collided, followed by a muffled groan was not something you hear in the upper deck. I could literally feel the body blows land when a linebacker smacked full speed into a running back.

From the upper deck, it all looks so sterile and painless. Down low, I found the hand-to-hand combat playing out ten feet in front of me to be gruesome and yet strangely inspiring. Those first fifteen minutes were an incredible, once-in-a-lifetime experience as I literally got lost watching the action. I did take care to watch the players and not the ball. I realized any one of these nineteen- or twenty-something-year-olds could cause major damage if they ran out of bounds and into an unsuspecting neurologist.

Somewhere in the middle of the first half, an MSU player, Josh Rouse, number forty-four, dove over a pile to attempt a tackle on a punt return by Western Michigan. He landed headfirst with a *whoomph* on the ground and seemed slightly dazed as he struggled to get to one knee. He eventually made it to his feet, and, although his movements were slower than I would have expected, I didn't give it much more thought. When he started to walk over to the sideline, from where I was watching, he looked fine. I went back to watching the action, as it was breathtaking from up close.

I became absorbed with the fans on one side of the stadium chanting "Go Green," followed a second later by "Go White" from the other side. After a great play, the marching band chimed in with short bursts of the fight song. The players moved so quickly; on the field in front of me, on the sidelines behind me, and on both sides of me, they were in a constant, blurry swirl of action. I was amazed at the up-tempo chaos I was in the middle of. I somehow lost sight of Sally and could not locate Jeff. Everybody and everything seemed to be constantly on the move. Players were hustling on and off the field. Eleven people might run off and another eleven back on the field. It was all moving so incredibly fast.

I was guilty of watching it all, dealing with the crowd noise, and trying to figure out who was doing what. I was totally distracted and not doing what I should have been at that moment. My job was simply to notice players coming off the field and determine if they were injured. But I just didn't have the presence of mind to do that. I forgot my role. I did notice that Rouse had walked off the field a bit slowly, and I wondered whether he might have a significant injury, but, crucially, I did not act on my instincts. It was all occurring too fast; it was so loud and confusing, and in any case it was too crowded to do anything other than avoid getting walloped by a player running out of bounds.

In retrospect, I simply did not do the job Jeff Monroe was trying to get me in shape to do. The reality is that on that play when Jeff Rouse walked slowly off the field, I saw something that, as a brain doctor, I knew was suspicious, but I called no one's attention to it. Things were just happening too fast for me to follow. Fortunately, Sally and Jeff did do their job.

Caught up in watching football at ground level from ten feet away, I did not realize both athletic trainers and Dr. Randy Pearson were examining Rouse at the training table set up at the fifty-yard line and behind the bench. Instead, I was wandering around at the fifteen yard line trying to understand what was happening. All I saw were those chaotic streams of huge people moving up and down the sidelines, some going on and others coming off the field.

The sideline training table is where potentially seriously injured players are taken to be evaluated. I simply didn't remember the routine in the swirl of action, even though Jeff had explained it a dozen times during summer practices. I should have met the medical team and Josh Rouse at that table to help evaluate his status. Sadly, I was a no-show. About fifteen minutes later, I was still wandering around trying to understand it all when Jeff found me. He tapped me on the shoulder and said, "It's go time, Dave."

I said, "Jeff what do you mean, 'go time'?"

Jeff responded with his sterile, clinical voice. No southern drawl, no insider jokes, and definitely no friendly abuse. He was all business. I had never seen him that way before. He said, "We have a potential major injury, and you are needed in the locker room. Rouse seems hurt. We need you."

As I moved down the sidelines toward the north end zone and into the tunnel that led down to the Spartan dressing room, I got that nervous feeling again.

"Jeff, what is this all about? Why are we going to the locker room?"

"Dave, be quiet now. Our player was hurt on that punt. I don't think it was a concussion. I am not sure, but he isn't right. Josh has a really stiff neck. His muscles are sort of rigid and he's in the locker room. We just got X-rays and I need you to look at them and then examine him."

Josh Rouse had appeared in thirty-five career games and was a three-year letter winner. In 2008, as a junior, he played in all thirteen games at fullback, almost always as a blocking back. I vividly recalled seeing his first-ever pass reception for a touchdown at the Michigan game that year in Ann Arbor in front of a 110,000 Wolverines. I had been in the stands with Laurie and my son, Matt. We had not beaten U of M since the beginning of the decade. Worse, after a close loss to the Wolverines in 2007, Mike Hart, a Michigan football player, called MSU the University of Michigan's "little brother" out of disrespect on national TV.

The 2008 MSU–Michigan game was the first opportunity for the Spartans to seek revenge after that often-played sound bite. Michigan State was ahead of Michigan 28–21 and driving for the decisive score with less than four minutes remaining in the game. I watched as Josh Rouse sneaked out of the backfield on third down and into the left side of the end zone.

"He's open!" I shouted from the very top of the north end zone stands to no one in particular. "Hoyer, throw him the damn ball!"

On that play, Coach Dantonio had called for Rouse to fake a block and come out of the backfield to catch a pass. Rouse had never caught a ball as a Spartan, and the element of surprise seemed to catch everyone off guard. I noticed no Wolverine even bothered covering him. It was a brilliant maneuver. He was totally ignored until he was standing in the end zone, alone. MSU's quarterback spotted him and threw a perfect pass for a seven-yard score to give MSU the lead 35–21 with three minutes and six seconds left.

The Wolverine fans let out a collective groan because there was not enough time for Michigan to catch up.

"I think we just won!" I yelled with my hands over my head, giving the universal signal for a touchdown. That gave MSU an insurmountable, fourteen-point lead and allowed the Spartans to beat U of M for the first time in seven years. As we were seated among fifteen hundred MSU football fans in the designated visitors' area, my son thought it apropos to lead our small section with a distinctive cheer to serenade the Michigan crowd that was now headed for the exits.

"Little Sisters!" *clap* . . . *clap* . . . *clap* "Little Sisters!" *clap* . . . *clap* . . . *clap* "Little Sisters!" *clap* . . . *clap* . . . *clap* went the chant as people in our small MSU cheering section rose to their feet.

The next year, 2009, was supposed to be Rouse's breakout year. Sadly, he missed that entire season because of a freak injury to his big toe. He could have graduated but chose to stay in school, take an injury "redshirt" year, and successfully get NCAA permission to play one final season, in 2010. This past summer, the sportswriters described what it actually took for him to work his way back from that toe injury. Josh was quoted as saying it was his "military school background and his well-grounded faith" that helped him through the darkest moments of his rehabilitation.

I suspect it was both those traits—but also his undying passion for Spartan football. The newspaper articles talked about how hard he had to work to find his way back to the field, quoting him as saying his motivation was "to help my brothers." Reading his story inspired me, but now I was about to meet him up close, as a neurologist.

Jeff was very quiet as we walked into the locker room. He was not his usual self when he looked around and then asked his student athletic trainers, "Where is Rouse?"

It was clear to me something bad had happened. Just behind me and now coming into the locker room was Dr. Mike Shingles along with Sally Nogle. Sally was stone-faced and silent. I felt her tension. As we all looked around for Rouse, I saw those three anti-quated X-ray boxes, now with the radiology images of a cervical spine. I gasped when I looked at them but did not say a word. It was eerily quiet. I heard water running in the background but ignored who could have been taking a shower. The X-rays had caught my attention and from a distance they didn't seem right. "Where did you move Rouse?" came Jeff's question, this time with urgency.

I walked closer to look at the X-rays more carefully. A portion of the second cervical vertebra bone seemed just a bit off-center. The odontoid process or "dens" is a small protuberance of the C2 bone that juts up toward the skull and fits into the first cervical vertebrae. That bony extension is just in front of the spinal cord and allows for the rotation of the head. This is always pointed straight upward toward the first vertebrae (the atlas) at the top of the spine and located just below the skull and of course the brain.

I felt stupid because I had forgotten my glasses in the car. When I squinted to look things over, the dens did not look aligned appropriately with the other parts of the vertebra. It appeared slightly off-center and pitched forward just a bit, even leaning too close to the spinal cord. I finally concluded the dens was fractured and in a potentially dangerous position. This could be a subtle fracture dislocation, called a "hangman's fracture variant" because that specific bony defect of the dens typically happens during a hanging, usually resulting in sudden death.

I stopped, dropped my head, but then turned and looked at Jeff. I said with just a hint of sarcasm to my mentor, "Monroe, why on earth would you or anyone have X-rays of a hangman's fracture in a football locker room. That is macabre. Why would you do such a thing?"

Jeff was unemotional, clinical, and quietly asked, "Dave, are you sure?"

I responded, "Well, yes, I am sure. It sure looks like it."

Mike Shingles then moved closer for a look and he turned back toward us and said, "Jeff, looks like it." I said nothing further and none of us moved as we all looked at each other for a few seconds. Meanwhile in the background, I again heard that sound of water and a voice softly singing some modern-day slow and sad ballad. Mike turned toward me with a frown. He then asked, "Jeff, what is with this?"

Jeff asked again, "Dave, Mike are you both sure?"

I said, "Yes. That is what this is," and Mike nodded his head *yes*.

Jeff turned and stared at his two postgraduate athletic training students. One responded, "He had a concussion and wanted a shower. So the students took him in there."

Jeff did not raise his voice at all. He tightened his face and said very slowly to his staff, "Go get him in here."

A few seconds later, the singing stopped and all you could hear in that cave of a locker room was the *drip, drip, drip* of a showerhead slowly leaking out the last remains of water. Nobody said a word. Our starting fullback, now dressed in only a towel and soaking wet, walked slowly into the training room. He was guided carefully by two young, athletic training students on either side of him.

As Josh dripped water everywhere as he walked, I noticed he was trim and hard-bodied with thick neck muscles and "washboard" abdominals. His trapezius, the muscle at the back of his neck, was truly impressive, and I had a fleeting thought that those muscles might actually save him if we could somehow get him safely attached to a backboard for a race to the emergency room. He was walking fine, although a bit stiffly and far too slowly toward the training table. I also noticed he held his head perfectly straight, not turning it left or right, nor bending it in any direction.

He inched his way closer to the examining table and moved his hands, but not his head or his eyes. His fingers traced along the table to find the edge as he was trying to sit down. It was clear he was not willing to look down to see it. I suspected all of this was because of terrifying neck pain or worse, maybe weakness that intensified whenever he moved his neck. Jeff turned to Mike and me and said, "He is getting worse by the minute."

Maybe because of my gray hair, Rouse thought I was someone important. He looked right at me, moving only his eyes but not his neck and asked, "Doc, is it bad?"

Sally put her hand on his shoulder and said, "This is Dr. David Kaufman. He is our lead neurologist here at Michigan State and takes care of brains and spinal cords. That guy over there is Dr. Michael Shingles. You remember him because he is one of our orthopedic surgeons. He helped take care of you and that toe all last season. Josh, take a seat on the table."

Josh moved very carefully, holding his shoulders up high and very close to his ears. His very slow and very deliberate movements almost reminded me of patients I had seen with Parkinson's disease from the hips on up. Josh resisted essentially all unneeded motion in his upper body and always kept his neck totally rigid.

He carefully felt for the table under him with desperate searching movements of his fingers as he eased himself down the three or four inches to the flat surface. His pain was obvious, yet, like so many other football players I had already seen during practice, he did not mention that at all. He seemed intent on enduring the discomfort while asking me quietly, "What's next?"

"Do you mind if I examine you?" I said leaning in.

"No, go ahead, Doc," was Josh's quiet, unhurried response.

I noticed immediately he was still unwilling to turn his head at all. More worrisome, he continued to keep his neck very straight and rigid. Sally looked right at me after feeling his neck muscles and said, "Dave, the muscles in his neck are really stiff."

She thinned her lips and took in a deep breath. I took that as a sign that now even Sally, coolest of the cool, was worried.

I did my standard neurologic exam to be sure what we were actually dealing with. I documented Rouse had good cognition. He could wiggle his fingers and toes normally and his eye movements both saccadic (quick) and pursuit (slow) were fine. The other cranial nerves were normal except for a little issue with protruding his tongue. He was breathing fine, and his color was good.

He was able to move his arms and legs normally, but not his neck. He never moved that. He would only turn his eyes when he looked at me. The neck muscles on inspection were not supple or even life-like. Rather, they were rock hard and in clear spasm. He had all the signs of a severe neck injury, except this one could well be a true high spine fracture and a potential killer.

He said once again, "Doc, what is it?"

Not wishing to expose the entire situation to him at that vulnerable moment, I simply said, "Son, we need to get an MRI on your neck, and you're done for today."

Unexpectedly, he burst into tears. "I worked so hard to get back after my toe last year. I gave it everything, Doc. Now you are telling me I am done?"

I tried to recover the situation quickly so he did not move any more than he should. Yet now he was uncontrollably sobbing. So, I quickly added, "Josh, you are done, but maybe only for today. That's all. Today." I repeated slowly. "We need to figure out what else is going on quickly and then decide. But you are done for today."

Rouse immediately regained his poise, yet his words and his voice revealed his true feelings.

"Doc, I worked so hard to get back so I could play. I wanted to be with my brothers in my last year." He stopped, took a deep breath, and then added, "I'm sorry, I got a little emotional there."

At that moment, I finally recognized the depth of despair I had caused. He cared little about the pain, nor did he have any clue about his dance with death going on at that very moment. He was inconsolable simply because I told him he was about to miss the rest of one game, but maybe I had a look on my face that implied something longer. That was all that was on his mind, that and the effort to rejoin his brothers on the football field.

On my side of the conversation, I ignored all of this and thought only about the tug-of-war his spinal cord was having with gravity. I stabilized his head with one hand around his neck just under his chin and the other holding the back of his neck until we could summon the EMTs into the locker room. He let me know the pain was far less after I did that.

Sally gently touched her student-athlete's shoulder and said in her most reassuring voice, "Look Josh, right now we need to get you to the hospital and make sure we have everything we need to get you healthy. We are a little concerned about your neck. We just want to be sure you are okay. Understood?"

I knew right then that Sally Nogle was the best team mother any athlete could possibly have. She displayed the uncanny ability to remove Josh Rouse's fear almost immediately. She stabilized his emotion, allowing us to do what needed to be done.

EMT Karl Dahlke had been assigned to Spartan Stadium and football games for years because of his remarkable record of achievement in acute situations. He was rushed into the room by Jeff Monroe and Randy Pearson. Karl, known for his calm and professional demeanor, was his usual poised self and immediately understood the situation.

Karl said what we all understood. Turning to Josh, Karl was calm as he told him, "We need to put you in this collar. Then we are all going to slide this board under you as we lay you flat on the table."

Josh said he understood. Karl and Mike Shingles placed the hard cervical collar carefully around our fullback's neck, properly stabilizing it as I slowly slid my hands away from Rouse. Then all of us gently lowered him onto the table, where Karl had put the trauma board. Randy, Jeff, and Mike closed the attached black stabilizer cushions around his head and neck for further protection. Sally belted him onto the board, and we all carried him to the ambulance. Off he went to Sparrow Hospital's emergency room, three miles away.

I see now that I could have blown it with that sports neurology situation. Saying—even implying—an elite athlete's playing days were over was the wrong way to stabilize the situation. Josh, in a panic, could have turned toward me to ask questions, bent over to start to cry, or whatever, thereby endangering his life.

But I got lucky. Rouse instead listened to the calming voice of Sally and he stayed solid. Jeff, Randy, and Mike, all veterans, knew exactly what to do. I was simply the guy who decided maybe he should put his hands around the player's neck in a position to reduce the weight of his head tugging on his broken high cervical spine. What a moment for a sports neurologist covering his first game.

It was not until right then that I fully realized that these football players train themselves to be disciplined, to be utterly controlled, and to endure pain without complaint. I also became aware how important every single game was to them. Telling a football player he is going to miss even one game was like amputating something very special from his life. Implying his playing days were over prior to stabilizing a severely fractured neck was just plain dumb.

I learned the way I needed to deliver news as a sports neurologist was very different from how I worked as a clinical neurologist. I immediately knew I would never forget that athlete's face or his reaction when I blurted out, "You are done," even if I was trying to say "for the day." I also knew I would never forget his resolve and courage after only a ten-second talk with Sally.

As the ambulance sped off to Sparrow Hospital's Level I trauma center, I called the ER and the neurosurgeon on call, Chris Abood. I let Chris know what was coming as we all hustled back out onto the playing field. Jeff turned to me and said, "Nice job, Dave. I thought, everything considered, you did fine."

That was the first and only time Jeff Monroe ever said anything nice to me related to my work as a sports neurologist. Yet that was okay with me. At the moment of truth for that one student-athlete, and at my first game, I diagnosed and helped stabilize one of Jeff's players. As the rest of the game went on, Jeff became even tougher on me. He told me where to stand, how to respond to situations, and how to look over the field on each play and at each player.

I accepted that tutoring gladly, as I understood he was doing his best to teach me. My journey from academic neurologist to real sports neurologist had begun and in the most dramatic way imaginable. In a strange way, I also now fully understood and embraced it was no longer *his* boys that we were all trying to shield. They were *mine* now, too.

The Sparrow ER was ready for our fullback. Dr Abood made sure Josh's neck was indeed fully stabilized, then guided the trauma team and our injured player into the MRI unit within seconds of arrival. The MRI confirmed the diagnosis of a fracture dislocation of the dens. Ranji Samaraweera, from neuroradiology, sent the key image to my smartphone, as I was the "referring physician."

I showed the image to both Sally and Jeff; it demonstrated the clearly fractured dens leaning ever so closely to Josh's spinal cord. We shook our heads. I took a deep breath and started looking—far more carefully this time —toward the field for the next injured player.

At the end of the third period, Jeff said, "Kaufman, Coach D. wants to see that MRI scan."

"What?" I responded.

Jeff gave me his famous look of disdain, shook his head, and spoke each word very slowly as if he were talking to a five-year-old. "I . . . need . . . to . . . bring . . . Coach . . . Dantonio . . . over . . . to . . . you. He . . . wants . . . to . . . see . . . what . . . Josh . . . is . . . up . . . against." Then he added, without the sarcasm, "Dave, Coach D. actually is a rare one. He is a coach that deeply cares about his players. Get used to that. Just talk to Coach and tell him what is going on and what will happen to Josh. Just talk to him."

"You want me to talk to Coach D.?" I asked, feeling the butterflies rising up in my abdomen once again.

# CHAPTER FIVE

# Head Coach Mark Dantonio: The Alchemist

**A**s Mark Dantonio started to walk toward me, I began to fight that queasy feeling. I did have a lot going on today. Over the last three hours, I'd been at my first game on the field with seventy-five thousand screaming people in attendance. The game was on national TV. I had just diagnosed Coach D.'s starting fullback with a high cervical fractured spine, helped stabilize him, and sent him off for a ninety-mile-an-hour, three-mile trip to the ER. I had a lovely chat with the Sparrow Hospital chair of neurosurgery, who let me know if Rouse survived the intubation, the anesthesia, and the actual operation on his spine, he should live, and there was a "nice" chance there would only be limited neurologic deficits.

Now the MSU head football coach wanted to talk to me, and during a game. Oh, my. It was otherwise just a fine, leisurely late summer's day of practicing neurology outdoors in the midst of football sideline mayhem. That seat in the upper deck, where I would have been sitting with friends and family, quietly sharing a soda with Laurie, began to look better and better as this day went on.

As Coach D. got closer, I suddenly remembered I had talked with him once before, four years earlier. In 2007, when he first arrived on campus, we were introduced by MSU Trustee Faylene Owen. Faylene had invited Laurie, and me, along with fifteen or so people, to her home for a Sunday brunch. The group represented all sorts of university types: there were MSU vice presidents, East Lansing political figures, a few faculty, and some donors, all there to meet Coach D. I had no clue why the passionate and wonderful Faylene Owen wanted Laurie and me there, although we were delighted to go.

I had about three minutes with Coach D. in Faylene's kitchen. I found him alone, drinking a glass of orange juice while he was leaning against the refrigerator. I walked over to try and exchange a few words. He saw me coming and looked away, maybe to ward me off, I thought. I guessed he was thinking, "Oh no, not another one asking me if we will win."

Immediately, I sensed he was either shy or, more likely, an over-worked celebrity sending the signal that he did not feel like talking. Naturally, I was too boneheaded to pick up on either possibility. In that brief kitchen interaction exchange, Coach D. was anything but casual. He was an inch or two shorter than me, trim and athletic, with jet black hair. I noted a soulful, introspective, calm, spiritual way about him.

He was understated but articulate, credible, and poised. We talked about what the change was like coming to Lansing, what it was like to be a football coach and other small talk. I came away from that three-minute discussion deeply impressed by the aura of logic and respectability he projected without any pretense or effort. That interaction surprised me.

Back in the day when writing sports for the *Daily Cardinal*, virtually all the coaches I interviewed at Wisconsin were provocative personalities. Most were raconteurs, loud and fun-loving, sometimes to a fault. Coach D. was, in a word, dignified. I had never seen that quality before in a college coach. His aura, strong sense of fair play, and spirituality were all new territory in a football coach from my view. Frankly, the net effect was intimidating but impressive.

I also remembered I'd had a brief exchange with him, for maybe two minutes, in a hospital corridor during the past year. He was visiting Father John "Jake" Foglio after Father Jake had been in a serious car accident. Many of us were summoned to care for the aging priest, and he pulled through. I literally bumped into Coach D. as I was leaving Father Jake's room. He inquired about Father Jake's prognosis in a delicate and hopeful way, as one might ask about one's own father.

Yet now, Coach D. was walking over to talk with me again. This time, his face was maybe that of a man worried about his own son. That look reminded me of the change I had to undergo: from academic neurologist to sports neurologist and at warp speed. I did my best to be neither nervous nor excited. I silently took three deep breaths and I found my voice.

Jeff Monroe introduced me as a "visiting sports neurologist" to the coach. Mark Dantonio responded, "I know who Dr. Kaufman is, Jeff." That stunned me a bit. I quickly found the MRI images on my smartphone, showed Coach D. the fracture, and explained, "This confirms Josh has a fractured dens, slipping toward his spinal cord, a so-called hangman's fracture variant."

I then calmly revealed that Josh would no doubt need a delicate surgery in the next day or so. If the operation were successful, he would survive; he might even be fine physically. Coach Dantonio looked at me and then the MRI image, and his eyes and face said it all; *How could something this terrible happen to one of my boys?*

He seemed horrified as I pointed out the clearly dislocated dens on the MRI view. The dislocation was about two millimeters away from the high spinal cord. MRI technology has the ability to show spinal cord, bone, and tissue. It is so much more powerful than plain X-rays. I could now clearly see the intimate relationship of the frac-tured dens to the spinal cord. So could Coach D., along with the doctors and athletic trainers staring over my shoulder.

Coach D. looked at me again. I sensed through his quiet poise that he was deeply shaken and worried for his student-athlete. He looked back down at the images one more time, turned to me, then Jeff, and quietly said, "You never know when you are playing your last game—in football, or in life."

Dantonio shook his head and looked down at the ground for just a second. Then he gathered himself, took a shallow breath, and silently turned to walk back to his team. His players were already huddling, getting ready for the fourth quarter. We all understood Coach Dantonio owed his attention to them at this moment, not to the drama playing out at Sparrow Hospital's ER three miles away.

I understood right then why Coach Dantonio had already gained the respect of even the most cynical MSU faculty who had spent any length of time with him. Even though that interaction between the coach and me was silent except for those few words, with a simple facial gesture and the look of sorrow on his face, Coach D. had won my loyalty forever. Sportswriters had reported that Mark Dantonio had a calm, omnipresent stoicism, a quiet dignity. Yet they also let the public know he possessed a warrior's passion deep inside, displayed only during exceptional moments. Jeff Monroe reiterated all that. "Dave, Coach D. has passion," Jeff once told me just after Dantonio arrived at MSU in 2007. "Mark knows how to inspire his players when it's called for."

Coach found that passion whenever anything related to MSU was insulted. This was especially true when that disrespect was at the hands of a diminutive running back from the University of Michigan, Mike Hart. That Wolverine was foolish enough to refer to MSU as U of M's "little brother" live on TV, right after the Spartans suffered a last-second loss to Michigan on November 3, 2007. MSU had not beaten U of M in football since 1999. In Dantonio's first game against the Wolverines as head coach, Michigan State was ahead 24–21 deep into the fourth quarter. Then Michigan's Mario Manningham caught a Chad Henne 31-yard touchdown pass with two minutes and twenty-eight second left in the fourth quarter, resulting in a the 28–24 win for Michigan, and breaking MSU's heart.

In the live interview after the game, Mike Hart stated, "I was just laughing. I thought it was funny. They [the Spartans] got excited. It's good. Sometimes you get your little brother excited when you're playing basketball and let him get the lead. Then you just come back and take it back."

I remember seeing that exchange on TV. A sportswriter followed up with "Mike, are you saying MSU is Michigan's 'little brother'?" Hart's response was an immediate "Yep," followed quickly by a snicker and then a sarcastic laugh. It was that televised laugh that enraged everyone associated with Spartan Nation, including veteran tenured faculty at MSU. The clip was played throughout the state of Michigan, over and over, for months.

The following week, during Coach D.'s scheduled media inter-action, he was asked about Hart's comment. Dantonio responded with his warrior ethos hidden just beneath the surface. "I find a lot of the things they [U of M] do amusing," he answered. "They need to check themselves sometimes. Let's just remember, pride comes before the fall. . . . They want to mock us. I'm telling them, it's not over. They want to print that crap all over their locker room. It's not over and it'll never be over here. It's just starting. . . . I'm very proud of our football team, and I'm very proud of the way our football team handled themselves after the game as well. You don't have to disre-spect people. If they want to make a mockery of it, so be it. Their time will come."

Spartan Nation and MSU as a whole learned right then that Coach D. possessed an uncanny talent: He was an alchemist. He had the ability to create inspiration from disrespect. When he said, "It's not over, and it'll never be over here. It's just starting," Dantonio, football coach or not, found a way to speak for an entire university tired of being in the University of Michigan's shadow. He not only lifted his team but, in my view as an MSU faculty member, he lifted an entire university and all of Spartan Nation.

One week after that statement from Dantonio, MSU Trustee Faylene Owen invited me to give a warm-up talk at a fundraiser for my university at a friend's "house" in southeast Michigan. It was, in reality, the biggest mansion I was ever in. Down in the four-thousand-square-foot, magnificently appointed "basement," three hundred of Faylene's dearest Detroit-area friends and MSU alumni were packed in among thirty different tables having dinner. Mark Hollis had just been named athletic director and was the main attraction. Faylene thought it would be a good fund-raising event to introduce Hollis to her friends. In a fitting piece of timing, this event was taking place just a few days after Coach D.'s now nationally televised retort about the U of M "little brother" statement.

At the head table during the dinner, Hollis leaned over and confided in me, "You know, Professor Kaufman, I thought Coach Dantonio may have gone a little overboard with his statement criticizing that student-athlete from U of M after our game with them last week. What do you think? I mean, as a tenured MSU professor and all?

I realized I was sitting next to Coach D.'s boss, but I spoke from the heart even without knowing much about Coach D. I said, "May I speak candidly, Mr. Hollis?"

After he nodded yes, I added, "Frankly, it was the greatest, most accurate public statement I had ever seen an MSU staff or faculty give about the reality of U of M arrogance. May I be so bold as to suggest during your talk tonight with these well-placed MSU alumni, you ask them that question and see their response?"

He gave me a quick look of confusion, followed by one of amusement, like he had thought of an idea. Soon after, I was introduced by Faylene and gave a ten-minute talk about what it was like to be an MSU faculty member and how important alumni donations were to our university. I was nice and dull, living up to my professional role as a very stodgy medical school professor.

Then Hollis stood up and said, "Spartans! I am taking a poll. How many people here thought Coach Dantonio was doing the right thing when he criticized Mike Hart for calling MSU the University of Michigan's 'little brother'? Please let me know with a show of hands."

A few hands went up, and then some polite applause started. Soon after, table after table of these very affluent MSU alumni started clapping and then rose to their feet. At first, the clapping was nice and polite, like my spiel. But after everybody was standing, they looked around, and suddenly the applause turned thunderous, followed by big-time cheering. Hollis eventually was able to quiet the crowd. He turned toward me and Faylene and said, to the crowd's amusement, "Well, there you go, Professor Kaufman. We have our answer."

Dantonio became a master at using any Wolverine disrespect to drive his players forward. Coach D. never shied away from controversy with the University of Michigan. He embraced it. By doing so, he lit a fire that was palpable across the MSU campus. Best of all, Dantonio did it with a bravado that assured people there was indeed a powerful warrior inside the heart of a man who also had unquestioned dignity. A rare combination indeed.

I do not think I am overstating the importance of Coach D.'s response to Mike Hart's comment in 2007. The vibe around campus was immediate and visceral. It was repeated by faculty in both private and public conversations on our MSU campus. Usually, it went something like, "What exactly does U of M—or anyone, for that matter—have that MSU does not? We can do the same things as anyone else, including U of M, and maybe better."

There is no doubt the University of Michigan is one of the country's great universities. The problem was that the Wolverines were so very arrogant about their prominence and, frankly, everything else. Even their beloved fight song talks about being the "leaders and the best." Michigan State was, from its inception, a land grant institution, devoted to the common people and the farmers of Michigan, not the aristocrats or elitists. I suspect a natural rivalry sprang up based on that divide.

As MSU began to rise, the University of Michigan always seemed to do its best to hold it back, whether through competition for state appropriations, or, eventually MSU's attempts to gain entrance into the Big Ten after World War II. The disrespect MSU felt whenever it interacted with the University of Michigan only became worse over the next six decades.

It was obvious from his first days as head football coach at MSU that Coach Dantonio understood the divide between the two universities was far more than just an athletic rivalry. In reality, it reflected overall institutional disrespect. He somehow found a way to use that reality to challenge his team to rise up and overtake the University of Michigan's decades-long superiority in football. But he did so much more.

It always struck me as remarkable that one person, especially an athletic coach, could actually inspire an entire university. I sensed it was Mark Dantonio's ability to make a person believe not only in him, but, more importantly, believe in themselves. Slowly but surely, Dantonio's public persona and attitude of finding "some type of way" to win began to turn the state of Michigan from Wolverine blue to Spartan green.

A key, of course, was Coach D.'s ability to back up that very public display of indignation toward the Wolverines. The next year, 2008, was the first time MSU started to win games against its archrival in almost a decade. Ironically, Josh Rouse's first-ever touchdown sealed that victory at Ann Arbor in 2008. Then the Spartans beat the Wolverines again in 2009, and, although Dantonio was only 22–17 overall at MSU, the recruits started to come to East Lansing, big time.

So what was it about Dantonio that allowed him to inspire not only football players but faculty and staff at MSU? Perhaps the answer was best explained by my own wife. She was once asked at a faculty cocktail party to explain why Coach D. was so inspirational. Laurie simply stated, "He simply has all the attributes that people admire. He is inspiring, has ideals, determination, and morals."

Yet I knew he also had street credibility, especially when things got tough. He made the people around him believe "ideas and ideals" still counted. Publicly, Coach D. made it clear, his true loves were his family and God, followed by teaching his players to have success and well-being in life, not just sports. He was extremely loyal to his coaching staff and those associated with his team. It was also obvious he loved football, and Michigan State University.

Coach D's public persona also had an amazing effect: people trusted him even if they never met him. That was maybe his greatest gift. Whatever the formula, the alchemy was unique and palpable. People in the Lansing community, along with MSU's fifty thousand students, thirteen thousand staff and faculty, plus 640,000 living alumni and their families were to grow closer and closer to him as the years progressed.

# CHAPTER SIX

## *A Love Lost*

The game with Western Michigan ended in a runaway victory for MSU. The crowd was unaware of the events surrounding the effort to save Josh's life. That struggle was still occurring three miles away at Sparrow Hospital. Sparrow is a remarkably sophisticated institution, especially considering it is situated in the middle of a city of only one hundred thousand people. It is a Level I trauma unit, meaning it was instantly ready for any sort of mayhem that could be brought in from the highway, a knife-versus-gun fight, or a football field.

Sparrow has an outstanding emergency room, where I had taken my own family many times. My own son, Matt, had developed a brain bleed right after he was born. He spent weeks in the neonatal intensive care unit until he fully recovered. Ever since then I had deep respect for the physicians, nurses, staff, and administrators who had been recruited to Sparrow to care for the people of Lansing. I took great pride in working among them.

It had 24–7–365 neurology in house. I was the chair of neurology there as well as at MSU and had helped build neurology from the ground up over the past three decades. Sparrow radiology had multiple MRI units and, perhaps most important for our fullback, five outstanding neurosurgeons accessible at all times. I personally had deep respect for each neurosurgeon. Once Josh was stabilized at the stadium, I thought our guy would be okay if he could be transported successfully without losing his airway. He could then be fully stabilized in the ER.

Karl Dahlke and his EMT crew did their job and got Josh to the ER safely. Josh was moved into trauma bay 1 without incident. Sparrow nurses and the MSU trauma surgeons were waiting for him. They did not have to remove much clothing; once the blanket was removed, they realized he was still dressed only in that towel from the locker-room shower at Spartan stadium.

They rechecked his Miami J collar to be sure it was secure. His vital signs were taken efficiently by the triage nurse and two large-bore IVs were started, as is standard in any trauma case. This was the same protocol they would have gone through for any person with a high cervical neck fracture, whether the result of an automobile accident or a football injury. He had been stabilized successfully.

Blood was drawn and a head-to-toe CT scan was done, according to the standard trauma-team routine. The key was organizing and then doing that urgent MRI scan to document the nature of the fracture. It was concluded without much fuss. Josh's vitals remained stable, neurologically he was intact, and his airway was maintained.

An unstable C2 neck fracture with dislocation was documented, but no other spinal cord injury appeared on the MRI. He was taken back to the calm sterility of trauma bay 1 to await therapeutic decisions. Rouse was comfortable and now in a place about as far away as he could get from that cave that served as MSU's stadium locker room.

The triage decision was to maintain stabilization but to wait until the next morning, a Sunday, for neurosurgery to attempt to screw the dens back in place. That judgment would allow for the "first team" neurosurgery scrub nurses and technicians to adapt to an unscheduled, early-Sunday-morning surgery more easily after a good night's sleep. It would also allow time for two well-rested neurosurgeons to plan and then execute the delicate surgery. Transport carefully moved Josh to the Neuro-ICU located on the sixth floor of the Newman tower.

Jeff had already called Josh's father, who was in town for the game. The elder Rouse came to the hospital immediately to be with his son. He talked with the neurosurgeons about the situation, but now he wanted input from Jeff to be sure he was doing the right thing for Josh. This request surprised me a bit until I realized Jeff was always seen as the on-field "dad" for so many of these student-athletes. After the game was over, Jeff asked me to come with him to talk with Mr. Rouse, and I agreed.

I just had spoken at length with Dr. Chris Abood, the neuro-surgeon who would be responsible for planning and executing a successful operation. I had known Chris since he graduated from Notre Dame in 1987 and became a brilliant medical student at MSU. After his extensive postgraduate training, he chose to come back to his beloved hometown of Lansing to help his community. The two of us had shared many patients over many years, and I had complete confidence in him.

I realized Josh had been stabilized and the neurosurgeons now had the time needed to adapt and calculate the best surgical approach. Typically in this situation there would be an entry wound through the anterior neck. A key would be to avoid the vital arteries and other structures there to get to the fractured verte-brae. The only issue of course was given the fractured dens location near the cervical spine, the possibility of complete paralysis or even death was a potential complication. Chris took all the time needed to assure me that screwing the dens back into place with just a little innovation in the surgical approach was a feasible procedure from his view.

I asked Chris if he was confident he could get it done. Chris calmly said, "Dave, it is doable with only minimal adaption after the entrance wound is placed. It will then be straightforward, as long as there are no anesthesia or blood pressure issues. If we avoid that, he should get an excellent result, and your player should be able to overcome this mishap and go on with his life.

After hanging up the phone with Chris, I felt quite secure. I had a relationship with Chris in which we spoke very plainly with each other. I felt for the first time that, with a little luck, Josh might actu-ally be okay. Jeff and I then met with Mr. Rouse in the Neuro-ICU conference room. I knew that room very well; I had spoken to many spouses, children, and their friends about both the good and the very bad things that can occur in a Neuro-ICU.

Mr. Rouse was the spitting image of his son. He was forthright and direct: "Dr. Kaufman, I have a fixed wing aircraft to fly my son to Phoenix, to Barrow Neurologic Institute. There is a neurosurgeon there that I have a good relationship with, and he is prepared to accept the transfer."

Jeff looked at me to say something. I was as direct as I could be with a man worried sick about his son.

"Mr. Rouse, I have no doubt you have the funds, connections, and the will to do that for your son. I know you are afraid Josh will become paralyzed or worse during the surgery. I have had a very sick son myself once admitted to this hospital. I know, at the moment of truth like this, you need to be sure he will get the very best. I personally think we have that available for him here.

"We can and we will put him back on a stretcher, move him into an elevator, transfer him down to the ground, get him to an ambulance and then transport him over the roads to the airport if that is what you want. Following that he will have to go through a takeoff, a five-hour plane ride, and then a landing followed by transport to another hospital over city streets in Phoenix with a bunch of cars. Sir, whatever advantage they might theoretically have over there in Phoenix, it is my judgement that is outweighed by the risk of that sort of prolonged transport."

He looked at me and asked, "How can you be so sure your neuro-surgeons can do this for my boy?"

I thought a bit and then said, "I imagine you also have played sports, Mr. Rouse."

He said," Yes, I have."

"Well, sir, in a locker room, when you have a teammate you've known for a long time and you trust, and that person tells you he can get something done, and he has never let you down before, you tend to trust that teammate. Does that make sense?"

Mr. Rouse said, "Go on, Dr. Kaufman."

"Well, it is my strong belief that is what we have in this situation here. My medical teammates are straightforward people. They know what they can do and what they have issues with. They have assured me they have confidence they will get this done. I also believe moving your son is risky and, worst case, might border on reckless, from my view. If you need to do it, we understand, and will do our best to make it as safe as we know how."

Mr. Rouse said nothing for a long time. He looked at me and then at Jeff and then back at me. He responded, "No. That isn't needed, Dr. Kaufman. I heard what I needed to hear. When are your guys going to do the surgery, and where can I stay this evening?"

I got home very late that night. Laurie, who had been sitting in the upper deck of the stadium with many family friends, was of course completely unaware of the chaos and the near-death experience I had helped stabilize and triage my first day as the Spartans' embedded team neurologist. As I walked through the door, in her usual upbeat way, she asked, "Well, Dave, how did your first game down on the field go? Anything interesting to talk about?"

I collected myself and choked out "memorable," as I sat down and started to cry.

The next day Dr. Chris Abood met again with Josh Rouse and his dad. Father Jake also made an appearance, to help settle the fullback and his dad down just a bit. Then Josh was taken away to the operating room. While waiting the four agonizing hours for Josh to make it out of surgery, I had an epiphany. I suddenly realized MSU football did not need me as a fan when I was on the field. In that context I was of no value to them. Instead, I had to work as hard as I knew how to be a competent sports neurologist when I was among them. Only then would I be of any value to this team.

A few minutes after noon, word came down that Josh was out of surgery, talking and moving all four extremities perfectly. That gifted neurosurgeon, on a Sunday morning, well-rested, and with his A-team of surgical nurses and technicians in place, pinned that C2 fractured dens back into place, simple as could be. That stabilized Josh's high cervical spine, thereby ending the emergency, and assuring all of us that Josh would live a normal life.

The next morning, young Josh was sitting up. By lunch, he got to his feet and, with the Miami J collar in place, walked around the Neuro-ICU. The coaches and players had already been to see him by the time Jeff and I walked in with Father Jake. Josh did not dwell on the reality that his playing days were over. He understood that fact without asking. It seemed like Josh had already begun to overcome his life-threatening experience and did not ask "why me?" He only asked for more specific details about the Spartan win over Western Michigan. He smiled broadly when we went over the short replay clips, which very conveniently happened to be on TV.

As the conversation went on, it was apparent Josh would be able to cope with the reality that he had played his last football game. We talked about how life takes different twists and turns, and he wondered out loud if coaching or maybe business might be fulfilling. Never once did he ask how close that broken piece of dens had come to destroying his spinal cord and ending his life. Nor did any of us feel it necessary to share that specific detail with him. When the talking was over, he decided to watch Monday Night Football and munched on some popcorn I had liberated from the hospital's cafeteria.

By the following Saturday, despite the near on-field calamity seven days before, the team traveled to Detroit, normal as could be, to play the Florida Atlantic Owls at Ford Field. There I witnessed my first concussion occur live since that Fundamentals of Football incident from four decades before. I took careful note of how the MSU player was handled by the sports medicine team. The player was attended to on the field by Jeff and Sally and helped to the side-line. Coaching made the position change smoothly as soon as Sally whispered something to Coach D.

On the way off the field Jeff made eye contact with his physicians as the signal he needed us. To me it appeared the issue was clearly a concussion, also called a mild traumatic brain injury (mTBI), based on the way the player had a significant imbalance when he tried to walk by himself. The player was taken to the training table and was attended to by lead team physician Randy Pearson. Within a few seconds, it was obvious that indeed an mTBI had occurred. Dr. Pearson let the athletic trainers know the player was disqualified from further competition that day.

I had taught my medical students over the years that a mild traumatic brain injury was a disruption in the brain's normal physiology due to a force imparted to the central nervous system. Loss of consciousness occurs in only 9 percent of cases. In the other 91 percent there is an abnormality in memory, cognition, speed of thought, balance, eye movements, weakness in the extremities, incoordination, or similar neurologic dysfunction.

Postevent, patients sometimes had symptoms surprisingly similar to those of a migraine. In addition to the usual headache, people could have major problems with bright lights (photophobia) and loud sounds (phonophobia). After an mTBI, a patient who used the word "dizzy" often seemed to have a prolonged course of recovery. However, every concussion was different, just as every patient was different.

Having suffered more than one concussion myself, I also taught my medical students mTBI symptoms could be unpredictable based on "my own personal experience." I suffered my worst mTBI while I was playing goalie on Lake Lansing without a helmet. I fell on the ice trying to prevent my ten-year-old son, Matt, from scoring a goal. I was actually knocked out, and, as I came to, I was very confused. It was the way you might feel if you were hungover the morning after a very serious New Year's Eve party. Everything moved very slowly. My thinking was way off, as was my balance. I noted a really bad headache. I was nauseated and nearly vomited as part of the entire ordeal.

Then, after about twenty minutes, I abruptly came back to full consciousness. I was absolutely normal again, as if a light switch had turned on. Although my headache remained, the confusion was totally gone. It was one of the most unusual things I had ever experienced.

In 85–90 percent of mTBI, patients appear to get relief from most major symptoms in anywhere from a few minutes to several hours. Yet I had also cared for patients after auto accidents where symptoms went on for a week or far longer. These "postconcussion syndrome" issues were very troubling, as patients reported horrible symptoms. Even worse, they complained that no one seemed to believe their symptoms even existed because they looked so "normal."

What worried me, as I thought about it more, was that on the football field I was not going to have the luxury of being able to perform an intricate neurologic examination behind closed doors, in the quiet and sterility of my MSU medical offices. I was going to have to see and examine these patients in real time and in front of seventy-five thousand screaming people. As I let that thought sink in, I began to appreciate what it meant that Randy Pearson had done this routinely for the last twenty years and did not allow that reality to bother him one bit.

As I finished watching the Spartans clobber the Owls 30–17, I began to think more and more about mTBI and how I might help my MSU football team with this issue. When I got home that evening, I realized I had to lose my love for college football and become more of a detached brain doctor. I started reading the sports neurology literature with a renewed sense of urgency. Even though I was now intimately aware neck injuries could occur, I knew my main job would center on diagnosing occult concussions and treating postconcussion syndrome. I would also have to quickly learn about mTBI's two evil cousins—second impact syndrome and chronic traumatic encephalopathy (CTE), which was swirling in a growing controversy—if I wanted to be of value to my university's student-athletes.

# CHAPTER SEVEN

# *The Loyal Sons of Notre Dame: A Last Request?*

Traditionally, the athletic trainers, team physicians and players who have been injured hold a training room session the Sunday after a game from eleven in the morning to one in the afternoon. This was the time to analyze who was injured, how it happened, the treatments they needed, and if they would be ready to practice and play the next week. It soon became obvious that Sunday training room event was among the most important duties we had. After a relatively easy win over the Florida Atlantic team, the level of activity was fairly light. There were no major injuries and not a lot of issues to be concerned about.

That suddenly changed when my good friend and orthopedic surgeon Mark Kirkland called me from his home in Iowa. I was instantly transported back, to the time when we were young, and he and his brother Brian (a University of Notre Dame graduate) and I were all in medical school together.

"Hey, Mark! Big man! You be sounding good! Except, for a second, it's almost like you were going to use your surgeon's voice. That always worried me. What up?"

Mark said nothing for what seemed like an eternity. Then he somehow choked out in a whisper, "Dave, I need you and Laurie to know: Brian is probably dying."

I nearly laughed and said, "Mark. Mark, stop. Don't joke like that. Don't ever joke like that. What are you talking about?"

"Dave, Brian has survived a bone marrow transplant at the Cleveland Clinic to try and cure his leukemia. They actually allowed him out of the hospital a few months ago. He never really told anyone but me and Joseph about the cancer until a few weeks ago. He's been awfully sick. He is trying hard to pull through. Brian doesn't want anyone to know. They just got him to his feet the past few weeks."

Mark continued, "He was talking about funeral arrangements, writing a will, and crap like that. I told him flat-out to find something to look forward to rather than talk about stuff like that. Brian then said, 'Okay. I understand. But Mark, help me figure out how to get to one more Notre Dame football game?'

"Dave, whenever I called him these past few weeks, that was all he talked about. His spouse Joseph and I tried to get seats for them in South Bend, but they told us there was no way someone that sick can be safe in a crowd at Notre Dame."

I was crushed after hearing all of this. "Mark, does Brian have any shot at recovery?" I asked.

"Sure, Dave. A guy as tough as Brian always has a shot," came the unconvincing reply from his brother. "I was thinking maybe you and Laurie with Joseph, could come up with a plan to get him to one more Irish football game. They want to try for it in East Lansing, at the game coming up this Saturday. With you and Laurie being professors and all, we wondered if you could come up with some sort of isolated seats, maybe even in a section where he could be safe from the crowd?"

Choking back tears, Mark asked, "Dave, can you try?"

Mark's words trailed away many times as he spoke, and he had to stop talking to compose himself. He wondered whether I would have the will to try. Would I have the will to help Brian fulfill maybe his last wish of me, namely one more Notre Dame football game? Would I consider helping my lifelong friend, who had helped countless thousands of people in his role as an emergency medicine physician?

I simply said, "Mark, I'm on it."

That is the way it is with people who have had an intense shared experience, be it medical school or, I suspect, playing a collision sport. The more intense the experience, the closer the bond. When asked for a favor, you have to deliver. Unfortunately, when I hung up the phone, I began to think, "Uh-oh. What kind of shot would a guy like me actually have to find protected seating for something as important as a night game with Notre Dame?"

I worked up the courage to walk over and talk to Sally Nogle while she was providing a treatment to one of our linemen's injured shoulders. I told Sally the whole story. She heard me go on and on about Brian. I told her how he helped me through medical school, the trip we took to Notre Dame to see "Touchdown Jesus" and the Grotto.

I talked about his visit with me to Madison, Wisconsin, to see the *Daily Cardinal* offices, Lake Mendota, State Street, and all the rest. I finally told Sally about Brian's leukemia and his very iffy survival chances after his bone marrow transplant. I told her every single detail. It took a half an hour and she listened without saying a word.

Then Sally flashed that soft, gentle smile only a mom can provide and said, "This won't be easy, Dave. You need to get to associate athletic director Jim Pignataro early tomorrow and explain the whole story. Everything. Jim will understand. Remind him you are now one of our sports medicine team members. Dave, we are talking Notre Dame at night during a season we are going to win a lot. It'll be tough. Just do your best."

With that, I hung my head. When she saw this, Sally gently added: "Dave, I understand. It may or may not be his dying wish. We get requests like this more than you realize. Every story from an alum that is in bad shape and just wants to see one more game . . . well, it just warms your heart."

With that, it finally hit me once more how special football is to so many people, even those facing what Brian Kirkland was up against. Sally added, "It gives all of us such respect for the way college football is such an important part of our society."

She explained the rules for such a request and what I needed to emphasize when I got an audience with the associate AD. Sally then advised, "Really, you only have one shot. But you can do this. I know you."

I actually believed her. The next day, I found my way to Jim Pignataro's remarkably small office in the ancient Jennison Field House. After we shook hands, I sat down and just blurted out, "Mr. Pignataro, I need two tickets in a special isolated section for Notre Dame."

He just stared at me and did not blink for a very long time. His mouth hung open just a bit and I saw his knuckles get red and then white as he gripped the edge of his desk. I took a deep breath and finally added, "Mr. Pignataro, I am so sorry to ask, but I need help for a Notre Dame alum that wants to fulfill maybe his last wish. They tell me he is dying from leukemia."

At that, Jim Pignataro's face softened. He stopped gripping the edge of his desk and he slowly nodded his head, implying he now understood a little better. I told him the whole story. Then he leaned forward and said, "Dr. Kaufman, I get it. Potentially, his dying wish of you."

Any game with Notre Dame was always a landmark, wherever and whomever they played, but especially at night in front of a national TV audience. Athletically, the Irish remained an independent, while every other team of any note belonged to a conference. Notre Dame had a stand-alone TV deal with NBC, so the Irish did not, in theory, need to share any media attention or revenue with anyone.

Notre Dame also got a very special deal with the eleven-member board of managers for the College Football Championship Subdivision. There was one member for each of the ten major conferences. (For example, a huge conference like the Big Ten is represented by one executive.) The eleventh member of that committee was there to represent only one team, the Irish. This unique allowance was for a program that actually had not won a major New Year's Bowl game for the fifteen years from 1995 to 2010.

Still, "Irish football" is more than just football. The team represents a truly outstanding institution with a remarkable national following. I think Lou Holtz, the last Notre Dame coach to win a national championship, in 1988, said it best when he pointed out, "For those who know Notre Dame, no explanation's necessary. For those who don't, no explanation will suffice."

I guess over the years I became one of those who believed that Notre Dame is indeed special. The school's academic requirements are exceptional, as are the vast majority of their students, faculty, staff, and alumni. They have also earned the gratitude of the old guard at MSU. Notre Dame helped the Spartans when they were trying to get into the Big Ten after the Second World War. The University of Chicago dropped football in 1939 and officially left the Big Ten in 1946. After the war there was a mad dash by other universities to join. However, a special relationship had developed between Michigan State and Notre Dame that helped MSU win that race.

Back then, MSU was officially called the Michigan State College of Agriculture or MSC. The "Aggies," as they were known, were trying hard to get national visibility. Acceptance into the Big Ten, an elite academic and athletic conference, would clearly signal that MSC had "arrived" on the national scene.

Sadly, MSC was being blocked by relentless lobbying from the University of Michigan. Typically, U of M referred to its in-state rival as "Moo U," a degrading term implying Michigan State was "just" an ag school and nothing more. They argued MSC should never be allowed among the elite universities in the Big Ten. People in East Lansing understood changing that perception was paramount. The issue was: how to do it, and how fast?

During the 1940s, the MSC president was John Hannah, and he was convinced winning football games could get Michigan State some of the national recognition needed to get into the Big Ten. Hannah signed the innovative Clarence "Biggy" Munn as his football coach in 1947. He was aware the NCAA had begun discussions about the possibility of allowing scholarships to student-athletes despite the protests of some major universities like the University of Michigan.

Munn and Hannah realized the promise of providing scholarships to cover college costs could lure top players to MSC. This innovation worked, and many top athletes gravitated toward East Lansing during those pivotal years in Michigan State's attempt to join the Big Ten Conference.

The University of Michigan denounced these scholarships as a "thinly veiled payment to amateur players," according to old news clippings. However, MSC's athletic-scholarship program was a landmark advance for student-athletes and soon became the national norm. MSC was among the first to do it, which allowed outstanding players to be recruited.

Father John J. Cavanaugh, then president of Notre Dame, appointed Father Theodore Hesburgh as his heir apparent after the war. In the 1940s, President Hannah and Father Ted developed a fondness for each other. They talked about MSC's dream of joining the Big Ten, and they agreed it had the research activity needed to qualify. However, the "Moo U" whispering campaign by the Wolverines hurt the Spartans badly.

Hannah realized football's popularity might get the national visibility needed to get over the top. He and Father Hesburgh agreed back in 1943 that, starting in 1948, Notre Dame would play MSU in football. On October 9, 1948, the Irish won that first game 26–7, but MSU's success in engaging with Notre Dame was soon parlayed into national relevance.

Despite the active protest of the University of Michigan's president Alexander Ruthven, MSC was indeed admitted to the Big Ten in 1949. Alumni money poured in to help expand the faculty, the GI Bill brought in students, and the university expanded dramatically during the postwar years.

By 1950, under the governance of the NCAA, colleges were allowed to provide scholarships as a way to compensate prospective student-athletes. As head coach at MSC from 1947 to 1953, Munn had a remarkable 54–9–2 record, including his two undefeated teams in 1951 and 1952. He was the American Football Coaches Association's

Coach of the Year in 1952, the same year the team won their first of six national championships over a fifteen-year period.

Hugh "Duffy" Daugherty was handed the coaching job in 1954 after Biggie Munn became athletic director. Daugherty and Munn doubled down on the idea of athletic scholarships. By 1964 the college became Michigan State University. Coach Daugherty went out of his way to recruit Black student-athletes from the segregated south. That was significant because no one else in the Big Ten was doing that on a consistent basis.

David Squires, in The Undefeated, (a website that covers sports and race), wrote: "The catalyst for true integration of college football began with the success of Michigan State's 1965 and 1966 national championship teams, which featured 20 Black players."

That article went on to reveal that many of these twenty were not allowed to play for their home universities, like Alabama, Texas, or Mississippi. The group included stars like Bubba Smith, Gene Washington, and George Webster. Duffy Daugherty brought them all to MSU, which provided opportunity in college football for athletes of all ethnic backgrounds. It appears that altered the direction not only of MSU, but, ultimately, of all college football.

As a sportswriter in the late 1960s and early 1970s at the University of Wisconsin, I was aware of the important advance Michigan State created at a remarkable moment in America's evolving cultural consciousness. Up until the early and mid-1960s, very few Big Ten schools had Black student-athletes on their rosters.

I once had a conversation about this with Father Jake during one of our road trips. He said, "You know, Dave, even though MSU led the way in initiating these opportunities, we are hardly ever acknowledged for accomplishing it. I never understood that."

When I asked the priest about why it is MSU never reminds the world about that, he said "Dave, you have been around MSU long enough to know that is not the way we do things here." Then Father Jake added with a smile, "To brag about something like that is just not our style. You and I belong to a university that wants to be elite without being elitist."

Notre Dame's long-term success along with MSU's rise to football prominence led to the famous November 19, 1966, "Game of the Century" in East Lansing. Both were undefeated and ranked first and second. The ABC broadcast had more than 33 million viewers, implying it was one of the highest watched television events of all time. The game ended in a 10–10 tie, a fitting ending for two schools that admired each other then—and that continue to do so.

My deep admiration for Notre Dame had been cemented well before the 2010 night game I was desperately trying to get Brian Kirkland into safely. I had met many Notre Dame graduates along the way, including Chris Abood, the neurosurgeon who saved Josh Rouse's life. Then there was my sports editor at the *Daily Cardinal*, Jim Lefebvre. He was what I call a born-again Notre Dame fan. Jim and his wife Joanne's two daughters went to Notre Dame and played in the Irish Marching Band. Jim eventually took on a prominent role as executive director of the Knute Rockne Society. Although both Chris and Jim have exceptional Notre Dame stories, the best example of true Irish football loyalty, of course, still belonged to Brian Kirkland.

Brian was among the brightest of us all in medical school. I met him during my first day at the Philadelphia College of Osteopathic Medicine in 1974. He was a devoted Notre Dame football fan and a proud Irish alum to his very core. His brother, Mark, had played fullback for Villanova as an undergrad, and he was also in our same med-school class.

Laurie, the Kirkland brothers, and I all became fast friends. After late afternoon and nighttime study sessions we all drank a lot of beer (except for Laurie) at the Five Points bar in our Philadelphia neighborhood. I shared my knowledge of neuroanatomy and neurophysiology, and in return Brian frightened all of us with creepy tales of horrible infectious bacterial diseases that could kill you nice and slowly, like the tiny "Naegleria fowleri" and "Dracunculus medinensis."

Brian had this impish, elf-like smile that was permanently etched on his face. He was also relentlessly sarcastic to friend and foe alike. Cynical but lovable, he directed his limitless humanity to those who truly needed him during his work as a doctor in the emergency room at Cleveland Clinic.

Brian's best attribute was his football IQ. It was legendary. On January 1, 1978, Brian forced dozens of classmates to his home to watch the national championship game that pitted Notre Dame against top-ranked Texas. The Longhorns were led by Heisman Trophy–winner Earl Campbell, while the Irish had a junior quarterback by the name of Joe Montana.

Throughout the game, I could see Brian actually feel the body blows as he moved and ducked with every running play. He leaped to his feet, triumphant, after every Notre Dame touchdown. His beloved Irish won the Cotton Bowl Classic 38–10. Then he, Mark, Laurie, and I along with dozens of others, celebrated until dawn with one of those legendary medical school parties.

After graduation, the four of us scattered for more training. Brian went to Cleveland Clinic for internal medicine, Mark to Pennsylvania Hospital for Orthopedics, and Laurie and I back to our alma mater at the University of Wisconsin. I did my neurology residency while Laurie started her endocrine fellowships before we both moved on to the Harvard system for more training. All was well with the four of us as we went through time. We frequently talked on the phone and occasionally saw each other at weddings or reunions. Personally and professionally, things were turning out great for each of us. That was until Mark Kirkland called me to let me know his brother was looking death in the eye.

When I left Jim Pignataro's office that Monday, I was the proud possessor of two seats in the "special zone" at Spartan Stadium for the 2010 Notre Dame night game. This "special" stadium section was separated from any sustained exposure to the crowd. That was essential to allow Brian to avoid at least some danger to his newly created immune system. I was on top of the world, feeling victorious, simply because I was holding two tickets to a college football game.

I really didn't understand what I had accomplished until I called Brian that evening. I simply said, "Brian, tell Joseph you are both all set for Saturday's Notre Dame game in East Lansing."

I heard nothing on the other end for a very long time. Then Joseph picked up the phone and said, "Dave, Brian is crying. Is it good news, or do I have to kill someone?"

Joseph (also a Notre Dame alumni) had been inseparable from Brian for two decades. He told me how Brian had been through it, enduring chemotherapy, experimental whole-body radiation, and then a bone marrow transplant. In sporting terms, that regimen was a true "Hail Mary"—a last-ditch effort to rescue someone from death. Brian survived and was only now slowly improving after months of being desperately ill.

Joseph said, "Dave, the thought of one more Notre Dame game actually helped Brian look forward these last few months. It was like a beacon of hope. You're the best. We'll see you Friday."

When Brian struggled through our front door at week's end, Laurie and I gasped. All his hair was gone and he was essentially skin and bones. He flopped down onto our green living room sofa exhausted.

"What are we dealing with?" I asked.

Brian said, "They told me my original blood work showed numerous immatures, you know, 'blast' cells. Acute Lymphoblastic Leukemia, Philadelphia chromosome positive."

Laurie turned to me horrified. "By fall last year, I was hurting badly and I asked for time off from chemo to return to Notre Dame to meet with [Notre Dame's iconic leader] Father Hesburgh. He greeted us warmly, but he knew how badly I was doing. We talked a long time. Eventually, he told me to call on a higher order than just medicine. Then he gave me his blessing and I knew I needed to find things to look forward to as a way to try and survive chemo, radiation, and then the transplant."

Joseph added, "That October evening Brian and I walked around the Notre Dame campus and watched the Fighting Irish Band practice outdoors. We teared up when we heard 'The Victory March' and vowed that it would not be Brian's last time. Then we had to go back to the Cleveland Clinic for whole body radiation and then the bone marrow transplant. It was a tough winter and spring. Next thing I know, we are here."

I understood Brian had looked death right in the eye these past few months and refused to take a backward step. Laurie and I hugged him, and we all helped him up the stairs to get a proper night's sleep. He was so excited about making it to at least one more Norte Dame game. He tried for a smile, nodded his head, maybe too weak to say anything. I hung my head and I teared up.

Then he whispered in an exhausted voice, "Dave, thanks. I really needed something to look forward to keep me going. I know you and Laurie think I'm dying, but this is not my 'Farewell Tour.' It's just my first major venture at the beginning of a long rehabilitation."

I lifted my head up at that and looked at him, much closer this time, and, I must say, I believed him. Before disappearing into the guest room, Brian added, "You know the best thing? We spent yesterday at Notre Dame and finally found Father Hesburgh. He was so pleased I was alive. We shared several stories about life and then he wished us well for our drive up to East Lansing to see this game."

The next morning dawned warm and sunny. Brian's profound weight loss showed up mostly in his face, especially around his eyes. Yet that afternoon at Blondie's Barn, he began to pack away eggs, toast, ham, and bacon. That gave me hope.

"Getting my appetite back, Dave. Pretty soon I will be as fat as you!"

Everyone laughed but me. I feigned chest pain while grabbing a strip of bacon off Brian's plate. It felt so good to see my close friend looking forward rather than thinking about the horror he had just come through.

I thought to myself: Maybe that's one of the things about football's allure. It is an event to look forward to. Ritualistic and tribal, yes. Brutal, no doubt. But it was also enough of a cultural happening to create positive memories, especially of one's youth. It also served as an excellent excuse to bring friends and family together. The game was enough of a spectacle to give people and entire communities something to look forward to. In this case, it had clearly helped Brian get up every morning this past, horrible summer to do the work necessary to live. "Looking forward to something, anything was a key for me," he said.

Looking forward engenders hope, and hope is one of the most valued things a physician can provide. This MSU–Notre Dame spectacular at night—complete with bands and a motivated, sold-out crowd—provided Brian with that elusive sense of hope so needed by someone desperately ill. This was the only medicine I could provide to my lifelong friend, and I was fiercely proud of my university's ability to deliver it.

As Laurie paid the check, Brian whispered, "Dave and Laurie, thanks for all of this. All Joseph and I want is a good game, really. I learned so much about life during this last year. I am just trying for the experience of one more game. We really don't care who wins. We just want it to be close and exciting. Thanks so much."

Driving toward campus in the early evening dusk, none of us said much. I dropped everyone off at the foot of Spartan Stadium, and as I turned to drive to the locker room I saw Joseph and Laurie help Brian struggle to the stadium elevator. On a sultry late summer's night, despite everything, Brian and his Joseph were among the more than seventy-five thousand who would see one more MSU–Notre Dame football game. All I hoped for was a memory-maker for my friend. Fate delivered.

# CHAPTER EIGHT
## *The Honorary Captain*

I ronically, Josh Rouse was back in that same Spartan Stadium locker room for the Notre Dame game two weeks after his near-fatal injury. He was urging his teammates, who had won the first two games of the season, to get ready to face the mighty Fighting Irish. I was amazed at how natural it was for Josh to be walking among his brothers, talking strategy as everyone was getting game ready. Josh's successful surgery had led to a rapid recovery with no neurologic deficits. He would be required to wear that Miami J collar for three more months to allow the C2 bone fracture to fully heal. Other than that—and a surprisingly small scar on his right anterior neck—there was nothing visible to tell the tale of his fight with death.

Rouse was also wearing number 44, his green game-day jersey, as he reminded his teammates how important tonight's game was. He went player to player, whispering a shared secret to one while accepting a fist bump from another. He was methodically moving among them to ease the pregame jitters. Yet, by his very presence, he was inspiring them to play in front of a rare nighttime crowd of seventy-five thousand along with a prime-time TV audience of millions. Every Spartan player had placed a small "44" decal on the back of his helmet in Rouse's honor. Although now "retired," Josh was anointed by his teammates as the team's honorary captain and he was all smiles.

After warm-ups, everyone assembled to get last-minute instructions from Coach D. about the task ahead. The message was brief but clear: win tonight, and the entire nation would be forced to pay attention, after so many years, to Spartan football once again. Everyone understood. The team lined up in the tunnel, quiet at first, as they were all thinking about the task ahead. I noticed a rare smile crossing Jeff's face as he watched Josh work his way through his football brethren to the front of the swarm. As Rouse passed through them, I began to hear them shouting his name as encouragement and appreciation of all he had just gone through to be with them once again. Josh finally made his way to the front and took his place next to Coach Dantonio to lead the team out of the tunnel.

Josh turned around to look at everyone and yelled, "Are you ready?"

The team's return volley was shouts of their own, as they started jumping. Although his playing days were over, Rouse's life as a graduate assistant coach for this team had begun.

I was struck by the paradox of someone so seriously injured, now gladly returning as quickly as he could to the same location that almost cost him his life, simply to be with his teammates. His presence served as a reminder to everyone in that tunnel about what they coveted most: the chance to play just one more game of football. As the Spartans were getting ready to run into the stadium, Mark Dantonio and his now-retired fullback were standing at the tunnel's entrance to the field.

As everyone followed Coach D. and Josh into the night air, they were greeted by that wall of noise from the crowd. I reflected upon Coach Dantonio's words when we talked about Rouse's situation just two weeks prior: "You never know when you are playing your last game."

Josh, hard cervical collar, and all, was still able to trot a few feet out of the tunnel leading his team forward with Coach D. As the Spartans poured onto the field, the crowd rose to its feet to celebrate Josh Rouse and the Spartans.

I teared up as I looked high above the field to the "special zone" seating section and found Brian and Joseph, nice and comfortable at the thirty-yard line. It was a perfect seat: well away from the crowd, covered, safe, and secure. I realized I did not care if I was about to witness a good game—or a close game or even a blowout Irish victory against MSU.

I had fulfilled my duty to provide a longtime friend with the gift of hope created by a simple football game. Then I turned back to watch a twenty-two-year-old student-athlete reclaim his life by slowly jogging back onto the field to assist with the coin toss, fittingly at almost the same spot where he broke his neck only a few weeks before.

I thought I had enough treasured memories from those two pregame observations to last a lifetime. Such surreal events as a near-death experience, ending in triumph two weeks later in that same locker room and on that same field, cannot be truly appreciated from the comfort and distance of the upper deck. Maybe that's a good thing, as I suspect very few could tolerate witnessing such a thing. Who really wants to know a young man came within three or four millimeters of total paralysis or far worse, while playing a sport for free? I realized there must be a spiritual attraction to a sport like football for the people that endure such risk and do it gladly.

I mentioned this realization to Father Jake just prior to the national anthem. Years earlier, well before my on-field involvement with the team, I had come to respect Father Jake for the integrity and insights he provided to medical students as their professor of spirituality. Surely, as football team clergy for so many years, he had seen similar events comparable to what had happened to Josh.

His response was insightful. "Dave, football is totally engrained in the culture of our society. It means so much to so many people. I think it must be deeply woven into the very soul of so many communities nationwide. What Josh Rouse now represents to Michigan State University, his teammates, mid-Michigan, and to you and me is just an example of how special the bond of football can be among a community."

Then he added, with a wry smile, "Besides, we are going to need everyone's help tonight to beat these Irish."

The game was a terrific matchup. Both MSU and Notre Dame had truly outstanding offenses. The teams traded touchdowns back and forth in a hard-fought but remarkably clean game. As we approached the end of the fourth quarter, I was emotionally drained by trying to figure out if the Spartans could keep up with the passing and running attack of the Irish. Somehow at the end of regulation, it was actually tied at 28 apiece. The Spartan defense stiffened during the first overtime, holding the Irish to a field goal, which made it 31–28.

The ball was given to the Spartans at the Irish twenty-five-yard line as required by the overtime rule. If they did not score, MSU would lose. A field goal would send the game into another overtime. A touchdown would bring a Spartan victory to end one of the most memorable days I had ever lived. Sadly for Sparty, the Irish defense held. On third down, Cousins was sacked back at the Notre Dame thirty-one-yard line.

Yet after the play, I was not disappointed or even sad. It would be an impossible field goal try into the wind. I was just happy, realizing Brian and Joseph had seen a fiercely contested Notre Dame–MSU game that went into overtime. *One for the ages*, I thought.

Now it was the sophomore field goal kicker, Dan Conroy, whose moment had come. He would try for a tie to force that second overtime. In this, his first year as a starter, could he actually kick a forty-seven-yard field goal this important? This would be a tough kick at a tough time for anyone, let alone a redshirt sophomore. The week before, he had hit three field goals including a fifty-yarder (albeit indoors) to help MSU beat the overmatched Florida Atlantic team 30–17. But the Notre Dame game was Conroy's first "big game." Would he be tough enough to meet the moment against Notre Dame? Given the stiff wind, it seemed to me an impossible task.

*We are doomed*, I thought. I just hoped the kid didn't fall apart for the rest of the year from embarrassment when he missed it.

Coach D. gathered the field-goal team around him. The holder for field goals was Aaron Bates, a former high-school quarterback, and a cool customer. He had been elected a captain by his teammates, the first punter in MSU football history to ever do that. It was interesting to watch Aaron after the time-out: He showed little emotion. I noticed Conroy had a bemused and quizzical look on this face.

Bates looked at Coach Dantonio one last time. The young athlete raised his right hand above his head and then made it into a fist. I wondered if it was some kind of signal. Then Bates nodded *yes* toward Coach D, as the captain slowly trotted onto the field to hold for Conroy's field goal attempt.

The teams lined up, the ball was snapped, and suddenly Bates rose from his field-goal holder's position with the ball. From my location, I could not tell what he was thinking. Then it dawned on me: It was a fake! Did this winner-take-all gamble have any chance for success? The way everyone was moving, it looked like it was supposed to be a short throw to Le'Veon Bell just across the first down marker in the right flat.

But Bell fell after he collided with two defenders. That allowed the Spartans' tight end, Charlie Gantt, to escape from any coverage in the confusion; he was all alone just a step from the end zone. Bates saw him. Cool and calm, Bates threw a perfect pass to Gantt, who caught it, danced untouched through the end zone, and into Spartan football immortality. Pandemonium!

The play was called "Little Giants" after a 1994 Warner Bros. movie of the same name. That movie depicted little kids using deception and trickery to pull off a victory against their bigger tougher rivals to win the game. When people asked weeks later about the risk that he took on that play, Coach D. told them matter-of-factly, "Dan Conroy was essentially in his first year kicking for us. He would have to try that long kick just at the outside of his range during the earliest days of his college career. I thought, 'Let me take the responsibility for the loss instead of him.' So, we decided to run 'Little Giants.' I guess we were ready."

That decision demonstrated the gentlemanly side of Coach D. If the field goal failed, Conroy could have lost his confidence and never developed his career the way he could have. This way, Conroy was totally shielded from failure by his coach. The play was successfully executed based on lots of preparation, and what seemed to be at the time, luck. Or was it luck? I believe to this day: Coach D. was a unique motivator. Over and over, such trick plays always seemed to work for him and the Spartans. Somehow, he knew the way to instill the will to win in his players, and they always seemed to respond.

# CHAPTER NINE

# *Best Call of the Night*

Coach D.'s fame as an effective risk-taker was assured with "Little Giants". I could not help but think what everyone else thought after seeing that victory. At last, after so many years, we had a very special coach leading talented people forward at a special time. Maybe one more Rose Bowl could occur for MSU in my lifetime!

Mark Dantonio left the field with the joy of a man who had just delivered big time. Later, in the locker room, after Coach D.'s post-game radio show, everyone including me was gone except for Sally and Jeff. Coach D. apparently complained to Jeff about some pain in his mid-sternum, his elbows with some minor stomach discomfort.

As was explained to me later that night, Jeff called Sally. Soon after Coach D. became more uncomfortable and Jeff wasn't really sure what it was. "Maybe indigestion or some mild costochondral pain, from where you were hit on the sidelines during the game?" he asked the coach.

The reply was, "No, Jeff, I don't think so."

Jeff was concerned and stayed with Coach D., while Sally hurried out into the night to find Randy. Randy had left several minutes before, but he fortunately had only made it a few blocks before Sally found him. He had been slowly walking to his car, which was parked, as always, across from the stadium at the Duffy building. After that amazing ending, Randy, like everyone else, was enjoying the electrifying win by accepting, in his words, "more than a few drinks from motivated tailgaters." If Randy hadn't been celebrating, surely, he would have been more than a mile away in his car, snarled in postgame traffic, unable to move anywhere.

Back in the locker room, after yet another bout of "cramps," Coach's wife, Becky, happened to walk in looking for her husband. She was widely regarded on campus as Coach D.'s "unfair advantage." She was wonderful and wise, beautiful, lithe, and warm—but, above all, tough. She was also, by all accounts, the relentless leader of the Dantonio household.

Mark Dantonio, unlike virtually every other big-time college football coach, did not have an agent. Instead, he had Becky to help him think through his most important professional and life decisions. She was also outstanding at protecting her husband, their two teenage daughters, and any member of the extended Spartan football family. That night, after "Little Giants," Becky showed up at exactly at the right moment to help her husband make the best call of the night.

Jeff Monroe and Becky briefly talked about the pain. She immediately insisted an ambulance get her husband to the hospital. I wonder how many men have died talking their wives out of calling for an ambulance, saying, "It's just some gas." Coach D. probably knew it was not going to be worthwhile to argue with Becky. However, he did insist, "No. No ambulance. Let's find another way."

Just then, Randy burst into the locker room with Sally. He took Dantonio's blood pressure and listened to his heartbeat, and another family discussion occurred. I imagine it went something like, "Becky, no ambulance and that's it." I can also imagine Becky Dantonio looking at her husband then at Dr. Pearson to state her case. As legend has it, a compromise was forged. Becky would drive the family car, Coach D. in the front seat next to her, and Randy in the back seat, calling ahead to pave the way. I suspect Randy was also praying he would not need to do CPR as the car went barreling down Michigan Avenue, like a runaway freight train, covering the three miles to Sparrow Hospital in minutes.

Randy Pearson had been with the team for two decades by this time. I had worked with him in the past on the medicine floors at Sparrow. I learned long ago his best quality was his ability to keep things simple no matter the situation and with absolutely no panic. While Becky probably hit ninety miles per hour down Michigan Avenue, Randy must have been on his cell phone, gently persuading the Sparrow triage nurse in his usual calm and cool manner to get the head of the emergency room to drop what they were doing and talk to him. Once alerted by Randy, the ER personnel began to gear up, yet again, for another MSU football figure tempting death. This time, it was not a broken neck in a fullback, but instead the head coach with an apparent evolving heart attack, occurring just after a once-in-a-lifetime finish to an MSU–Notre Dame game.

Now it was up to Sparrow's cardiology team to move into action. Once Coach D. was inside the ER, Becky's suspicion that it was a heart attack was quickly confirmed. Randy's call ahead allowed the invasive cardiac cath team to assemble quickly. Within minutes, Coach D. was in the Sparrow Heart Cath Lab, allowing the on-call cardiologist to thread a catheter into Coach D.'s heart.

I was totally unaware of any of this; we were taking Brian back to our house. In the back of the car, Brian deliriously repeated, "It's the game of a lifetime. I'll never forget it."

Brian was utterly content to drag himself up the stairs of our home and into bed. He was way too exhausted to do anything but be grateful for the opportunity to see his beloved Irish one more time. Later that evening, Laurie, Joseph, and I decided to wait for Jeff with his fiancée and our friend, Joyce DeJong, at her home.

While waiting for Jeff to appear, Joseph told us how this was such a thrill for Brian and him to see such a special game. "Brian and I really did not care who won or lost. I swear. We just wanted one more game to see our beloved Irish and our band. It was one of those events that will always be with us. No matter how long Brian lives, I guarantee you he will talk about this game. It meant the world to him."

He added, "Dave, other than the Irish, Brian and I are now Sparty fans forever. What a coach to call that play! What a team to make it happen! A fake field goal, where they lose the game if it fails! Thanks for somehow finding a way for Brian. It meant so much to him and to me."

Just as Joseph walked over to give Laurie and me a hug, Jeff burst into the house. I recognized that same look of horror on his face he flashed only two weeks before when our fullback almost died.

"Jeff, what is it?" I said.

Jeff told us the story he'd seen unfold in the locker room just an hour before.

"Coach D. was probably having a heart attack," he said. "He must be at Sparrow by now. He was okay when they took off in the car. Randy was with them. Dave, can you find out if he made it to the ER?"

We all looked at each other as I wondered how this could possibly happen now—why to Mark Dantonio, of all people, and why at such a moment of triumph? A special evening shared with lifelong friends just stopped. All we could think about was the scene going on a few miles away in the middle of the Sparrow Heart Cath lab as the cardiology team worked to save a life.

As luck would have it, that was not the end of this college football story. Coach Dantonio's stenotic coronary artery was opened in plenty of time to prevent any true damage or cardiac dysrhythmia, assuring his rescue. A Becky Dantonio handoff to Randy Pearson, followed by a lateral to the ER personnel and then a pass to cardiology saved the Spartan coach. That was by far the most impressive play that happened that night. Only a few people truly understood the real miracle that evening: it was Becky Dantonio who made the best call of the night in Spartan Stadium, when she persuaded her husband, a proud and dignified man, to endure a trip to the ER.

Within hours of his cardiac procedure, Coach D. was his usual self. His "Little Giants" call, which surely will be remembered by generations of Spartans fans, was essentially insignificant compared to the life and death decision made by him, his wife, Jeff and Sally, and Dr. Randy Pearson. That event and the one involving Josh Rouse two weeks before had a deeply profound effect on me.

I had been allowed to observe the very heavy, behind-the-scenes price that coaches, student-athletes, and their families sometimes had to pay to participate in this sport of college football. The emotional cost was simply astronomical. Although horrified by the life and death events in that old locker room within weeks of my joining the football medical team, I also felt a sense of sincere honor that I was allowed to see any of this up close, and, in my own way, help whenever I could. Yet I also found myself wondering long and hard about why people played and coached such a brutal sport.

# CHAPTER TEN

## *Truth or Consequences*

Postcatheterization, Coach D. did very well. However, he had to remain in the hospital and missed the next game, another victory, against Northern Colorado. He then reluctantly agreed to sit in the MSU press box on October 2, 2010, as the Spartans beat the eleventh-ranked Wisconsin Badgers 34–24 to open the Big Ten season. MSU was now 5-0.

I had the strangest experience during that game against the Badgers: Will Gholston, a crowd favorite, looked me in the eye and I thought may have not told me the entire truth about a potential concussion. After Will had made a particularly difficult tackle, he had lain flat on his back on the field for what seemed like an eternity. He eventually got up and walked over to the sidelines to be checked.

After the usual triage, Randy asked for my opinion. I did an extensive evaluation, especially focused on cognition and the vestibular ocular system, in addition to all the other elements of a proper neurologic examination. Will seemed fine, but why would he lie on the ground so long after the play? After thinking about that, I looked back up at Will and wondered.

On cue, after my neurologic examination was done, Jeff came over and said, "Dave, do you think Will is in or out? Defense is going to go back out after Bates's punt."

I looked up at Gholston and asked, "Big man, are you good? Why did you lie on the ground so long after that play?"

With a sly look, half grin, half smile, he responded, "Doc, I must have needed to take a play off. I am doin' fine. I just came off to catch my wind, that's all."

He looked down at me and saw my frown.

"Will, are you sure?" I said again, looking up at him.

He spoke with added intensity, sprinkled with just a little anger. "Look, Doc, I am good. And I ain't got no damn concussion! I am good!"

"Dave, I don't like it. His personality's off," Jeff said after hearing the exchange. Gholston had always been among the nicest and most respectful young men I had ever been around.

I laughed and told Jeff, "Personality? He looks okay and he says he is okay. Let him go back out to play."

I was too naïve at that stage of my career as a sports neurologist to realize an elite student-athlete might do absolutely anything, even not telling the truth, to be allowed to play even one more down of football. So Will Gholston went back onto the field and, to me, he played great. But Jeff said, "Dave, he is playing slower than usual. His personality is off just a little bit. I get that everyone's exam, even yours, was normal, but I know my guys. Let's check him carefully after the game."

I agreed, then thought about it. *His personality is off just a little.* I wondered, *where is that listed in the Sports Concussion Assessment Tool (SCAT) testing protocol?*

After the victory, there was the usual raucous locker room celebration. The 5-0 Spartans counted out the thirty-four points scored, followed by the MSU fight song. Then the speakers blasted out the latest hip-hop with the players singing and dancing to celebrate a big win, Will Gholston included. Seeing that, and after a thorough postgame reexamination, I felt much better about the call I made on Big Will.

The next day was a typical postgame Sunday morning. All players that thought they were injured had to report to the treatment room to be rechecked to be certain they were okay. Most were there just to celebrate being 5-0 for the first time in anyone's memory and eat the habit-forming, extra special chicken wings Dr. Mike Shingles always supplied after a victory as "motivation." Dozens of able-bodied players flooded the treatment room playing and laughing with each other and trying to get to the chicken wings.

Frankly, it seemed like an old-time college party that had extended into Sunday morning, and I couldn't have been happier. There I was, elbowing players out of the way to get my fair share of those wings, gobbling them down while talking with players and the assembled doctors and athletic trainers. All that, plus we had the Michigan Wolverines up next week. The place was buzzing with excitement, and I was euphoric.

Then Will Gholston walked in, wearing enormously large, almost clown-sized, Spartan Green–framed sunglass with totally dark lenses, so you couldn't see his eyes. Everyone looked up, and we all broke out into laughter as soon as we saw those huge sunglasses on the giant defensive end. Will popped a right hand up to his forehead to comically salute the crowd in recognition of their laughter. He was also wearing an enormously bright smile that seemed to take over his whole face. Everyone went back to talking, laughing, and eating, as did I, until Will walked over to Jeff and me.

He whispered, "Jeff, I wasn't sure anything was actually wrong during the game. I did not realize I had a concussion. Now I got a headache, a bad one. I vomited last night. These lights are killing me. Everything is slowed down and the noise in here is horrible. I must have got a concussion. I know it now."

Hearing this, I was sick. I said, "Will! Big Man! You were supposed to tell me when I checked you out during the game. I am there to protect you. I am supposed to be your shield. Why didn't you let me know? Why didn't you tell me?"

He responded slower than usual. "Doc, I just did not know. I didn't realize it, but, man . . . I wasn't this way during the game. No way. I didn't think anything was actually wrong during the game. It's on me. I wanted to be playin' in there with my people. I was good enough to play. I'll be good in a few days, but I am hurting bad now."

I finally noticed the absence of his typical upbeat personality. During the game that maybe was the clue he had indeed suffered an mTBI. I realized I did not diagnose an mTBI because I did not understand the importance of personality change as a subtle clue someone might have a concussion.

That event taught me several important lessons: Number one, concussion symptoms can actually emerge the day after a game. Next, I did not realize an mTBI can change personality, and that might be the only clue. Lastly, Will taught me players sometimes will underestimate what is wrong with them or, in the extreme, sometimes not tell the truth, if it allows them to play. They gladly accept the consequences unless you are there to prevent it. I promised myself I would look as hard as I knew how at every player every time even if they denied they had any symptoms of a concussion.

I had so much to learn. Jeff took me into a room and sat me down. "Dave," he said gently, "Like any rookie on my team—or any team—you're going to miss a few things. Maybe this was one of them. Let's just learn from it. You're coming along fine. Faster than I expected. Just keep learning. Start going to more practices to learn more about your players, their personality, and, frankly, their intellect. This team needs you. Besides, we got those blue bellies coming up next week. Now is no time to get moody on me. Just keep doin' your best."

With those parental remarks, Jeff rescued me from the valley of despair, and I thanked him. He left and I sat alone for a few minutes thinking about all of this. Eventually, I realized the time to feel sorry for myself was over. I got up, took a deep breath, and rejoined my medical staff team members.

That is how a six-foot seven-inch surefire future NFL player taught me one of the basics about concussion. That is also why a proper sports neurologist should get to know the personality of the players by going to practices.

Jeff Kovan, head of the sports medicine fellowship at MSU, then came over to also help settle me down. Kovan said, "Dave, everyone thinks you are doing fine. Let me talk to you about a few things, Big Will just did not know if he may have had an issue. It happens. As long as he and you learn from it. But you also have to realize some other player may look you in the eye and not be truthful about a concussion, just to play one more down. Two more things, Dave. If a player ever tells you they do not want to go back into the game, that is when you need to be really worried about something very serious has occurred to that student-athlete. When that happens the player needs to leave the game. Also, players will pretend to actually have a concussion during practice to get out of work. Learn that reality also."

After about an hour, I was doing better. As always, the medical staff gathered at the end of the Sunday training room to determine who could practice, who might be able to play, and who had to sit for the next game. That would then be reported by Jeff and Sally to Coach D. By the end of training room, the mood of the players and all of us had changed from supercharged excitement back down to the cold hard business in front of us. The "twenty-four-hour rule" was in effect. You have twenty-four hours to be euphoric after a big win or devastated after a loss. Then it is over. You have to be disciplined to tell yourself they "all count one" and then move on to prepare for the next opponent. In keeping with that rule, everyone began to put the big Wisconsin win behind them and gear up for rivalry game next week against the Wolverines.

On my ride home that Sunday, I thought about the reality that there were so many things I did not fully understand as a rookie side-line sports neurologist. Way up in the upper deck or on TV, to any sports fan, football is such a splendid game. No fuss. No bleeding. No concussions. No pain. No career-ending knee injuries. No crying moms or disheartened sons after an injury. What I had learned within these first two months was that football is not a contact sport. It is a truly brutal, collision sport played by violent but very disciplined young men.

Off the field, almost all of the players were wonderful people, poised and controlled, up until game time. Then they would "let the lion out of the cage," as Coach D. would say. Even when sitting in the upper deck, I understood violence was part of it all. I wasn't a total idiot. I just did not understand how bad the violence could be until I came down for that closer look. Up close, I realized football is absolutely organized but chaotic mayhem at first blush. The pounding these student-athletes take is horrific.

On every play, twenty-two men smash into each other to impose their will on the other. Almost everyone ends up on the ground every play, many times after running full speed (ten to twenty miles an hour) into each other. It seemed like World War I trench warfare fought with only bare hands, shoulders, and the helmet as weapons. After all, having at least three or four doctors plus two athletic trainers (along with ten athletic training students) on each sideline at every game might be a giveaway that people are going to get hurt.

As I turned onto my street by Lake Lansing and parked the car in the garage, I thought about how concussions and orthopedic injuries occur so frequently in football. Folks viewing from the upper deck cannot truly understand how violent an event they are experiencing. I realized Randy was right when he told me on my very first day, "Dave, we need to teach players to recognize a concussion in themselves and other players. We also need to make them understand the consequences of not revealing if they have had an mTBI."

I realized Randy was absolutely right. A simple tutorial by him at the beginning of every season would be a great way to make the game a little safer. It could be the key to help prevent "second impact syndrome," a dangerous event when a second concussion occurs before the first one has had a chance to heal. As I walked into the house and sat down in my study, I became more determined than ever to become even less of a sports fan and more of a proper sports neurologist.

# CHAPTER ELEVEN

# *Concussion's Two Wicked Cousins: Second Impact Syndrome (SIS) and Chronic Traumatic Encephalopathy (CTE)*

**A**s a rookie on the football medical team, I eventually understood my true value was to help the players avoid the very rare occurrence of second impact syndrome (SIS). The literature suggested SIS was caused by severe brain swelling from a second mTBI occurring soon after the first. This syndrome had been reported mostly in younger individuals, particularly those under the age of twenty. Theoretically, the cause was loss of autoregulation (bodily control) of blood vessels in an injured brain. That could eventually cause uncontrollable swelling of brain tissue.

The key was to avoid such an event altogether because, although rare, SIS can be fatal. Successful treatment requires rapid diagnosis and control of brain swelling. Doctors often resort to intubation, hyperventilation, and osmotic agents because heroic neurosurgery, such as a hemi-craniotomy (removal of half the skull), has usually proven ineffective. Outcome, as we say, was usually quite poor.

I was on the field to serve as another pair of eyes, to make sure no one had a "silent" mTBI. I was also the last line of arbitration in cases when it was unclear whether a concussion had actually occurred. Sally, Randy, Jeff, Mike, and I had many discussions about our protocols to prevent such a calamity. We all realized what was at stake.

When I first joined the sports medicine team, our group also had many debates related to chronic traumatic encephalopathy. We all understood that repeated subconcussive hits to the head could cause an alteration of normal brain physiology. That also meant CTE could theoretically occur in any person who played any contact sport, especially collision sports like football, hockey, and rugby.

The five of us were aware of Dr. Bennet Omalu's 2002 autopsy study on Mike Webster and his subsequent publication. I saw Webster play center for the Badgers in the early 1970s when I was at Wisconsin. "Iron Mike" was drafted into the NFL and played 245 games from 1974 to 1990 (all but two years with the Pittsburgh Steelers). He was enshrined in the Hall of Fame in 1997 and died in Pittsburgh of a heart attack in 2002 at age fifty. Prior to his death, he had well-documented issues with reduced intellect, depression, mood swings, and, eventually, drug abuse.

By coincidence, Omalu happened to be the pathologist on duty, so he was called to perform Webster's autopsy. Like anyone in Pittsburgh who followed sports, Omalu was aware of Webster's cognitive and emotional problems. Using his own funding to do brain-tissue analysis, Omalu observed large amounts of abnormal tau protein and other unexpected changes and his findings were published.[2]

[2] Bennet I. Omalu, et al. "Chronic Traumatic Encephalopathy in a National Football League Player," Neurosurgery 57, no. 1 (July 2005): 128–134. https://doi.org/10.1227/01.neu.0000163407.92769.ed.

He described clinical and pathological features similar to a disease described back in 1928, when a physician named Harrison Martland observed the same thing in boxers. Martland's autopsies were done on (nonhelmeted) prizefighters who had developed speech issues, slower movements, and confusion. They were called "punch drunk." Martland's eventually coined the term "dementia pugilistica," meaning abnormal brain function (dementia) in boxers (pugilistica). His article, "Punch Drunk," is commonly referenced in the traumatic brain injury literature.

More than seven decades after Martland's seminal discovery, Omalu's case report on Mike Webster made an important new contribution: doctors had assumed that the risk of dementia pugilistica was confined to players with no head protection. Omalu noted a similar disease in an athlete who played a helmeted sport, namely football. The term "chronic traumatic encephalopathy" was used by Omalu to describe the condition he found in Webster. Shockingly, he demonstrated that such brain abnormality could indeed occur in a sport other than boxing, even when athletes used head protection.

By the time I joined the MSU football medical team, CTE was all over the media. Initially, we wondered if it was just typical journalism hype; however, as a neurologist, I was soon convinced by the medical literature that CTE in football players was indeed real.

The major question then became, "Is CTE inevitable for football players?" That statement alone made people afraid, and many families stopped allowing their children to play football. Soon hockey, rugby, and even soccer were on the list of sports that families were afraid to let their children play. That reaction struck me as regrettable. At MSU, we all wondered what the true risks of CTE were and whether they actually outweighed the social and physical fitness benefits of participating in team sports.

Articles ran not just on sports pages, but on the front pages of newspapers and covers of magazines. The Boston University Concussion Study Group started reporting that a huge majority of former professional football players they autopsied had CTE. Many sportswriters did not understand this finding was in a "biased" (self-reported) sample, and some reporters inappropriately concluded CTE was indeed "inevitable" if you played football. Sadly, well-publicized professional football player suicides, and some controversial sports-writing contributed to widespread public fear of the sport. By 2010, a true public panic was brewing, one that threatened to eventually turn the sport of football into something unrecognizable—or maybe even kill it all together.

I understood the public panic; newspaper articles about CTE made the disease seem very common. Yet, when I thought about it a bit more, I realized hundreds of thousands of amateurs and thousands of professionals played contact sports in the United States and most were doing very well, even after age seventy or eighty. I thought that developing "clinically significant" CTE was not anywhere near "inevitable" and, in fact, probably unusual.

As I looked into CTE more, I found that genetic predilection may be a factor, based on a gene known as APOE. APOE helps in the synthesis of apolipoprotein E, which, among other things, helps reduce clumps of amyloid, (a protein identified with Alzheimer's and other diseases that cause brain cell death), in an almost detergent-like fashion. The emerging science implied that if APOE malfunctioned or at least one APOE epsilon 4 allele was absent, increasing amounts of beta amyloid might occur in the brain, which might make the possibility of CTE higher.

Other clinical investigations emerged, implying that several other factors might also contribute to developing CTE: a prior history of ADHD, migraine, and use of alcohol or drugs. Additional basic science studies began to look at other potential causes: autoimmune, neurochemical, abnormal cell biology, or a neuroendocrinology abnormality. The presence and importance of Tau in CTE cases was also eventually recognized.[3] Neurologists quickly understood that if we could determine who was at high risk for CTE, we could help people manage their personal risk more scientifically.

Neuroepidemiologists pointed out that determining how many hits might cause CTE in specific individuals would be invaluable

[3] Kaufman SK, Svirsky S, Cherry JD, McKee AC, Diamond MI. Tau seeding in chronic traumatic encephalopathy parallels disease severity. Acta Neuropathol. 2021 Dec;142(6):951-960.doi:10.1007/s00401-021-02373-5.

for personalizing risk management. Data like that could allow an individual to retire prior to a dangerous number of blows to the head. But I eventually realized that obtaining such personalized data would be very hard, given the long timespan from youth football to the typical age an athlete might develop signs and symptoms of CTE. It could take twenty years or more—perhaps as long as fifty years—of careful follow-up.

A proper prospective study (analyzing a group in real time on a go-forward basis) would also need to use multiple standardized testing: neuropsychological testing, advanced MRI, PET scanning, and the like. It would probably also require frequent blood draws for serum biomarkers as they emerged over the years. Autopsy evaluations would be required for 100 percent assurance that any clinical development of a neurodegenerative process or a frank dementia was actually due to CTE, rather than from an unrelated brain disease. Although theoretically doable, it would be as hard a study as had ever been done, and the time and cost would be astronomical.

Retrospective CTE studies (looking backward at a group after the diagnosis is known) are far less scientific than a prospective study. Prospective studies are the gold standard in science; they reduce the number of false assumptions and more carefully eliminate bias or preconceived notions about outcome. Yet retrospective or very short prospective studies were all we had to go on to determine the true clinical risk of CTE.

A Mayo Clinic retrospective study looked at the rate of development of neurodegenerative diseases (like Alzheimer's and Parkinson's disease) in high school football players from Olmstead County in Minnesota from the 1950s and 1960s. The study compared them with band members from that same geographical area and era. Interestingly, there was no difference in outcomes between, say, a left offensive tackle and a piccolo player. Football players and band members both developed these neurodegenerative diseases at a similar pace. This is not the end of the story, however, as similar studies from different cohorts have also shown different results. Furthermore, in the last five or six decades, players have become bigger and faster, thereby generating more force on impact especially when the head is involved.

Early on, I realized how doubtful it was we would ever scientifically understand who is truly at risk for neurodegenerative disease or CTE with statistical certainty in American football players unless some unique biomarker became available. That possibility did intrigue me even before I joined the football team's medical staff. I understood that CTE at its worst was a horribly devastating and debilitating disease. But as a clinician and neuroscientist, I found one conclusion obvious: clinically relevant CTE must be relatively uncommon. Sally and Jeff frequently pointed out that the vast majority of alumni who played football for MSU were living normal lives. Similar findings were also present with other college football program alumni.

The MSU football medical team also began to wonder if CTE occurred with different levels of "clinical expression." In other words, could a person with widespread CTE have few or no issues with activities of daily living—or vice versa. Could a person have severe behavioral manifestations of CTE—horrible mood swings, violent outbursts, cognitive impairment, loss of memory, deep depression, even suicide—with only "mild" CTE discovered on autopsy?

Very early on the five of us also began to wonder if there was something more we could do to help answer some of these unknown things about mTBI, CTE, and second impact syndrome. We went to MSU's Department of Radiology to see if there was some kind of technique to study connectivity of various brain systems. It struck us that dysconnectivity of the normal physiology of the major brain systems was perhaps the reason people had significant clinical symptoms following an mTBI.

An MSU physicist, David Zhu, agreed to guide us in a project using a special type of MRI scan called "functional MRI" (fMRI). He thought the fMRI technique might help us understand CNS connectivity better in acute concussion. Once our protocols were set, and the Institutional Review Board agreed, we were allowed to do fMRI on players who consented to be tested after a concussion.

Then all we had to do was stand on the sidelines and wait for the inevitable.

# CHAPTER TWELVE

# *The Big House; Hail to the Victor*

I felt getting our fMRI concussion research project going just after I joined the team was among the more important things I was going to do at MSU. But in week six of the season, I realized there was something that was even more urgent, at least for a week.

Michigan State football was preparing for its annual game against the University of Michigan. This year's game was in Ann Arbor and it had added significance, as both teams were undefeated, a circumstance that had happened only once before in the 103 previous games between the schools. MSU was ranked seventeenth and Michigan eighteenth nationally. This game was always circled by the Spartans at the beginning of the year. The winner got statewide bragging rights (even among neuro-ophthalmologists), an important head start on recruiting top football talent statewide, and the Paul Bunyan Trophy.

In addition, MSU had defeated the Wolverines in the two games since Mike Hart's "little brother" statement in 2007. One more win in 2010 would be the trifecta, and all of a sudden, Spartans could correctly claim they had the Wolverines' number, tilting statewide recruitment significantly toward MSU. Coach D. preached every day after practice that when the team was in Ann Arbor, they "have to be the rock" to win. He must have used the term "be the rock" half a dozen times or more with the team during the week leading up to the game.

Cardiology agreed to allow Coach Dantonio to travel to Ann Arbor, but only if he stayed in the press box. Although it must have been very hard for Coach D. to agree, he publicly promised to be a "good patient." We all bused down to Ann Arbor on Friday, and our first stop was the "Big House," the University of Michigan's name for its enormous football stadium. The entrance to the visitors' locker room was no more than twenty feet from the street-level entrance.

I found it surprising the Wolverine dressing room was located right across from the visitor's locker room at the base of a fifteen-foot-wide, one-block-long tunnel that led down to the playing field. I wondered how often a spirited battle of words, or worse, had broken out between the rival teams when the trip back up from the field within that tunnel had not been carefully orchestrated.

While the Spartan players were dressing, I walked the long tunnel under the stands into the Big House. At ground level, I was astonished by how enormous the stadium actually was. The structure was a gigantic bowl set deep into the ground. The building surrounding the outside of the stadium was surprisingly short, maybe two stories at most. But once you got inside the seating area, the rows of seats down to the playing field seemed to go on forever. With a capacity of nearly 110,000, it is usually considered the biggest stadium in North America. It had served the Wolverines well, helping the University of Michigan become the winningest college football program of all time.

The players eventually filtered down the tunnel. Once on the field they linked arms and, starting at one goal line, they walked together to the other; this walk of the field was an MSU tradition. The players were then given thirty minutes to loosen up. The receivers played touch football, but with absolutely no running allowed. It was hysterical to see lightning-fast receivers like Mark Dell, Keyshawn Martin, Bennie Fowler, and B. J. Cunningham catch a football and then try to "out speed walk" each other toward an imaginary goal line. Eventually, the team reassembled for a discussion with Coach D., after which we all jumped back onto the buses for a short ride to the hotel.

The team stayed at a beautiful golf resort in Ypsilanti, about fifteen minutes away from the Big House. We were greeted warmly by the Eastern Michigan University undergrads, who worked as bellhops and servers within the four-star restaurant. The adjacent golf course was beautiful with its immaculate greens, and the sun glistening off the water of the nearby river was magnificent. It struck me that this was hardly noticed by anyone except the rookies like me. As this was my first true road game, I was delighted to discover I was rooming with Father Jake.

Everybody, as usual, had strict assignments for the evening, except for the physicians. Sally and Jeff were assigned to the training room, and along with their fellows and athletic training students, delivered various treatments to the players. The players themselves had a series of meetings. After the team meal, the players and coaches gathered together for a required movie. Following that, a strict curfew was enforced by Ken Mannie himself. I would not want to be absent from my room during a bed check by Coach Mannie.

After the players had completed any medical treatments and returned to their rooms for the night, the entire medical team, including Father Jake, went out for a late evening dinner, as was their tradition. One of the great pluses of traveling with the football team was that everyone got a per diem to purchase a proper set of daily meals. It was hard to believe. I was driven the sixty-three miles down to Ann Arbor in a comfy bus, with a police escort, and then handed money to pay for my food. As I counted out the seventy-two dollars, I turned to Father Jake and said, "All this, plus money? Unbelievable."

Mike Shingles always scouted out the best restaurant available. I was told he had the knack of ordering just the right thing. Tonight, he started the six of us off with cocktails and wine along with two gigantic seafood towers consisting of shellfish, lobster, shrimp, and crabmeat. He got additional appetizers for the table, including some sort of lobster macaroni, roasted brussels sprouts, and an order of specially prepared french fries. Then came different cuts of beef with various types of potatoes, veggies, and some sort of mystery—a delicious specialty of the house. Mike insisted on a sumptuous dessert for everyone before he personally picked up the tab.

Back at the hotel, after our third Scotch, Father Jake forced all of us to listen to him sing a few songs. But once we got back to our room, the old priest suddenly became serious.

"Dave," he said, "We need a special homily for tomorrow's pregame."

I did not realize that prior to every game Father Jake held a Mass for the players and coaches. He asked if I would be comfortable helping him think through what he should talk about, given everything the team had already been through this year.

"Dave, I could use a little advice from you about what I should talk about tomorrow. Can you give me your best quote from the Bible? It would also mean a lot to me if you came to the Mass."

I assured our team clergy maybe my background was just a little different than his formal divinity training, but I knew enough to respect the word. "Father Jake, I'm your guy. I don't know much about the Bible, but maybe I can help with something. Did you know the first description of cardio-pulmonary resuscitation, or CPR, was recorded in the Bible?"

"I didn't know you were a Biblical scholar!" he responded. "Of course I am aware, Dave. Did you think I missed the story about the little shepherd boy?"

"Right!" I said. "Father Jake, then you know! Second Kings, chapter four. The little shepherd boy went unconscious and died. His mother, heartbroken, summoned Elijah. As we both know, Elijah was considered a pretty capable doctor. Well, Elijah showed up and analyzed the situation. He then placed his face upon the face of that shepherd boy and 'breathed the breath of life' into the child, resuscitating him! I keep that story in mind every time I hear a Code Blue called at Sparrow, although I move slower and slower to those as I have aged."

The old priest winked and gave me a knowing smile, and then quoted some of his favorite passages. After a while, the priest fell silent, thinking to himself. He eventually looked up at me and asked, "Dave, I need something special for the homily tomorrow. I have an idea. Would you listen as I try and put it together for tomorrow's Mass?"

How could I say no? Father Jake told me he was getting old enough to realize each time he could make it to a football game, it had to be considered special, especially when it was against the University of Michigan.

"Dave, you need to appreciate every single one of these. Every single one. You're still sort of young, so it hasn't hit you yet that one of these days we are going to be calling Elijah to help you. You never know when you are going to be at your last game."

I had an immediate flashback to when Coach Dantonio said the same thing as he and his medical team looked at the MRI of Josh Rouse's broken neck.

"Dave," Father Jake continued, "you know, I think about that reality a lot lately. I wonder if this might actually be my last MSU–Michigan football game. I try to make every one of these special. So should you."

Father Jake and I both grew quiet at that reflection. I thought to myself, here is a man who was deep into his eighties. He had graduated from MSU, seen war as a marine, then decided to become a priest. He had invested his entire adult life at Michigan State University, including teaching at both of MSU's medical schools. I felt honored that he would seek out my opinion on anything, let alone what to say to these young men before such an important game.

I realized Father Jake wanted to craft the perfect homily to fit this occasion. He worked on it deep into the night. He talked about various biblical subjects almost like he was probing the depth of my knowledge. We talked about Ruth, Jesus, Moses, and many other heroic biblical figures.

"Dave," he said at last, "we got a big game tomorrow in a big place filled with those Wolverines. We are huge underdogs for that game. I wonder if it might be appropriate to talk about David confronting Goliath and the Philistine army."

I knew the players would immediately identify with it prior to playing a behemoth such as U of M, especially in front of their screaming fans in this special year. I simply smiled and Father Jake said, "Good. I think so, too."

The old priest kept fine-tuning the homily for hours, talking to me about each phrase, changing this word or that word until, eventually, I fell asleep.

I was awakened early on game day by Father Jake roaming around the room, dressing after his shower. After breakfast with the team doctors, I found my way to the back of a large meeting hall to listen to the homily Father Jake had worked so hard on the night before. The plan was straightforward. Coach D. would precede Father Jake, then Father Jake would offer his "simple prayer." After that, the guys would board the buses for the Big House to face the U of M football team in front of 110,000 raucous Wolverines. Everyone understood the importance of the game, as the winner would have an inside track to the Big Ten championship.

After Coach D. quietly gave final instructions to his team, he called on Father Jake to provide his blessing. Graceful despite his age, the priest gently walked to the front of the room. He seemed so small and frail compared with the enormous players he was walking past. He started his homily quietly at first, speaking softly and directly from memory. He spoke each sentence slowly and distinctly, making it clear his words carried Biblical importance.

"The Israelites came to face the Philistines. They had among them a youth named David, who had courage and the will to succeed. David had gathered five rocks from amongst the rivers and plains his army had traveled. Each had been carefully chosen, as he knew they represented the hopes and dreams of the Israelites. He carefully placed them in the satchel he carried along with the sling he had practiced with for so many years. As they came upon the Philistines, David moved forward to take his position at the head of the army.

"The Philistine army came forward to confront the Israelites. They had at their head a giant, a Goliath. The giant came forward and stood just yards apart from David. It was understood if the young Israelite lost, his people would become enslaved by the Philistines. Yet if David was triumphant and somehow defeated the Goliath, the Israelites would keep their land."

Not a word was spoken in the hall as Father Jake sped up the tempo and raised his voice just slightly.

"Goliath stood beyond a height of six feet and one half. His armor was heavy and glistening in the sun. His arrogance on full display. Goliath looked down and then past David and asked in his booming voice, 'Where is your warrior, so I might kill him?' David, a mere sixteen-year-old, was thin and appeared meek and unworthy to the Philistine. Although he came dressed as a shepherd, David answered, 'I am the warrior you seek.'"

Now just a little faster and a little louder, Father Jake added, "Goliath bent backward and delivered a rolling, boisterous laugh. The giant said, 'I am here to destroy a warrior, not slaughter a boy. Israelites, show me your warrior. But do it now or I will kill this tiny one.'

"David said nothing, nor did any within his army behind him, as he chose his favorite among the five rocks he had gathered. He placed it in his hand, feeling its weight and smoothness, except at the pointed edge. With his other hand, he took out his sling and placed the rock within it. Then Goliath boomed, 'Is there no other than this child?' as he picked up his gigantic sword and walked toward the youth."

Father Jake spoke louder and louder, then stood ramrod straight and looked into the eyes of the players sitting just a few feet in front of him. Almost shouting, the priest said, "David stood unafraid. He began to twirl the sling with that special rock inside, first slowly, and then faster and faster still. When the giant was done laughing, David let loose the rock and it flew, striking Goliath square in his forehead, embedding itself into the Philistine's skull.

"The giant fell at that spot on his back, staring up with a frozen and stunned face while looking at the sky. David rushed upon the giant, grabbed Goliath's enormous sword, and cut off the Philistine's head with a single *swoosh*. David grabbed the dead Philistine's severed head, then turned to the Israelites and showed them the giant's startled face. Goliath's eyes were still staring straight ahead, but with the life drained out of them."

Father Jake then quietly turned with his back to the team, bent over, touched the floor, and mimed grabbing the fallen Goliath's severed head by its hair. He then turned back toward the players, symbolically holding up the head of the fallen giant. He slowly moved his arm straight out to the players, pretending to show the head to them. He moved his arm first to his left and then to the right, as David might have actually done for his Israelites. With this, the entire room came to its feet as cheering and then hollering erupted from the hundred or so people assembled. The yelling grew louder and louder until the priest called for quiet.

The yelling slowly died down; Father Jake had more to say. He turned to Coach Dantonio. In measured, almost slow-motion fashion, Father Jake took a black pumice rock from his shirt pocket. It was about the size of a large dark walnut with a clear sharp point at one end. Father Jake held it just above his eyes with his right hand as he showed it first to Coach Dantonio and then the players.

"Coach, as you know, I traveled to sub-Saharan Africa this past summer. Before I left, you made me promise to bring you something back, something symbolic from my travels. That was many months ago, and already this team has been through a lot this year, as have you. I think you may have actually thought I forgot my promise, but I didn't. I took this rock from the foothills of Mount Kilimanjaro. I was told it came from that mountain the last time it erupted, so many centuries ago. I bring it to you now, when we need to slay this giant we are going to play today."

With that, the priest handed over that perfectly shaped black volcanic rock to Coach D., who, just a few weeks after a heart attack, was back among people he loved.

"Coach," Father Jake concluded, "be the rock we need you to be today."

I am a brain doctor, hard and cynical. My job is to care for people who are afflicted with the worst things life can bring. Yet I found myself moved to tears as the players silently walked forward and huddled around Father Jake and their coach in quiet reflection of what they had just witnessed.

Taking the MSU team buses from Ypsilanti through Ann Arbor and into the stadium parking lot prior to an MSU–U-M game was quite an adventure. Having been put in a Biblical mood by Father Jake, I would describe the Wolverine fans in Ann Arbor as ungracious emissaries of Beelzebub. I learned new and remarkably exotic ways to use a variety of profanities, courtesy of the Wolverine undergrads. Occasionally the harsh language was accompanied by a gesture involving a specific finger or even the display of an undergraduate's bare skin above their gluteus maximus. All this was expected given how even an academically elite university like Michigan had, over the years, developed such an attitude against anything MSU.

Prior to game time, the Spartan dressing room seemed very quiet, yet the boys did not seem tight or nervous. I thought maybe instead of talking they were reflecting on what had to be done to achieve victory. My small talk with some of the players in the medical area implied they were quietly confident. But I just wasn't sure about the feeling in the locker room. Were the guys anxious and nervous, or were they preparing to "be the rock"?

Father Jake set me straight: "Dave, they aren't tight or worried. I have seen this before. They have their game faces on. We'll be fine."

I was still learning the nuances of my role. In the past, when I had tried making small talk with the players prior to a game like this, I would say something like, "Are you all right?" Jeff had heard me do that before the Wisconsin game, and he jumped all over me.

"Dave, what are you doing? Do not ask a player if they are 'all right.' Especially on game day. What is wrong with you? That is a way to get inside their head and in a very bad way. They might start thinking, 'Hey, am I all right? Maybe my knee isn't what it should be. Maybe I ought to sit down or get it checked out.' Dave, be very careful what you say to a player especially on game day. Don't use that phrase anymore. Find another. Understand?"

After that exchange with Jeff at the Wisconsin game, I was shattered, but Father Jake picked up the pieces.

"Dave, Monroe is a good man as you know. He gets a little, shall we say, excitable. Maybe you can come up with a different phrase to make that small talk with the guys to help settle them down like, 'Are you good?' Try that phrase out instead."

Father Jake had a way to solve virtually any dispute and make things right. He was a master at it. Legend had it that he was able to pacify warring faculty, Board of Trustee members, deans, provosts, lawmakers, bishops, undergrads, you name it. Fortunately for this football team, there was not a person in that locker room who did not respect that five-foot-two tower of virtue.

Prior to today's Michigan game, Father Jake was in the process of making the rounds in the locker room, talking to the guys, listening to what they had to say, and soothing whatever might be on their mind. I, of course, was nervous as hell but standing in a corner of the medical area to be sure I was not on some stool rocking back and forth like a panicky child, as I had before game one. Eventually our six foot two, 288 pound all-Big Ten nose guard, Jerel Worthy, came into the medical area to get an ankle retaped. When he came in, I said almost absentmindedly, "Big man, you good?"

"Damn good, Doc," came the response. Then he flashed a broad grin and made it clear he understood what the Big House was all about and how important victory was today.

Jeff, standing right next to me, did not look up from the lumbar spine adjustment he was giving to our star running back, Edwin Baker. He did smile when he heard Jerel's response. A few minutes later, he wandered by me and said, "You're learning."

Most of the boys in that locker room had been here before. They were riding a two-game win streak over the Wolverines. The seniors all recalled Mike Hart's "little brother" statement back three years earlier. They let the younger players know they needed to remember Michigan's arrogance and respond to it with their play, not with words.

Kirk Cousins walked among his teammates, who were gathered in small groups prior to warm-ups. "We need this win," he said. "We want to be able to walk the streets of Michigan with our heads high and make sure the Wolverines know we have beaten them three in a row. We need today."

On October 9, 2010, I ran onto the field behind the Spartan football team. It was unreal: We were greeted by a 110,000 people who rose as one to greet the Spartan team with a chorus of boos. Every fan seemed to have a little yellow pom-pom, which they were shaking in unison to the Michigan fight song, "Hail to the Victors."

After MSU was on the field, the Wolverines left the locker-room tunnel and ran across the field toward their bench. They all went under their traditional big blue sign held up by two enormous poles at midfield. They all leapt up to touch it for luck. I had seen that occur a dozen times on television but somehow it was far more inspiring to see it live at field level.

The game went back and forth until my old dancing partner, Le'Veon Bell, scored on a forty-one-yard run for the Spartans, allowing them to take the lead 14–10. Dan Conroy followed up with a field goal twenty-three seconds before halftime to make it 17–10.

Scoring right before the half against an archrival in a close game—there is no greater motivator. The locker room was electric. Everyone was talking it up, and it seemed the guys were primed to beat the blue bellies to make it a third time in a row. All we had to do was keep up the momentum. MSU had not won three in a row against Michigan since Lyndon Johnson was president nearly a half-century earlier.

Of course, in the training area of the locker room, I was thinking of all the ways we could fail. While giving halftime back and neck treatments, Sally turned to me and said, "Dave, the first score of the third quarter will tell us everything. If it's us, we are going to do it!"

That assertion calmed me down; I absolutely believed her. After inspiring words from Coach D. about legacy, out the boys went, riding high. The Wolverine fans were slightly less jubilant than they had been pregame, knowing their team had a true fight on its hands. I secretly hoped Mike Hart, who left the University of Michigan in 2007, was seeing all of this on TV because I just had that feeling we were going to win.

Cousins found Mark Dell for a forty-one-yard touchdown pass after only two minutes and twenty-eight seconds into the quarter.

The small contingent of about forty-five hundred Spartan fans in the north end zone went nuts, yelling and screaming, making the only noise in the otherwise silent Big House.

The MSU band followed with the Spartan fight song, and all was right with the world. Eight minutes later, MSU's Larry Caper scored again to make it 31–10. Father Jake wandered over to me to say, "We got enough to win if we don't fall asleep."

Michigan's talented quarterback, Dennard Robinson, scored at the start of the fourth quarter, but then the Spartans took total control with a twenty-eight-yard field goal to make it 34–17. With six minutes left in the game, Michigan had the ball at its own forty-yard line on fourth down, needing six yards for a first down. U of M coach Rich Rodriquez surprisingly decided to punt the ball, down seventeen points with time evaporating. With that act, he admitted the game was over and all he wanted was to end the game with a score that was not embarrassing.

The Michigan faithful started to boo loudly and then got up and began to leave the stadium. It struck me right then that no one among the Wolverine faithful would want Rodriquez back as the Wolverine coach next year. After the punt, as the Wolverine fans exited the stadium within minutes, the Spartan cheering section climbed to their feet and started chanting and clapping.

"Little sisters!" *clap, clap, clap.* "Little sisters!" *clap, clap, clap.* "Little sisters!" *clap, clap, clap.*

Following the victory, our football equipment head, Mr. Nick, was quick to bring the Paul Bunyan trophy out of the locker room and onto the field. Following his lead, the players decided to carry it all around the Big House's field, the first time the trophy had ever been displayed outside of the locker room after the game in anyone's memory. The Spartans deserved it. Three in a row against an outstanding archrival was pretty incredible.

I watched close up as Paul was passed from player to player, each one raising it over his head in total joy. I thought, what could be better than watching your players, victorious over their archrival, walking around the Big House in total euphoria, holding up the four-foot-tall carved and painted wooden trophy. One of the players put his helmet onto the head of Paul Bunyan. That made it clear, after this third victory in a row, that Paul and all of the state of Michigan were Spartans, at least on this day.

After the game, I noticed that everyone seemed to enjoy lingering outside of the buses for a long time to talk. They wanted to share the moment with parents, family, and friends, and also to savor the victory on your opponent's soil. Very tribal, I thought, but very well-deserved.

We eventually did get our postgame boxed meals and boarded the six Dean Trailway buses for home. The usual sixty-minute ride took about two and a half hours because of game-day traffic. But it seemed like the ride was over in five minutes. Everyone was euphoric—athletic trainers, TV commentators, Catholic priest, team doctors, and team neurologist included.

With this win, Michigan State was now 6–0. MSU had not done that in the previous forty-three years and had not had such a convincing win over the Wolverines in the twenty-six years I'd been on campus prior to this game.

In week seven, Michigan State defeated Illinois 26–6 and rose in the rankings to number seven in the nation. The Spartans were now 7–0 for the first time since 1966, the year they last won the national championship. During both the U of M and Illinois games, Coach D. was relegated to the press box, on doctor's orders. But the team found some type of way to win. Next up was a game in Evanston against the resurgent 5–1 Northwestern Wildcats during their homecoming festival.

# CHAPTER THIRTEEN

# *M.A.S.H. Unit*

I t had been four weeks since Coach D.'s cardiac event, but he kept his players' motivation sky-high. Northwestern was to be his first game back on the sideline since the "Little Giants" game against Notre Dame. Thinking like a fan, I could not comprehend how this football team, so awash in mediocrity for the past two decades, was now going undefeated into the last part of the year. I thought maybe it was Coach Dantonio's calm and stoic spirituality, amplified by the urgency of his quarterback, Kirk Cousins. Maybe it was that aggressive defense created by Coach Pat Narduzzi and led by linebackers Greg Jones and newcomer Max Bullough. Whatever the chemistry, it was working.

During pregame warm-ups at Northwestern icy cold rain pelted us like little spiked icicles. I was delighted to see Coach D. actually on the field, but I silently prayed he was not overdoing it. Prior to kickoff, I was struck by how very quiet the locker room was, sort of like church. Perhaps the guys were exhausted after the emotional win over the Wolverines the week before. Maybe, even worse, they were underestimating Northwestern. It was eerie. The players seemed down and the coaches detached. The team was certainly not its usual pregame raucous self.

Immediately after the opening kickoff, the Spartans were getting uncharacteristically beaten up physically. Northwestern came out hitting and within minutes caused multiple injuries. One after the other, MSU players came limping over to the sidelines. As I watched the orthopedic surgeons and athletic trainers scramble, it quickly looked like a M.A.S.H. unit on the sidelines. Equally troubling, Northwestern was scoring, almost at will.

I was stunned at how badly things could get so quickly for a team that was 7–0 and now in the top ten nationally. I just watched the score against the Spartans mount. I also had a helpless feeling as I saw the number of leg injuries being suffered. Finally, as Jeff was helping his third player to the training table in the first ten minutes of the game, I asked how I could help. His response was direct. "Dave, just try real hard to stay out of the way. We got big trouble right now. We'll call you when you're needed."

Calm and cool, Sally Nogle helped each injured player cope as he limped or was carried to the training table for analysis. Jeff and Sally had to drag Keshawn Martin off the field. Keshawn was a chiseled specimen but quite thin. He was all about speed. "He runs like the wind, a game-breaker," is what Jeff had said when I first asked about the wide receiver weeks before. Jeff rarely gave his heart away to any student-athlete, but he made it clear that Keshawn was a special player. When he went down in the first few minutes, Jeff looked at me and shook his head, whispering, "Dave, we are in for it today."

Keshawn was in so much pain, it was unclear what was wrong. He hardly ever said anything to anyone, and now he was just grimacing with his eyes squeezed shut. Orthopedists Mike Shingles and Doug Dietzel pressed for a diagnosis. Everyone made it clear there was no need for a neurologist, and I got elbowed away. I saw the pain on Martin's face, but he never said a word to anyone, even though he was surrounded by physicians and athletic trainers.

I was told Keshawn typically could have been missing his entire kneecap and would never have made a sound. That was just the way he was, and that was why everyone was so worried. I tried again to speak with Keshawn, simply to provide comfort, but Jeff gave me a look that told me to back off. I turned and started looking for the next casualty. I found it hard to tolerate the fact that I simply did not have the sports medicine training to help anyone unless they suffered some sort of blow to the head or neck.

As the first-quarter body count got higher and higher, the steady, soaking icy rain became even worse. Jeff eventually came over to where I was standing with water dripping off my nose and soaking through the light wind breaker I was wearing. I was talking to one of the players standing by the bench to be sure he was okay after a hard hit. Jeff leaned in and again reminded me of one of the golden rules of being a sports neurologist.

"Dave," he said, "do not talk to the players. Let them come to you. You should literally have nothing to do with them unless they come to you or the athletic trainers call for you. We will let you know when we need you. Remember, don't touch, talk, or assist any player in any way. Wait your turn. Those concussions will roll in soon enough. So right now, remember, don't be a distraction."

*Don't be a distraction.* I got it. Another golden rule for a sideline doctor. Sadly, I was still too much of a fan, even after all I had seen. Yet as my first year with the team went on, I had matured enough to realize how important that phrase "don't be a distraction" actually was. I took a deep breath and turned back to look at the field of play frustrated.

I was still trying to figure out how to do my best for these Spartan student-athletes and my MSU medical teammates. We were getting annihilated on the road and in frigid rain. I was depressed; it is really hard for a doctor to do nothing. We are trained to provide comfort, care, education, wisdom, and, on rare occasions, dispense a cure. I concluded I still had a long way to go to feel I had truly earned my place on the medical staff of this team.

Suddenly, our all-American nose guard, Jerel Worthy, came running over to the sideline after a pileup. His helmet was off, and he was covering his right eye with his hand, absolutely screaming. He had intense right orbital pain after overcoming a blocking assignment from an overzealous Wildcat offensive lineman.

Sally called me over. "Okay, Dave, you're on. Help out Jerel."

As a neuro-ophthalmologist, I knew how to handle this one. The key was to be sure there was indeed no serious issue like a ruptured globe or retinal detachment. I urged Jerel to sit up and examined his eye carefully. I then distracted him from his pain by having him hold a four-by-four gauze pad over the eye and told him to keep both eyes closed.

I talked him through his pain by explaining it would slowly go away and his vision should be okay. As he improved, he eventually looked out from behind the gauze pad, blinked a few times, and then a smile came to his lips. I turned to Sally and gave a thumbs-up. "Thanks, Doc," said Jerel, as he walked over to his position coach. He was sent in on the next play.

Unfortunately, the score was now 17–0 Northwestern. The Wildcat fans were all whooping it up in the west stands despite the unrelenting rain. Yet I was ecstatic. I had actually diagnosed and helped a Spartan player get back on the field within minutes—by myself.

Sally then asked Randy and me to examine another player who had developed an intense electricity-like burning feeling down the entire length of his right arm. The student-athlete said the pain had come on right after a hard hit to his shoulder and neck. Randy asked me to confirm—which I did—that the student-athlete had no sign of a neurologic issue that would imply a fractured neck.

Then Randy explained the electric sting is like hitting the "funny bone," except much worse. He said it was called a "stinger" due to the stinging pain that envelops the entire arm. Randy predicted it would only last two to five minutes and then let up. He let us know the player could return to the field for the next series of downs and "without danger to themselves."

I suddenly realized, once again, things were moving too fast. It was almost as bad as my first game, but I was smarter now. I kept my focus and did my job. Fortunately, a TV time-out eventually occurred, allowing me to finally catch my breath. I realized I was in the middle of absolute, unrelenting mayhem. I looked over at the Northwestern side of the field and noted their smiling and laughing players were waving white towels to generate more fan enthusiasm.

I thought for sure we were doomed, but I had a secret smile, knowing I was more or less holding my own during a brutal moment for our MSU sports medicine team—and our players.

I thought for a second that maybe I was a help to the medical staff and therefore to my beloved Spartan football team. I also real-ized our team's win streak was about to end. Along with it, the dream of a Big Ten championship. That trip to the Rose Bowl was going to be lost unless something miraculous happened. Fortunately, momentum was about to change. I had lost hope. We were behind by seventeen points, caring for the injured nonstop, and it was raining cats and dogs. The only nice thing was the twenty thousand MSU fans at the game. The Spartan faithful were right behind the Spartan bench but they had watched the entire first part of the game without so much as a peep.

I had not taken any rain gear to Evanston and by the middle of the second quarter, I was soaked to the bone, shivering and miserable. Even worse we were getting beaten up on national TV. As the water dripped down my face and off my nose, I started to think, "What on earth am I doing here, rather than staying back home, nice and dry?"

Then the wind started to blow from Lake Michigan, and the air turned bitterly cold within minutes. I thought about sitting on a dry sofa, drinking a hot chocolate with those little marshmallows while warming up next to the fireplace. I just wanted this agony to be over. To compound all of this, there was a prolonged TV time-out just after a Wildcat punt.

As my shivering got worse, I thought about how crazy it was to agree to be a neurologist for a college football team. To compound my anger, the Northwestern announcer chirped, "We take this time out to honor our new Nobel Laureate, the Ida C. Cook Professor of Economics, Dale Mortensen! Professor Mortensen won the 2010 Nobel Prize in economics, earning him one third of the $1.5 million prize for his work on the analysis of 'Markets with Search Frictions,' revealing why so many are unemployed at the same time as there are so many job openings."

Professor Mortensen walked onto the field with great dignity and he was formally honored for receiving his Nobel Prize as the TV time-out wore on and on. Then, Northwestern President Schapiro, also an economist, seem to feel it was necessary to join his star professor on the field. He gave Mortensen a football jersey with the number 1 on it. "Okay, isn't that lovely. Good for him," I thought as my now nonstop shivering continued.

I tolerated all of this until Northwestern called an additional time-out, apparently to allow the full award ceremony to occur. The economics professor was given the microphone, and he proceeded to deliver a short speech right there while a football game was trying to restart. That's when I became angry. Honoring an academic during a football game, even for winning a Nobel Prize, was inappropriate given how horrendous the weather was. Then to allow the ceremony to go on endlessly was just plain wrong. I started to boo. Yes, I booed a Nobel Laureate—and as loudly as I could.

To my delight, others among the twenty thousand Spartan fans seated behind the MSU bench had this same thought. Slowly at first, and then with increased volume, Spartan fans also began to boo as the rain got heavier. For better or worse, this was the first significant sound the MSU fans had made since the game's opening kickoff. Undeniably, this was the most bizarre nonathletic scene I had ever seen on a football field. However, the good news was the MSU fans were now once again awake and actually making noise.

Ryan Field is set up so the fans are no more than ten feet from the players' bench, close enough to look around and find friends, if you were bored enough to do such a thing. As luck would have it, my old *Daily Cardinal* campus editor and close friend, Jim Podgers, was actually in the stands right behind the MSU bench, rooting for the Spartans. I knew he had turned into a Spartan fan since his lovely daughter, Hilary, decided she might want to go to MSU for college.

He called out to me during the chaos of the Nobel Laureate's walk off in the rain, and I spotted him at the forty-yard line. I felt compelled to leave the sidelines, walk up the four aluminum steps leading to the third row, to hug my old college chum who was now working in Chicago. I had not seen him for years, but, like great friends, we talked like it was old times.

"Dave," he said, "this is Northwestern's way of laughing at Sparty with a ridiculous speech by that Nobel Prize guy. The Spartans suck today. Do something."

"Podgers, you do something."

So Podgers and his three impressively drunk chums then started to chant, "Go Green!" Followed a second later by, "Go White!" as the

Nobel Laureate and his family concluded their leisurely exit from the field. To my amazement, Podgers' small entourage encouraged folks to pick up the chant and soon enough, that entire section was yelling back and forth to each other like crazed lunatics, "Go Green!" and responding, "Go White!"

The chant grew louder and louder and it swept over the entire stadium like an enormous wave of noise. Pretty soon, the twenty thousand MSU fans were on their feet screaming and yelling for MSU to do something, anything. It was a remarkable thing to behold.

I noticed Kirk Cousins then started to walk up and down behind the Spartan bench. He periodically stopped his pacing, bent over, and whispered something in the ear of one offensive lineman or another. They were all hunched over, trying to stay dry; they acknowledged whatever secret their quarterback whispered to them, some with a nod and others with a vigorous fist bump.

Then, a few seconds later, almost like a delayed reaction, each lineman sat up straight and began to tighten his helmet straps with that recognizable rapid *click, click, click* sound. I recognized what that action meant from previous games: They were checking their number-one weapon, their helmet, to be sure it was on good and tight. That action made me imagine soldiers checking their rifles before stepping off a landing craft and into battle. MSU's offensive linemen were getting ready to turn it up a notch, courtesy of whatever their quarterback had just whispered to them.

Suddenly, Cousins vaulted over the bench and stood right in front of his linemen. He started yelling something at them, and they all stood up as one and began chanting and yelling with him. The louder and angrier he got, the more the lineman seemed to respond. One by one, they came over and formed a circle around him as they moved off the bench and closer to the field. Even I could not escape the renewed energy the crowd provided, despite the reality that we were down 17–0.

Jeff walked over to me after I came back onto the sidelines. At first, I wondered if this was my last game on the sidelines, based on my impromptu attempts at cheerleading.

"Dave," he said, "I have a job for you. I need you to get hot dogs for the entire medical staff at halftime, because, somehow, we always ended up winning when we did that. Shingles usually gets them, but he's going to be too busy with all the injuries. If you do it, I'll find you some rain gear."

"Deal," I said, though I was skeptical of lucky hot dogs. While I was suiting up in my waterproof poncho, I watched as Jeff quietly spoke to a key receiver. I also watched Sally check on some of the offensive players about to go out, using soft and encouraging words. Then strength and conditioning coach Ken Mannie was making the same rounds as Jeff and Sally, speaking to different players in surprisingly quiet but encouraging language. This quiet side of Ken Mannie was effective. He had saved that gentle part of his personality for when it was needed the most. Now was that moment.

After the game restarted, MSU's offense took over, with five minutes left in the half. Everyone on the Spartan sideline seemed passionate again. As the rain was letting up, the noise created by the fans behind us grew louder as the Spartan offense lined up. Cousins started opening up the passing game allowing MSU to drive right down the field. With about three minutes left in the half, Cousins threw a strike over the middle to Mark Dell, who caught it in stride for a touchdown. The excitement on the bench was clear. People were mobbing each other, hugging like it was New Year's Eve.

The boys now had hope, courtesy of a Nobel Laureate taking his time to accept the gratitude of his cherished university while the Spartan bench, along with their fans, helped a 7–0 club rise to their feet.

After the touchdown, Jeff came over to me really excited and said, "Okay, now we've got some hope. I need you to do something for the medical staff."

"Sure," I asked, "what do you need from me, Jeff?"

"Well, Dave, we need you to get those halftime hot dogs."

"Where do I go?"

"There's a place just outside of the statium. About a block away. Get over there and bring back as many hot dogs as you can. Go over to Mike Shingles, tell him you need money, and let him know it is for Mustard's Last Stand."

I looked at Jeff thinking this was just crazy talk. Then he half-pushed, half-shoved me toward the orthopedic trauma surgeon extraordinaire and shouted over his shoulder as he was walking away, "Do it, my man."

Off I went, down the sideline to find a professor of orthopedic surgery to get cash to buy what Jeff described as the "lucky hot dogs." As I walked up to Mike, I thought, this is some crazy prank Jeff has sent me on. Mike and Sally were concluding a shoulder exam of yet another injured player. Mike looked up at me and asked, "Dave, what's up?" He said, half-jokingly but with a smile. "Are you also injured? Do you need a shoulder exam, too?"

"No," I retorted. "Jeff Monroe told me it is my job to go buy some hot dogs for us to eat at halftime. I was supposed to talk to you about it. I apologize. I know this sounds crazy."

"Wonderful!" Mike shouted. "Here's a hundred. Go over to the southwest corner of the stadium and walk across the street. Find Mustard's Last Stand. They have terrific Chicago-style hot dogs, and for cheap. Ask for the thirty-three dogs I ordered when we got off the bus. Make sure they come with all the toppings. Pickles, onions, sauerkraut, mustard, and maybe ketchup. Dave, if you leave now, you can make it back by the middle of halftime. Ask for the lady with tinted blue-white hair. She will be chain-smoking. She is about eighty or eighty-five years old. You can't miss her."

With that, he pressed a crisp hundred-dollar bill in my hand, patted me on the shoulder and said, "Dave, don't eat them all on the way back to the locker room."

Of all the places in the Big Ten, only at Ryan Field could you do such a thing. The stadium is surrounded by an affluent neighborhood in Evanston, making the stores within easy walking distance. So with two minutes and fifty-eight seconds remaining in the second period I made my way off the sideline, past the visitors' locker room, out the three-foot fence surrounding the stadium, and onto the sidewalk. The security guard assured me that, when it was time for me to return, he would remember "the six-foot three-inch goofball wearing totally green rain gear who went looking for hot dogs."

He pointed out Mustard's Last Stand, about 200 yards from where we were standing. I thought to myself, I just may be the most highly paid delivery boy in the history of humankind. I arrived at Mustard's Last Stand in about a minute. The game was still going on, and I could clearly hear the roar of the crowd. At Mustard's Last Stand that meant there would be no one waiting in line. I went to the outdoor serving area wearing my now very wet MSU rain poncho and asked, "Do you know where the young lass is that has prepared the Shingles order for thirty-three hot dogs?"

I was, of course, talking to the eighty-something-year-old lady with blue-white tinted hair and a cigarette drooping from her lips. With a straight face she said, "Well, that would be me. Are you going to eat all them thirty-three dogs here or are they to go?"

She did not laugh as she leaned forward with her cigarette about an inch from my chest. She seemed quite interested in the answer. I responded, "Mike Shingles sent me, and he said you would know about the order."

"Oh, yeah. We all know Dr. Shingles. He always comes over when we play you fellas. I am pissed it ain't Mike. He usually comes over to get these. Give Mike a big hello from all of us. By the way, do you have the cash?"

I handed over the hundred and told her to keep the change. She did not laugh, but she did refuse the one-dollar tip with great ceremony. She informed me that "Dr. Shingles had already taken care of us. Keep your dollar!"

Then she winked and eventually handed over thirty-three loaded Chicago-style hot dogs, with all of the trimmings. They were neatly wrapped in foil and organized inside a huge box. Mustard's Last Stand also supplied napkins, a lot more mustard, pickles and sauerkraut, and a zillion plastic forks and knives. The sweet smell was fabulous and the dogs were piping hot.

I struggled with the huge box that held the prized halftime treat. As I was walking away, she yelled, "Be careful now and don't eat them all on your way back to the locker room. And say hello to Dr. Shingles."

I made it back to the stadium as quickly as I could and easily found the guard who let me out of the gates. He just shook his head as I struggled with the enormous box filled with delicious-smelling hot dogs, trying hard not to drop it. As I walked the twenty feet from the gate to the Spartan locker room, my mouth was watering.

What I saw when I walked into the locker room was out of an action movie. The players had just come in for halftime. They were wet to the bone but animated. Everyone seemed to have an ice pack on their shoulders, ribs, or arms. I was holding that huge carton filled to the brim with food. I tried my best to move silently along the wall, past dozens of athletes sitting in the offense team's dressing area and do so without being noticed. The boys were listening quietly but intently to their offensive coordinator explaining the schemes the Wildcats were using to thwart the Spartan running game.

The offensive linemen were sitting on small stools or folding chairs scattered around the tiny, well-worn Northwestern excuse for a visitors locker room. The place smelled of damp walls and had electric wires dangling from the ceiling. There were also dust and paint chips falling from the ceiling, maybe due to the screaming coming from the defensive group huddled across the room.

Everyone was jammed into a space so small it made MSU's cave of a locker room look like heaven. It was by far the worst in the Big Ten, with the possible exception of the Spartan visitors' locker room. As I went by the offensive players' group, they all looked up to see where that sweet smell of Chicago-style hot dogs was coming from. I politely smiled as I walked toward the defensive unit that stood between me and the medical area. The next sixty seconds proved to be among the scariest I had lived to that moment.

# CHAPTER FOURTEEN

# *Summoning the Will to Win; a Love Rediscovered.*

I soon realized that, despite the huge box of hot dogs I was carrying, I had to tiptoe past the entire defensive unit to make it back to the medical area. There was no other way. That might have worked fine, except the guys were currently listening intently to every word defensive coordinator Pat Narduzzi was screaming to no one in particular. Narduzzi's black hair was combed straight back along with his deep-set dark eyes. His facial expression and his enormous leg and calf muscles made him look incredibly menacing, especially when infuriated, as he was right now.

Coach Pat Narduzzi was forty-four years old and the son of Bill Narduzzi, the head coach at Youngstown State University from 1975 to 1985. Pat actually played football as a freshman for his dad in 1985 before moving on. Twenty-five years later, he was widely acknowledged as a defensive genius. He had been with Coach D. since 2004, first at Cincinnati, then when they both moved to MSU in 2007. He was deeply respected by his players and fellow coaches based on his passion and unflagging desire to win. I was told by everyone he was a major key to success for the 2010 Spartans.

However, on this day, it was his defense's inconsistency that was causing Narduzzi's rage. Despite being 7–0, Narduzzi's boys had come out flat and uninspired in the first half. They were being embarrassed on national TV and, worse, their manhood was being challenged right now by their beloved coach. Not a pretty sight.

Narduzzi was a master motivator, he was beloved by his Spartans. That was obvious in the way they all talked about him at practice or when they were in the treatment room trying to recover from some leg or arm injury. They adored his passion and intense commitment. He had recruited and trained them all.

Coach Narduzzi was reviewing, in rapid fire, each defensive play from the first half using an old-style overhead projector. He would place plastic overlay sheets, already marked up with X's and O's, on the illuminator and then discuss the specifics of each man's responsibility on the play. He had created them in real time from his perch high above the action in the press box, where he always stayed for the first three quarters or so of the game before coming down to the field.

I moved silently past the rather calm offensive unit where Father Jake was talking to one of the running backs. I could see Narduzzi watching me out of the corner of his eye as I was attempting to maneuver that huge box, with the unmistakable hot dog scent past his defensive unit. As I moved closer, I did my best to become invisible, but no luck.

Coach Narduzzi's face was scrunched so tight it resembled a tight fist as he looked right at me. At first, he seemed to try to ignore the craziness of me gliding between him and his defensive players. He simply continued to yell even louder as I began to walk past him, but he soon just started to stare and everyone became totally quiet.

When I looked around from behind that box at his face, I did fear for my life, especially given the sudden, complete silence. I worked even harder to become a ghost as I tangoed around stretched-out legs and ice-pack-covered arms into the adjacent medical area. "My God. I'm safe," I thought as I entered the medical area located in a back room.

As I turned around to look, I saw Narduzzi pick up the overhead projector, bounce it off the ground and then attempt to do a drop kick of the device. It went about three feet and landed with a loud

*clang.* Everyone in the training room, Jeff and Sally included, stopped what they were doing and looked up as they heard the overhead projector hit the ground. They stared at me, recognizing what had just happened. I felt much better after Narduzzi started screaming again, and the athletic trainers went back to work. Randy and Mike came over to grab the box from me and to get started on their first halftime hot dog.

"Good," said Mike, "you're alive, Dave. Keep the change from the hundred."

Pat Narduzzi was as fiery, loud, and in-your-face as Coach D. was calm and spiritual. Pat had helped Coach D. build an exceptional defense and I interrupted Narduzzi while he was at work. Not a good thing. I proved to be a distraction and at a bad moment, the absolute worst thing a sports medicine doctor can do. Sally gave me her five-second stare of death, and then assured me if I ever did something like that again, I would be sent right back to academic neurology.

After I got my courage back up, I peeked out from the side of the training room. Pat had already retrieved the slightly mangled projector and put it back on its cart. Every defensive player was now riveted, at attention, and sitting ramrod-straight on their stools. I wished my med students listened to me that way. Mike, between mouthfuls of his second hot dog, assured me that the projector had taken quite a beating over the years.

Pat's players were mostly analyzing the X's and O's appearing on the wall, while sipping Gatorade silently. They gently nodded their heads at the coach's description and advice on how to recognize and handle things when they saw the same offensive alignments again. Pat was also teaching them about the unique formations Northwestern had used to ambush his vaunted defense. I was sure these rapid-order halftime adjustments must be a big part of his success.

After about four more minutes into his review of the first half plays, he surprisingly lowered his voice to just a whisper and moved a little closer to the boys sitting not more than two feet in front of him. He leaned forward.

"Men," said Pat in a barely audible voice, "these are the same players we beat up every time we play them. They are running the same plays they have been using for the last four years I have been here. The only difference is the formations they are using. They are simply doing that to confuse us. Do you get that?"

Then, suddenly, he screamed, "DO YOU GET THAT?"

With that, Pat Narduzzi, all six feet and 220 muscular pounds of him, wrestled the overhead projector off the cart again. He turned to his right, raised that poor projector over his head, and then threw it hard to the ground. It bounced up, and, with perfect form and follow-through, he drop-kicked the thing ten feet, where it smashed against the far wall, breaking into a dozen pieces. With that, his players leaped to their feet, screaming, and I ducked back into the medical room.

I found that the athletic trainers, team doctors, videographers, athletic training students, equipment managers, and others I could not identify had already grabbed one or two of Mustard's Last Stand's best product. Off to the side, I saw one of our starting linemen getting a lumbar spine manipulation from Sally Nogle. An audible crack could be heard with a sigh of relief coming from the player. Another lineman was getting what appeared to be an inspection of his right knee.

Just then Mike Shingles came with a hot dog and bun loaded with goodies and handed me my halftime reward. "Dave, get going with that first hot dog. Otherwise, you'll have a lot of catching up to do."

Crazy as it was, a player or two would also wander into the medical area, ignoring the hot dogs being consumed at a feverish pace by the entire medical team. They would get an ice pack or a minor treatment and did not comment on the sight of around fifteen people pushing each other aside, acting like locusts, as those thirty-three hot dogs disappeared.

Simultaneously, contusions were being treated with white gauze and then wrapped with green tape. The players with significant orthopedic events suffered at the outset of the game were now in street clothes. Two were on crutches, including Keshawn Martin.

They came in to get an ice pack along with some sympathy or to get their crutches adjusted. One also grabbed a hot dog.

After personally wolfing down two dogs in less than 120 seconds, I admitted to Randy that I was proud to be the one trusted to carry on the Mustard's Last Stand tradition. Mike, working on his third hot dog, looked over at me and with a half a piece of hot dog bun sticking slightly out of his mouth. I could barely understand him until he simply said, "Dave, I changed my mind. Where's my dollar?" Laughing, he then demanded I produce it.

I took the dollar out of my pocket and handed it over to the gazillionaire orthopedic surgeon with a feigned look of disgust. He smiled and asked me to sign it. Mike then carefully folded it with great ceremony before putting it into his wallet. "Dave, when I was your medical student you used to give me a dollar every time I answered a hard one in class. I've saved every one of them and I am going to save this one too."

As the doctors and athletic trainers finished up the halftime medical issues, we walked out of the training area over to where the players were congregating. The locker room was now jumping with energy. The players had concluded the offense and defense huddles with their specialty coaches and were talking it up while waiting for Coach D. to gather them together as a team.

At other halftimes, before he had his heart attack, Coach Dantonio had quietly said a word or two, pointed out a few items to concentrate on, and then sent the team out for the second half. They needed more than that today. On the road, losing 17–7 even after that touchdown late in the first half, I still wondered if we really had a chance.

Coach D. exchanged some last words with Pat Narduzzi and the other coaches. He then made his way over to where the players were standing with their backs toward the locker room door that led out to the field. Quarterback Kirk Cousins was in the very front of this group with his offensive linemen just behind him. The receivers and running backs were next and further toward the back were the defensive players.

At the very back was the "auxiliary staff," made up of Mr. Nick and the equipment managers, videographers, the team photographer, electricians, communications people, and athletic trainers. Even behind them was Father Jake, Randy, and Mike. Behind everyone else was the medical team neurologist: me. Father Jake came back to where I was standing, gave me a little poke in the ribs with a knobby finger, and looked up at me. "Dave, this is going to be Coach D. at his best. I feel it."

Everyone went quiet. Coach walked over to the front of the group, looked around at everybody, and said nothing for a few seconds. The quiet seemed like hours. Finally, in a low voice, he said, "OK, everybody, take a knee."

Cousins and the linemen bent down quickly onto one knee. They were followed slowly by each of the players. Then the coaches and some of the auxiliary staff went down to one knee. Coach D. looked around again and added with a little more insistence while focusing on his medical team, "I need everyone down on one knee. Everyone—and I mean everyone—take a knee. We have some work to do."

To my surprise, Father Jake went down to a knee and then waved at me to do the same. While I was watching all of this, I realized that even the doctors were getting down to a knee. That really surprised me. Father Jake waved with more urgency, summoning me down to the ground. I suddenly realized I was the only one left standing. Then Coach D. stared directly at me and, in a quiet but very measured and compelling voice, added, "I do need everyone down on one knee."

Down I knelt, next to Father Jake on one side and Randy and Mike on the other. Coach D. began to speak. He started softly.

"We are all one here. None of us would be in this room unless you belonged. You have all worked hard to be here, and you worked hard for us to be undefeated. Right now, we are up against it. On the road and losing in the rain and cold. We have been beat up. We came out flat. We were not ourselves. But everyone, make sure you understand this. We need to win this game to become champions. I know we are going to turn it around. I know something else, and right now I want everyone in this room to know it, too."

He stopped for effect for a few seconds. There was literally no sound in that room. Then he bent forward and down toward his quarterback and his linemen. You could barely hear him as he said, "You are a special team. I need you to understand and remember that. You are a special group of people, at a special place and at a special time in MSU's history."

With that, the players who had been on one knee staring at the ground, raised their heads just a little bit and looked into the eyes of their coach. Not once in the typical team huddles after hard practices and during other halftimes had I heard Coach D. talk like this. Nor had I ever heard him sound quite this way. He was, for lack of a better description, spiritual. Although speaking quietly and gently, he was using language and a tone that at once projected dignity but with that secret edginess of street credibility.

That combination made you instantly believe what he had to say was truth. Even as far back as the time I had that three-minute talk with him in Faylene Owen's kitchen, I recognized it was his innate credibility mixed with a sense of dignity that proved to be his supreme advantage when speaking from his heart. When he truly believed in something, you could tell. Even better, after he was done, you also found a way to believe in him and even more important, believe in yourself.

It did not matter if you were a middle linebacker, a running back, or a brain doctor. At that moment, in that locker room, it was easy to believe that somehow you were indeed special and that you would find some type of way to win. His words, his body language, and his demeanor made you absolutely believe you could do whatever was needed. I was enthralled.

"I saw the way we ended that half," he continued, "and I know you will win today because you are special. I know it. Today, we will win. Now, Kirk, take us back out to the field."

With that, Coach D. stepped aside, and Kirk Cousins stood where Coach D. had been just a second before. The junior quarterback also paused for effect and looked around at everyone. Then Cousins stared at each of his linemen, still on one knee. He then looked beyond them, to the people in the middle of the pack, then those behind them and even to the team doctors and team priest, all still on one knee.

Cousins shook his head up and down and then suddenly yelled, "Right now!"

With that, as if on cue, his offensive linemen looked up at him as one. They all stood up and, upon reaching their feet, shouted back in unison, "Right now!"

The young quarterback yelled "Spotlight!"

"SPOTLIGHT!" the team all screamed back to him as they scrambled to their feet.

"We will stand," said the quarterback.

"WE WILL STAND," was the answer.

"Stand and fight," he shouted.

"STAND AND FIGHT," echoed the team in response.

By now everyone—including the team medical staff—was on their feet.

"Now is the time," Cousins implored.

"NOW IS THE TIME," his team responded.

"Now or never," Cousins continued.

"NOW OR NEVER," came the confirming reply.

"Win today, win forever!" Cousins yelled.

"WIN TODAY, WIN FOREVER!"

"Who wins?"

"WE WIN!"

He asked again, louder, "Who wins?"

"WE WIN!"

Then one last time, Cousins bellowed, "Who wins?"

"SPARTANS WIN!"

"Let's go!" yelled Cousins, "Take it to them!"

Middle-aged and more than just a little plump, I ran along with everyone else down the ramp leading out onto the field. I, too, was inspired, and I was more than a little sad I did not have that helmet to put on to meet the Wildcats.

After dancing by defensive coordinator Pat Narduzzi with those thirty-three Chicago-style hot dogs, after observing Coach Narduzzi's subsequent drop-kick of that poor overhead projector, after hearing Coach D.'s dignified but street credible statement to his team and a bona fide Kirk Cousins rant, it struck me I had witnessed a pretty

special halftime. I also sensed it was a different Spartan squad that took the field for the second half.

MSU kicked off and squashed the Wildcats, quickly forcing a punt. Cousins and the offense rapidly moved the ball down the field to the Northwestern twenty-yard line. Randy casually said, "Ok, let's look for Bennie Fowler on a jet sweep."

I turned to look at our true freshman, as he entered the lineup. I thought, "What is Pearson talking about?" I only saw a skinny eighteen year old who was built just like a pogo stick: tall, active, but thin as a rail. If Bennie ever got hit by a linebacker, I was worried sick he would get cut in half. Bennie had played absolutely zero meaningful minutes in any Spartan game prior to this. However, with so many injuries today, his time to answer the bell had come. I held my breath. I really liked Bennie and did not want him to get injured during a day that had seen so many Spartans go down.

I had grown quite fond of him during our numerous talks this past summer on the football practice fields. He was from inside Detroit but went to school at Detroit Country Day, an intellectually elite suburban high school. Sports writers called him Dantonio's "prize catch." Benny had Hollywood good looks, dark caramel skin, and a winning smile. His down-to-earth, easygoing attitude belied his extraordinary intellect.

About thirty seconds into our first conversation three months before, Bennie impressed me as among the most articulate young men I had ever spoken with. He was as mature as a senior medical student. His leadership quality was obvious from the start of our practice field discussions.

Prior to today's game, while Bennie was getting his ankles taped, I asked him about his background and family. "My father travels a great deal for Ford Motor Company," he said, "and my mother is absolutely committed to helping improve education for Detroit's schoolchildren."

As we spoke, I again thought: Here is a true student-athlete with remarkable leadership skills even as a freshman. I also saw him as someone with an exceptional future when he was done playing football. After Bennie let me know he was "grateful to have an opportunity to talk," he jumped off the training table to get ready for warm-ups.

Father Jake came over to let me know Bennie was from a family of considerable wealth. His dad worked as a Ford Motor Group vice president for global quality, and his mother was in a leadership position with the Detroit school board. Father Jake also reminded me he was a top recruit and added that he was fairly sure Bennie Fowler would end up playing in the NFL and then go on to become huge in business, politics, or something similar.

I said, "Father Jake, how can a guy with a future like that play a sport with such inherent violence?"

The priest's response was quite direct. "Dave, you are a nice guy, but there is a lot you don't know about who plays football and why. There is a tremendous benefit to engaging in the ultimate team sport like football. There is camaraderie that lasts a lifetime. You learn how to work as a member of something far bigger than yourself. You learn that being part of an entity involved in a great struggle is a way to truly feel whole."

Jeff added "Dave, Ol' Bennie has the ability to relate to anybody. That includes the team recruits from the toughest neighborhoods. He's got street cred with them. He was also comfortable talking to you or even a guy like Joel Ferguson [chair of the MSU Board of Trustees]. Bennie gets along with anyone from anywhere. He'll be a big- time leader for us when he starts getting playing time."

After the TV time-out, sure enough, Bennie Fowler was inserted into the game. I did not fully understand Randy's deep appreciation of football talent and timing until Randy said with confidence, "Dave, I am telling you, watch for Bennie and that jet sweep on one of these plays."

Two snaps later, it happened. Fowler was lined up on the extreme left side of the formation. He had taken a step backward and gone into high-speed motion toward the right sideline a second before the snap. When Cousins got the ball, he faked a handoff to Baker, who nicely amplified the diversion tactic with an embellished swan dive over the center of the line. That drew all three Northwestern linebackers into the center of the defensive line to mistakenly try and stop a run up the middle.

Cousins then quickly turned and pitched the ball to Fowler. The chicanery worked; everyone converged on the man without the ball. Bennie was totally ignored until he went past Cousins with a *whoosh*, grabbed the pitch, and took off around right end.

Our six foot four, 315-pound, all-conference offensive guard, Joel Foreman, had already snuck out to the right edge after the snap of the ball. Foreman leveled some poor 175-pound intellectual playing cornerback. That "pancake" eliminated the only remaining human between Bennie and the Wildcat goal line. Fowler danced around Foreman's crushing block and went untouched for twenty-two yards into the end zone. The hole was so huge maybe even I could have scored.

The MSU fans erupted like a volcano. The roar was so spontaneous and so raucous it startled me. On the MSU sideline, people yelled and screamed louder and louder as the freshman danced and skipped his way back to the bench. He was mobbed in celebration of his first collegiate touchdown. That touchdown and extra point cut Northwestern's lead to 17–14 with only three minutes gone in the third quarter.

It was now up to Northwestern to match MSU's newfound momentum and intensity. The Wildcats, a 5–1 team, proved to be very tough, especially at home. Dan Persa, their lightning-fast QB, led them down the field, and within minutes they scored to get the lead back to ten. I was crushed. But the Spartans remained determined.

With time ticking away into the fourth quarter MSU got into Northwestern territory. Sadly, the Wildcats stopped the Spartans on third down at the thirty-five-yard line. There was about ten minutes left in the game. The Spartans lined up and Cousins kept calling signals using the word "hike" on three separate occasions, hoping for an offside call. The ball was never snapped, and a penalty was called for an MSU delay of game. "What a weird blunder for Cousins," I thought.

Coach D. called a time-out and then sent out the punt team. A kick down to the five-yard line or closer would allow the Spartans a shot at the vital score they needed to climb back in the game if they could hold the Wildcats after the punt. Sally and Jeff both grew quiet and looked at each other like two kids who were about to pull off a prank. They seemed to know something I didn't, as Jeff was smiling ear-to-ear. Randy leaned over and whispered in my ear, "Dave, remember Little Giants?"

I looked at him like he was crazy. Then the ball was hiked to Aaron Bates. Time slowed down to a crawl. Bates went into his typical punting stride but then suddenly stopped. He straightened up, looked downfield to his right, and just like against Notre Dame four weeks prior he threw a perfect pass to Bennie Fowler for a fifteen-yard gain for the first down. Jubilation!

Northwestern was bewildered. The Spartans quickly lined up and Cousins passed to B. J. Cunningham for the MSU touchdown. The extra point was good and just like that it was 24–21. The Spartan crowd went crazy.

Northwestern's Persa was not done. He drove his team down the field but eventually had to settle for a field goal to make it 27–21. I realized the next Spartan possession would determine whether we went home with an amazing comeback or were crushed in a last-minute loss to drop us out of contention for a Big Ten title. The Spartans received the kickoff backed up to their own twelve-yard line. Cousins orchestrated a five-minute 88 yard drive. He found B. J. Cunningham for a nine-yard acrobatic catch for a touchdown to take the lead 28–27.

There were two minutes left in the game and during the post-touchdown TV time-out, I again heard the Spartan defenders buckle their helmets extra tight with that *click-click-click* sound once again. They got up from the bench as one to receive last-minute instructions.

Standing on the sideline, with the MSU crowd right behind me, it was impossible to hear what Coach Narduzzi was saying. But everyone could see how animated he was as he implored his boys to do their job this one last time. Then his face turned calm, and he was no longer shouting as he whispered some instructions to his people.

Coach Dantonio leaned in and appeared to say only a word or two as the defense ran onto the field.

The ensuing kickoff went deep into the end zone with no runback. The Spartan defense held firm. The Wildcats could not gain an inch and turned the ball over on downs at their own twenty-five-yard line. With seconds to play, Cousins handed the ball to Edwin Baker, who ran through a dejected Wildcat team as an exclamation point on this remarkable road win to make it 35–27.

Nationally, when the score was flashed, it might have looked like a straightforward eight-point MSU road win. But any true MSU fan knew better. It was yet another miracle game designed and executed by Coach Dantonio, his coaches, and their players. As the boys ran off the field victorious, the Spartan fans were on their feet, yelling and screaming at the top of their lungs to celebrate victory. We were 8-0 for the first time in forty-four years.

My head was in the clouds, and I still did not believe what I had just experienced, and from as close up as any true sports fan could possibly get. Even more meaningful to me, it seemed like maybe I was now fully integrated into the medical team. It actually entered my mind I might have been of some small value to the team, all things considered.

As I was running with the pack across the football field, toward our locker room and through the wall of screaming, earthquake level noise created by our fans, I was on an emotional high. I was totally euphoric about what I had just witnessed. I knew it would be one of those unforgettable life moments.

That was when Jeff Monroe set the hook that allowed me to regain my love for college football until the day I die. He caught up to me about halfway to the locker room as we were both running off the field alongside the team. As he got closer, I saw he was incredibly excited as he whispered in my ear, "Dave, listen to those people cheering, and right now I need you to realize they are cheering for you!"

With that, he sprinted by me as the team went into the locker room to celebrate. Suddenly, I understood why players found the game so special despite its innate danger. On a day like today, anything good seemed possible. As a collective, once they made the decision to try, together they inspired each other to find the will to win. It was a lifetime lesson I would never forget be it sports, running a department of neurology at a Big Ten university, or living life. I was hooked. I suddenly felt I was part of something far bigger than myself and somehow that made me feel truly whole. I had indeed fallen back in love with college football.

When the yelling and screaming died down, Coach D. talked to his team about never giving up, ever. He then singled out Cousins as the most valuable player for today's win and told him, "Kirk, throw down your hat." Cousins put his helmet on the ground as was the tradition for the game's top player. Cousins then shouted out, "We just beat Northwestern 35–27!" He followed that with leading the team in the usual rapid counting of the points MSU had scored: one, two, three . . . , quickly reciting the numbers all the way up to thirty-five, accompanied by the entire team's clapping. Then came the fight song, followed by the raucous rap music played louder than ever, along with various players showing off their dance moves. After about fifteen minutes, people finally started to settle down and then went to get a shower.

Just a little later, I looked over and saw Coach D. alone in a tiny corner of the athletic training area. His postgame radio show was over, and he was sitting quietly, looking just a bit tired but with a very satisfied look on his face. It had been only a month since his heart attack, and this was his first game back on the field. Despite all of this, at halftime, he had found the words to inspire his players, the coaches and, perhaps, himself.

I again wondered about the physical and mental toll the game of football extracted from him and his wonderful wife and two daughters. It couldn't be easy. He had to love the game with all his heart to endure such chaotic turns of fortune. I realized now was not the time to try and talk to him about that. Yet it had to be very costly personally, given all the hours and all the stress he and his coaches endure to lead young men, student-athletes, in such a ruthless and violent game. Meanwhile, the rhythmic rap music was blasting out of the enormous speakers the team takes with them on the road.

What a juxtaposition to the inner calm a man like Coach D. appeared to have.

It looked like this incredible win actually allowed me to survive the hot dog blunder with Coach Narduzzi. Everyone in the athletic training area was alive and congratulating each other on the victory. Even Jeff was in a good mood, literally shaking my hand and thanking me for helping with Jerel Worthy's eye issue. It seemed like I was now an actual, accepted member of the medical team, holding my own and doing what was needed when called upon.

Flush with that newfound confidence, and ignoring the locker room chaos and noise, I summoned enough courage to walk over to Coach D. as he was sitting alone watching all of this. I asked him, "Coach, why did you deliberately take the delay of game penalty? Why not try a fourth-and-six pass play out of a real offensive formation? Or maybe even fake the punt, but at the thirty-five? Why take the penalty? You would have been five yards closer to the first down marker. What was that penalty all about?"

He smiled softly and said, "Well, that's an interesting question. We all saw it on film. Their left corner always goes back to help cover the punt in those close-to-the-goal-line punt situations. Anything from less than forty yards out, that corner always did the same thing, every time. He turns his back and runs to help his punt returner. Every time."

He looked at me a little like the coaches I had interviewed while writing sports in college so many years ago, but he went on. "We needed a play. A good punt by us still leaves them with the ball and us down by more than a touchdown. So we planned to take a delay of game penalty to make it seem like we wanted more room to punt the ball. When it became fourth and eleven, we thought they would forget about any possible fake. It worked. They took the 'cheese' and Bates closed the trap on them by making that throw to Fowler."

Coach D. added with an even bigger smile. "The name of that play is 'Mouse Trap.' Northwestern's punt coverage had to 'take the cheese' by backing off the line for mouse trap to work. And they did."

# CHAPTER FIFTEEN

# *Trying to Make Things Safer*

The sixty-minute flight home from Chicago seemed like it passed in two minutes. Dove Bars were passed around by Coach Folino, as was the habit after a win, and everyone was whooping it up. Father Jake, seated in front of me, waited until halfway through the flight to put his seat all the way back into my knees. I didn't care. We had won with a big-time show of determination and will. On Sunday, training room was raucous with trash talk and an extra tray of Dr. Shingle's very special chicken wings. The players came in one after the other with big smiles.

The only issue was another away game was coming up, this time against Iowa. When Sally mentioned how banged up MSU was, it got me thinking. Football is a game of attrition. A team is slowly whittled down during a season. You had to have great starting players, no doubt, but I now understood you needed a deep bench to be able to win later in the season.

Jeff came over and also set the tone. "We are going to have a time of it at Iowa," he said. "Another away game, we have all these guys on crutches. I don't know."

"Dave," he added, "before Thursday's practice, I want you to share with Coach D. how the concussion project using functional MRI is going. It might be best to do it this week rather than after Iowa."

Early on with the team, I thought it might be valuable to develop a tool that could help clinicians decide on the prognosis—and therefore the natural history—of a player with a concussion. I came upon the idea that functional MRI using blood flow to various parts of the brain during activity or thought might lead to a method to determine "connectivity" in a concussed brain. I knew from studies by other researchers on laboratory animals that reduced connectivity followed an mTBI. I wondered if that tool could be used in diagnosis, or even better, prognosis in student-athletes playing football.

I reviewed the idea with Randy, Jeff, and Sally, who were all very interested in developing such a radiographic biomarker. We were given permission by the MSU Department of Intercollegiate Athletics and the university's institutional review board to propose the study to the players, though none would be required to participate. I was pleasantly surprised when virtually the entire team agreed to sign permission slips to participate in the study. By mid-October, we already had a few players who suffered a concussion and were evaluated by serial fMRI over a month's time.

With the help of David Zhu from radiology and Tracy Covassin from kinesiology, we did initial exams within twenty-four hours of an mTBI, and then tested again at the one week and four-week marks. We found that within the first twenty-four hours of a concussion diagnosis, there was hyperconnectivity of brain systems, meaning the brain was more vigilant, more aware of surroundings. Then after one week, even though the clinical exam was normal, the brain showed hypoconnectivity; it was less vigilant, or less aware of surroundings. The results then trended back toward normal connectivity over a month's time, but not quite back to baseline levels established for age, gender, and physical fitness of normal volunteers with no history of an mTBI.

These early study subjects proved the concept that fMRI could be used as a tool in acute mTBI. Furthermore, it could measure acute brain activity in a fashion comparable to what I'd read in the animal literature. However, the stunning thing was even after a month, it appeared that "normal physiology" did not return to a player in some cases. We did not know the clinical significance of that finding, if any. But it was thought provoking. Prior to publishing the work in any journal, such as the *Journal of Neuro-Trauma*[4], we all agreed it was essential to review the findings with Coach Dantonio and other members of the Department of Intercollegiate Athletics.

I realized a major tension for any coach is a difficult decision: Is winning worth putting your players at increased risk—and is protecting your players worth putting winning at risk? How does a coach walk the fine line between those sorts of decisions? That was maybe where sports medicine doctors and athletic trainers truly earn their keep.

I was more than a little nervous on that Thursday, as I was about to show Coach Dantonio something he might or might not want to see about the dangers of his sport. I wondered if Coach Dantonio might not really want to deal with such data if it meant critical players would be sidelined for far longer than typically done. Or, conversely, would he be willing to embrace such medical information and the potential consequences of it, despite the fact that every opposing team he would face could easily avoid such issues.

I assumed going into that meeting it was possible once he saw these data, he might find it important to have me stay far away from the team and the players. However, I also realized we had to discuss this issue with Coach D. and let him come to his own conclusions and decision. Jeff had some large graphs made up to show the fMRI recovery trend of a player following an mTBI. I was then told we were to have the meeting in Coach D.'s office.

It was the first time I had been in the head football coach's office. It was magnificent. I had been in MSU President Lou Anna K. Simon's office on a few occasions, but that was nowhere near as glorious as Mark Dantonio's. Prior to the coach coming into our meeting, I whispered my observation about the room to Jeff, who responded, "Well, I hope Mark's office is nicer. First of all, he makes four times what President Simon does, has a far harder job, and has much tougher recruitment battles."

I was not sure if he was joking or not, but Jeff did flash that half-smile that always confused me. Before I could figure it out, in walked

[4] Zhu, et.al. 32 (5) August 2014 DOI:10.1089/neu.2014.3413)

Coach D. with his entourage. There were greetings all around and I was introduced to those who did not know me. Then I got up and gave my typical ten-minute scientific review as if I were presenting at the North American Neuro-Ophthalmology Society.

When I was done, I turned around and focused on the absolutely horrified face of Coach Dantonio. I again recognized that look instantly. It was the same one he used after I showed him Josh Rouse's hangman's fracture during my first game with the team.

Coach Dantonio cleared his throat. "Dr. Kaufman," he said, "let me be sure I understand. There is abnormality in the brain that you found with this functional MRI technique. That abnormality might last up to four weeks after a concussion. Am I correct?"

I assumed that my time with the team was now over. I would be going back to the upper deck to watch football games from this point forward. I didn't fear that and knew I had to respond using my background as a clinical researcher.

"These data," I said simply, "do imply that. However, we cannot verify the clinical significance of these findings. We need to do more work."

"Dr. Kaufman," said Dantonio, "please do more work. It means a lot to me. We have to find ways to make the game safer. Dr. Kaufman, I am pleased you are with us. Stay close and keep us up to date on this."

As Coach D. and his people got up to leave, I thought, "What a remarkable human being."

After that simple exchange, I had an ally in concussion research no matter where it took me. I also better understood why people respected Coach Dantonio so much. It was easy to summon the will to do your best for a man like that, every time. I felt privileged to be able to work with him and the team to try and make the game safer. As I left Coach D.'s office, I looked over at Jeff, who was wearing the smile of a proud dad.

# CHAPTER SIXTEEN

## *Pinked*

T he challenge with a sport as intense as football is the highs are very high, but the lows take you deep into the valley of despair. Despite the unbelievable victory against Northwestern the week before, the team was now down multiple players, and their absence was felt at the week's practice sessions. We were badly beaten up. Father Jake was quick to point out MSU had not won at Iowa for the past twenty-one years. But as the team prepared for the Hawkeyes on Halloween weekend, we were ranked fifth in the nation. Fifth!

MSU football had not seen anything like this since the Lyndon Johnson administration. Both a Big Ten championship and a trip to the Rose Bowl were right there to grab. Coach made that clear during the week of practice. A win meant there should be no way any pollster or even the Big Ten's byzantine decision-making system could deny the Spartans our dream of going to the Rose Bowl.

In 2010, the winner of the league was, by contract, always given an automatic berth to the holy grail: a warm and sunny trip to Pasadena in the winter, complete with a tour of Disneyland, Los Angeles night life for New Year's Eve, and then the Rose Parade followed by the Rose Bowl Game on New Year's Day. To virtually any Midwesterner who lives and dies with Big Ten football, the object every year was to go to "the Granddaddy of them all," the Rose Bowl.

Sure, being crowned as "mythical" national champions might be a nice thing, especially if you are from Alabama. And I know from experience that lots of Ohio State and Penn State fans felt that same way. But in 2010 there were no national playoffs in Division I football. So fans who grew up around the Great Lakes watching Big Ten football have always understood that the sustained week-after-week effort needed to win the rugged Big Ten and then that trip to California was the ultimate accomplishment.

There were great expectations for the Spartan Nation. Even Ohio State could not catch us. I thought Iowa would be down because the Hawkeyes had lost to Wisconsin the week before.

"A win at Iowa gets us up a game over everyone else," Jeff said, as if I needed reminding, "and we probably get the Roses."

As the team began to board the chartered jet, I could not be more pumped up. We all took the seats carefully assigned to us by Brad Lunsford, Coach D.'s executive assistant. Every away game Brad oversaw moving around two hundred people, their equipment and baggage to some distant city. That meant organizing travel for all the MSU players, coaches, equipment managers, video managers, communication experts, athletic trainers, one team priest, major donors, staff members of the athletic department, and three or four doctors.

It also included some sports equipment, athletic training gear, video cameras, and medical supplies. All the heavy football equipment, exercise bikes, special medical equipment, uniforms, and helmets were transported the day before by Glenn Edgett in an eighteen-wheeler and was set up prior to our arrival at the opponent's stadium. The players and most others packed a simple overnight bag, except for Randy, who always carried his doctor's medical bag and CPR equipment with him, even on the plane, "just in case."

The players boarded first, and the way people were seated on the plane was carefully orchestrated. It was always the same. The "big boys"—the offensive and defensive linemen—were seated in first class. This was not because they were the most important team members, (even though a great line is essential to a winning team). They were placed in first class because of their size. They are truly huge human beings and would have difficulty sitting anywhere else.

Right behind the first-class bulkhead, the linebackers and skill players sat in either the aisle or the window seat with no one in the

middle, giving each row the roominess of first class. All the rows from the bulkhead to the exit rows had that arrangement.

The coaches sat in the exit rows, usually three across. Coach D. invariably took an aisle seat on the right as you are walking down the plane from the entrance, with Coach Narduzzi typically flanking him in the left aisle seat. Next to them were their offensive or defensive coordinators and lead assistant coaches. The row behind the first exit row would have additional coaches. The group of "next men up" players were located behind the coaches, seated three across. The athletic trainers, Jeff and Sally, had the next row, given their importance to the team. They needed to be readily available if anybody had any medical issue during the flight.

After them came the equipment guru, Mr. Nick, and his people. Then the videographers, sports information people, communication folks, photographers, and team nutritionist. Many times, trustees, major donors, and important alums would be placed next. Among them typically is the lead team physician Dr. Pearson, our orthopedic surgeon Dr. Shingles and perhaps one of his fellow surgeons, like Dr. Dietzel. Then, after the doctors, almost at the very rear of the plane, would be the younger student athletic trainers and student managers.

Father Jake invariably would be seated in the next-to-last row on the left and by the window. In the very uncomfortable last row are the youngest of the equipment managers and athletic training students. Of course, all six feet three inches, 250 pounds of me was shoehorned into the last row corner seat right behind Father Jake. I wondered why I was always in a seat that did not have a window and no ability to move the seat backward.

"Dave," said Jeff when I asked him about it, "you occupy the worst seat in the worst row of the plane based on being the least important person on the plane."

To compound that, Jeff and Brad fully understood Father Jake's need to always put his seat all the way back after takeoff. As an attempt at negotiation, I eventually asked Brad why he personally felt it necessary to put me in the last row and in the worst seat on the plane.

"Well, Dave," he said with a wry smile, "your very good friend Jeff let me know you loved that seat, so I thought it made sense to place you there. You're welcome and have a nice flight!"

Even though I loved Father Jake with all my heart, that location was just not a good thing for a guy like me, especially since I had just a touch of claustrophobia. Although you could not imagine a better human being, Father Jake always reclined his seat all the way back immediately after takeoff, nestling it about an inch from my chest. He kept it that way for the rest of the trip. I had just barely enough space to breathe, and it didn't help that periodically I developed a panic attack that gave me a very rapid heartbeat.

I finally accepted this travel situation as "paying my dues." I soon realized I was so excited about the game ahead I was going to have a lot of difficulty handling my claustrophobia. I worked up the courage to tap Father Jake on his tiny shoulder.

"Father Jake, why exactly is it necessary for you to always put your seat all the way back and for the entire flight?"

Father Jake, half-asleep, looked at me through the opening between his reclined seat and the upright one beside him with his one open eye.

"Consider it your well-deserved penance, my son."

He then turned forward again, accepted a fist pound from the young, student athletic trainer next to him and fell asleep. That left me, an aging and plump neurologist, trying hard to catch my breath during an hour of agony as we flew to Iowa City.

The visiting locker room in Iowa was unique. It was large, with plenty of room for the players along with a nice-sized medical area, well separated from the dressing area to allow privacy. In my view it was pretty good with one interesting twist. Absolutely everything in the locker room was pink. Not sort of pink. Not close to pink. It was the hot pink of a high school prom corsage. Everything—including the sinks, toilet seats, walls, paper towel dispensers, and the toilet paper—was pink.

This color scheme was the brainchild of Hayden Fry, a master coach for the Hawkeyes during the end of the last century. Coach Fry apparently believed pink was a very "cooling color" and would reduce the passion of the players who used that visitors' locker room. Although the effectiveness of the pink color was more hype than reality, those teams under Fry had had inordinate success at home.

After the brief pink locker room visit, the guys walked the field. Arm in arm with Coach D., they silently moved the hundred yards down the field from one goal line to the other. I found that tradition stirring every time I watched it. That tradition reinforced the ethos that everyone belonged to this team and to each other. The symbolism that each player inexorably was linked to the player next to them was powerful. No one person was any better or any worse or less important.

After a lighthearted game of no-run touch football, everyone lined up on one sideline, as the coaches shouted out names. When called, players were expected to yell back who would be the next man up if an injury occurred. Randy let me know it was a way to reduce chaos after an injury. We all went into the locker room for one more look around. Everything seemed normal except all I saw was the pink.

On October 30, 2010, the Spartans were undefeated, 8-0, and leading the Big Ten. We were number five in the nation, and we faced number eighteen Iowa. As a reminder of what was at stake, the MSU coaches placed a green mat with a beautiful rose on it with the letters "PFRB" (Prepare For Rose Bowl) at the locker room entrance.

During pregame warm-ups, Father Jake and I walked around Iowa's Nile Clarke Kinnick Jr. Stadium, named for the 1939 Heisman trophy winner. It was the only college football stadium named after a Heisman Trophy winner, but I didn't understand why. I knew Kinnick stayed on at Iowa to attend law school rather than turn pro. Yet it didn't seem right to name the stadium for just one college football player. Initially it seemed like it took away from the team approach that makes football so special. I asked Father Jake about that.

"Dave," he said, looking at me with his soulful eyes, "Kinnick knew what was coming. He left law school and enlisted in the Naval Air Reserve as an aviator on December 4, 1941, three days before Pearl Harbor. He was assigned to the Lexington, a flat top [aircraft carrier]. By June of 1943, everyone was doing what they could to get ready for the island-hopping push toward Japan to try and end the war. During one of the training flights off the coast of South America, on June 2, Kinnick's plane got an oil leak. He tried an emergency water landing. They found the remains of his plane but never found his body. He was twenty-four and died serving his country during war. Why not name the stadium after him?"

Father Jake looked away and stared at the ground for just a bit. I suspected he may have been reflecting on his own experiences in the Marines during the Korean War. He did not need to speak another word. We remained silent even after we walked past the sixteen-foot statue of Nile Kinnick not dressed in a uniform but in his letterman's jacket carrying textbooks. I realized Iowa wanted him portrayed as the student-athlete and not just the football player. Then Father Jake showed me a sixteen-by-nine-foot bronze placard on the wall of the stadium; a reminder of Kinnick's game-winning touchdown (despite his broken ribs) against Notre Dame in 1939.

"Dave, you know, even to this day, the refs use the 'Nile Kinnick Coin' at the beginning of every Big Ten game to determine who kicks off. That's pretty special."

Kinnick Stadium has a capacity of 69,250. The first row is about seven feet from the players' area. A fan could literally whisper and be heard by the student-athletes on the bench. Right before kickoff, the trash talk started. I thought I might be of value by standing between the player being attacked and the front row "Hawkeye Hecklers." Then things got worse in a hurry.

Quarterback Rick Stanzi guided Iowa to a ten-point lead within minutes. Then with a few seconds left in the first quarter, the Spartans had driven deep into Iowa territory. Cousins underthrew a simple up-and-out sideline route, probably due to miscommunication with the receiver. Instead of MSU going in for a touchdown, Iowa's Tyler Sash intercepted the ball, lateraled to Micah Hyde who then went seventy-two yards to make it 17–0. You could see the entire Spartan sideline slump.

The hecklers started working on Cousins as soon as he came back to the bench, and they did not let up until halftime. By then

Cousins had thrown another interception from inside the Hawkeye twenty-yard line to stop another promising drive. That led to a Stanzi-to-Adam Robinson thirty-two-yard touchdown to make it 23–0. With one minute left in the half, another Robinson score made it 30–0. The Spartans were being crushed.

"Where is the Spartan offense?" I asked.

Jeff's abrupt reply was "Norm Parker."

Parker was Iowa's defensive coordinator, and his squad was swallowing the MSU offense whole. Parker was a celebrated defensive guru who had helped coach Kirk Ferentz guide Iowa to an impressive resurgence after the Hayden Fry era.

Jeff knew Norm Parker well. Born in Detroit, Parker had risen to defensive coordinator of the Spartans (1990–94) during his time with MSU from 1983 to 1994. And he was tough: He struggled with diabetes, and his right foot had been amputated just six weeks before this game. Yet here he was, back at work.

Over the years when I saw coaches sacrifice like this, I was amazed, but not surprised. Already, in my first season, I had seen Coach D. pull through his heart attack to coach again in a few weeks, but I was to learn that this sort of sacrifice is actually typical of coaches; they will go through almost anything to be with their team.

Halftime was not pretty. The MSU orthopedic surgeons administered Lidocaine and steroid injections into an A-C shoulder joint. They straightened and buddy-taped dislocated fingers and analyzed ankle injuries. There would be no magic trick plays, no last-minute lineup change to win this one. Coach D. assembled his team and said what needed to be said. He and the other coaches implored the boys to win the second half and play every play. After that, he said, we could regroup and go on.

Early in the third quarter, Kirk Cousins, having his worst game ever as a Spartan, threw his third interception. Iowa's Marvin McNutt scored on a seventy-two-yard catch-and-run with seven minutes and thirty-two second to go in the third quarter. The game mercifully ended, with a final score of 37–6, and the Hawkeye fans rushed the field to celebrate victory.

After the game, when we landed in Lansing, I asked Sally if we were done for the season. "Dave," she said, "They are just kids, and like kids, they are resilient. They should be fine by the end of tomorrow's training room. Coach D. is very good at the mental part of the game, maybe the best I have seen during my time at MSU. We'll regroup."

When I got home, I sat alone in a dark room for about two hours before I could talk to Laurie. I did not say much for the rest of the evening. There were four teams in the Big Ten with one league loss: Wisconsin, Ohio State, Iowa, and Michigan State. My only fear was that a defeat like ours after such high expectations could demoralize any team. MSU's dream of an undefeated season was in tatters. The risk now was that we would go into a tailspin and lose all desire to play, let alone win a championship.

Laurie eventually found me in my study and sat down in one of my overstuffed maroon leather chairs.

"I just looked at the entire Big Ten schedule," she said. "If we win out, it looks like there should be a two- or three-way tie for the Big Ten championship. We might not go to the Rose Bowl, but we could still get a Big Ten championship. Be sure they get that in their heads tomorrow at training room."

Laurie always surprised me with her football IQ. She pretended not to care about football or sports in general. But ever since that 1969 Wisconsin-Iowa game, I recognized her secret passion for sports. As usual, she was absolutely right. The coming week would tell a lot about this team's character.

If the players did not recover from their beating, it was over. If they could climb above the Iowa disaster, MSU still had a shot at the Big Ten championship, their first in twenty years. Sunday's training room, when the wounded came in for treatment, would be important. That would be the first opportunity to reset the team's course.

# CHAPTER SEVENTEEN

## *Muffled Agony*

**A**s always, the Sunday postgame training room at the Duffy Daugherty Football Building went from eleven in the morning to one in the afternoon. It is the focal point after games, which was both good and bad. Today I actually felt afraid to go. I just did not want to see the mess this loss had created.

When I arrived, things were indeed different than from the week before. This was my first loss as a team doctor, and I quickly gathered that the day after a loss was never good. Gloom hung over the training room like a fog. Everyone was down when they first arrived to see the medical staff. It was as quiet as a funeral. Nobody said anything to anyone.

Typically, when we win, the doctors arrive to an almost empty training room. After this first loss, I noticed that by eleven o'clock, it was already filled to the brim with the injured. Numerous players were already getting treatments, such as cold packs or soft tissue therapy, from the athletic training staff. Others were bunched together, having their vital signs taken, which was the first step to being allowed to see the doctors. Players kept coming in, most with some dubious complaint, or simply looking for sympathy. But others had significant issues that might require an MRI. The mood was somber and dark. Worst of all, there were none of those very special Dr. Mike Shingles chicken wings after a loss.

As I talked with them, I learned they just wanted some quiet time with their teammates. After a while, I sensed the somber mood might be lifting just a little as more teammates showed up for support.

Camaraderie seemed to do the trick. I was amazed how the guys began to return to their good-natured selves as they talked with one another. I realized the Sunday training room was not only needed to treat player injuries but also to allow a team's collective psyche to reorient. Today, a reorientation was sorely needed.

As the mood lightened, I, too, began to feel better. At around noon, Sally whispered in my ear, "Dave, they're resilient. Like we talked, really, they're just kids. They do better when everyone spends time with one another. You know, talking things over as teammates, maybe even like a big family, having fun with one another. We'll be alright." And I believed her.

The drill for the student-athletes seeking care was always the same after a win or a loss. They were triaged by the athletic trainers and the vitals were taken. Most players had already been seen and diagnosed on the sidelines or in the athletic trainers' room by the team physicians in Iowa City. I was amazed how Sally and Jeff remembered each nuance of the injury: how it happened, on which precise play, and at what time during the game.

The athletic trainers and physicians learned a lot in the training room about the student-athletes under their care. Were they tough or fragile? Stoic or complainers? Did they exaggerate their discomfort? Were they afraid and childlike, or were they mature?

I also realized how right Jeff and Randy had been when they told me that getting to know the athletes would help me identify occult concussions. Knowing players as people allowed me to detect the subtle personality changes that could imply an mTBI had occurred.

When a student-athlete came into the examination room, there would be a review of complaints, an examination by the appropriate physicians, and then a diagnosis. Sally and Jeff—and sometimes other athletic trainers—were always in the room looking out for their student-athletes. At times, we'd discuss whether we needed to get a player's parents on the phone. We determined the best diagnostic and therapeutic options, and then the player and the parents would decide how they wished to proceed. Then we would administer a needed shot into a shoulder joint, or order an MRI to obtain a diagnosis, or drain a swollen knee.

Sometimes, the player wasn't suffering from an orthopedic or athletic injury, but rather from some sort of upper respiratory issues, skin lesions, or other maladies common among college undergraduates. In that case, Randy would whisk the player away to an adjoining examination area with me and the appropriate athletic trainer in tow to determine the therapeutic strategy.

One of the things we feared most was a knee injury. The key was to identify the location of the injury: A medial collateral first degree ligament sprain is very different than an anterior cruciate tear. (The former heals up nicely, and folks are often ready to play within a week or two. The latter can end a career.)

A big linebacker came into the examination room complaining of his lingering medial collateral knee issue that was reinjured during the game. It had swollen up on the plane ride home from Iowa. The joint was stable enough on examination, but the knee needed to be drained. I was surprised that the procedure was done right away in the examination rooms by the surgeons.

This procedure has always struck me as barbaric. The student-athlete stayed in the ten-by-twelve-foot examining room on a typical, ER-like exam table that raises and lowers. The knee was illuminated by a bright, movable light that is a version of an operating room light. The player lays flat on the bed while the orthopedic surgeon carefully cleans his knee with an antiseptic and drapes a sterile covering over it.

A tray that hits about chest height when a physician is seated, called a Mayo stand, is prepared with three syringes and a long needle. The first syringe is filled with lidocaine. The surgeon empties its contents under the kneecap to numb the knee. Leaving the needle in place, the surgeon removes the syringe and attaches a second, empty syringe. The surgeon pulls back lightly on the syringe barrel and works the needle carefully around to remove fluid accumulated in the inflamed knee. A sample of that fluid is often sent to the laboratory for analysis. Typically, the surgeon will remove anywhere from 20 cc to 100 cc (about a third of a glass) of yellow, sometimes blood-tinged fluid. At last, the surgeon often swaps in a third and final syringe filled with a medication to assist with healing.

As a brain doctor, I don't drain knees. My role was to engage the student-athlete in some lighthearted discussion to take their mind off the procedure. I'd talk with them about home or school or a girlfriend. They usually seemed quite content to have the drainage done, as it typically relieves their discomfort. I never saw anyone complain, yell, cry, or anything similar during these procedures. Occasionally, I would be given the honor of placing the Band-Aid. The entire procedure would take five to ten minutes, and the players seemed far more comfortable as they left than when they first came into the examination room.

One of MSU's unfair advantages was the quality and camaraderie of the team physicians and the athletic trainers. We collaborated like clockwork. In between the good-natured ribbing, there was intense respect for each other all around. I didn't realize it isn't always that way at other universities or pro teams. In addition, we had an in-clinic fluoroscopy for simple diagnosis like a hand fracture versus a bruise. MSU also had absolutely superb availability of MRI scanning (even on Sundays) and musculoskeletal fellowship–trained radiologists to help with a "real time" interpretation of the MRI. That allowed diagnosis within minutes even on a Sunday morning. It was amazing to watch.

Sunday training room was pivotal in determining who was going to have a chance at being ready for next Saturday and who was done for the week or longer. Plans for the rest of the season could come down to who was lost after a game and who might still be able to return to play. Those Sunday assessments—especially with knee, ankle, and shoulder injuries—moved quickly. But these decisions were essential for the coaches, as they sought to create the game plan that would be needed to win the next game.

The speed and impact of those triage discussions on postgame Sundays seemed almost like battlefield decisions. Inwardly, I was impressed, that for the athletic trainers and physicians assembled, their decisions were never about winning or losing. They were always about the best outcome for the student-athlete.

Rarely, an athlete might get set up for surgery in the next day or two based on the exam and MRI finding. Parents would be called back after the MRI results were in; there would be much crying and wringing of hands as rehab plans for recovery were made. Sometimes the plan included a simple next-day arthroscopic surgery to see if the issue could be quickly remediated. That might allow the student-athlete to return within one to three weeks, saving his season.

Sometimes it meant more complicated surgery, followed by months of rehab to get ready for spring ball in four to six months. I found it remarkable most players would simply shrug their shoulders, take a breath, tighten their lips just a bit but go on when they were told they needed a significant surgery. They all just seemed to accept it as part of playing Division I football.

Next to come into the examination area was one of our starting offensive linemen, who was concerned that his shoulder did not feel quite right after the game. Linemen have read as much about the dangers of football as the rest of us. Yet I've never seen them complain about the sport they have chosen or the position they have been assigned to play. They live in virtual obscurity except when they screw up. They are the heart of the sport, absolutely essential for victory, yet so overlooked by the fans.

Sometimes after an exam of a painful shoulder, especially in offensive linemen, an injection of an anti-inflammatory into the shoulder joint might be done. That treatment strategy worked well in this case.

Offensive linemen are particularly vulnerable to shoulder capsule injury. This is based on having to literally punch their fists into on-rushing defensive linemen to throw them off balance. That technique was necessary to stop their opponent from overwhelming them on a "bullrush" technique or a spin move. If the offensive lineman failed to achieve his block, his opponent would skip by them for an open hit on the quarterback.

From the upper deck, I had never noticed that fistfights broke out between offensive and defensive linemen with every single passing play. Now, when I watch a game, even on TV, I try to be disciplined enough to look at this on-field barroom brawl, as four or five defensive players rush the quarterback, and five or six offensive linemen move to stop them on every pass play. The brutality inflicted on offensive linemen during pass protection is horrific.

During running plays, the tables are turned. Offensive linemen might drive into the defensive linemen's legs, trying to take out their knees. Sometimes on runs, two offensive linemen take on a single defensive linemen, to create a weakness or hole in the defensive line. When successful, a running back can slither through an opening in the defensive formation and into the open field.

Most people watch the running back. Very few notice the linemen. When the runner squirts through the line, it looks like some sort of miracle. But there is a price to pay: Linemen's shoulders, fingers, knees, and ankles take a pounding, game after game. So do their heads, and that's where I come in.

Good data are hard to come by, but by my unofficial count, blows to the head of a lineman seem to occur on about a third of plays. The key questions for me are: How many of these blows are actually "subconcussive events," that is, blows that do not cause a true concussion but transmit enough force through the helmet to affect the cell biology of the brain? And, just as crucially, is each man equally vulnerable to long-term sequalae, such as CTE?

Asked in a slightly different way: Is one player more at risk for long-term brain damage than another, based on genetics or associated health issues, such as migraine, underlying IQ, mental health, ADHD, alcohol use, etc.?

On the sidelines, one of my jobs is to look for potential silent concussions during this trench warfare. Surprisingly, I noticed that acute, game-ending mTBI among linemen seemed to be relatively unusual. I surmised that it might be related to the low velocity of hits among the linemen. These players usually do not take a long, running start prior to hitting each other. However, I worried that the combined effect of subconcussive blows—all game long, over the many games that made up a career—might lead some players to face issues in later life like CTE.

Dislocated or broken fingers among linemen were common discoveries at Sunday training room examinations. After the Iowa game, I noted one of our offensive linemen came in with a

particularly ugly-looking pinkie finger. It was bent at an awkward angle and swollen like a sausage.

"What happened?" Jeff asked him, "Why didn't you let us know you had an issue?"

"Well, Jeff, after a running play my finger was pointed the wrong way. Cousins pointed it out to me and said it looked like a dislocation. He is a premed type guy so I believed him. I just pulled on it and it sort of straightened out and I eventually got a Band-Aid. I didn't want to leave the field and tell you, 'Jeff, my little pinkie hurts.' So I just kept playing. The pain stopped soon enough, but the swelling started on the plane ride home. I thought maybe I should get it checked out."

Our training room X-ray unit immediately demonstrated the fracture dislocation. The orthopods reviewed the radiograph with the player and decided the bones were actually in good position.

"He also has a Tuft fracture," Doug Diezel said. "He'll need a finger splint and a hand wrap during practice and games but nothing further. With some buddy tape, he should be fine to practice tomorrow and hit on Tuesday."

As he was leaving the examination room, I asked the young man, "Should we call your parents?"

He just laughed. "Doc, if I called home every time I got a finger boo-boo, my mother would get crazy. Let's save the call for the big stuff." And out he went to get his finger fitted for the splint.

Some of the injuries during the Iowa game were serious, including an ankle sprain to our quarterback. After an X-ray showed no fracture to explain the swelling, it was diagnosed as a first- or second-degree sprain by the athletic trainers and confirmed by the orthopedists. I thought that was the logical reason why Kirk Cousins may have had his worst game of the year against Iowa. I shared that analysis with Cousins, who immediately corrected me.

"Dr. Kaufman," he said, "the issue was not my ankle. The problem yesterday was me. I have played well with worse injuries. I have got to be better if we want to get that Big Ten championship."

As Cousins left the examination room, I wondered out loud if he would somehow recover enough to play on the coming Saturday.

Everyone laughed. Sally turned to me and said, "Make no mistake, Dave. Kirk will play next week. As a matter of fact, when he is done here at MSU, he will also play on Sundays. And I suspect he'll be a game-changer."

I asked for a translation, and she added, "Kirk Cousins will play professionally in the NFL and eventually be declared a 'franchise player' for his team, well before he is done. I am sure of it."

Later in the day, Coach Dantonio made a surprise visit to the training room area. He came up to Jeff and asked, "Jeff, how bad?"

Jeff's response was simple. "Not as bad as it could have been. We'll be alright. Cousins has an ankle, but he is tough, as we know. There was a player with a messed-up finger, one or two low-grade knee sprains, mostly bruised egos. But we are still recovering from the Northwestern game for a few of the guys. We are sorting it out now, and we'll give you the run down at our one-thirty meeting."

Training room ended at one o'clock. The players in the treatment area walked out together in better spirits than when they came in—we all did. The boys began talking it up and joking around with one another as they got ready for their traditional Sunday stretch and run. Later that afternoon the coaches would gather with Jeff and Sally to see who was going to be ready for next Saturday and who might not.

Then the coaches would review film of the game just played, followed by viewing film on the next opponent. After a fast-food dinner, game planning would start with the coaching meetings usually going well past eleven at night, even on a Sunday. I thought to myself, Sunday is just another fourteen- to sixteen-hour workday for these coaches and the athletic trainers. Unbelievable.

The coaches' work on Sunday was not even half over, and here I was, leaving. I was happy that I could rest tonight and be with Laurie. I would only have sixteen patients the next day in my neuro-ophthalmology clinic, along with my daily administrative, education, and research responsibility. I suddenly realized, compared with the workload of the coaches, maybe I did have it easy.

# CHAPTER EIGHTEEN

# *Looking for the Promised Land*

T he loss to Iowa affected everyone on campus, even in my academic meetings at the medical school. After a satisfying win against a rival like the University of Michigan, even our grumpy dean would be in an upbeat mood. But at the eight o'clock Monday morning chairs' meeting after this Iowa loss, the dean was in a particularly dark place. No one and no department was safe from his complaints about real or imaginary issues.

I also found myself being abrupt with anyone I talked to. Staff, faculty, fellows, residents, nurses, even my beloved medical students were not spared. Around midday people began to duck into hallways to avoid me. By three o'clock my closest fellow faculty members, Eric Eggenberger and Jayne Ward, pulled me aside and pointed out that I was not myself. They made me realize that I was behaving like an idiot over one lousy football game.

True to Sally's prediction, this 2010 MSU football team endured its first loss of the season but began to pick up the pieces as they all collectively rallied. The typical hard-hitting Tuesday practice was pitched at an even higher tempo. Practices under Coach D. comprised anywhere between twelve and eighteen "periods," each lasting three to ten minutes. There were "soft periods," like field goal practice, when most people were on the sidelines taking a breather, and there were "hard periods," like pitting the number one defense against the number two offense, or vice-versa, in an on-field scrimmage.

Usually, Coach D. ran the "hard periods" at about three-quarter speed, to reduce the wear and tear on players. But occasionally they would "go live," meaning number one defense against number one offense and number two against number two; these were at full speed, all out. With forty-four people going all out on the two practice fields, the likelihood of injuries or an mTBI was even higher, given the reality there were four times as many players on the field as were ever in a game. At this Tuesday practice, there were a lot more of the "live" periods scheduled than usual, so I held my breath. This practice was far more grueling than the ones I had seen during the year, and that got me worried.

I asked Jeff about the intensity of this practice.

"Is it punishment?" I asked.

"Coach D. is so crafty, Dave," Jeff said, laughing. "He is being brutal today so they could not find any time to feel sorry for themselves. All they care about today is to hit. They are healing up after that loss. I can see it. We'll be fine. Wait until we put them in front of those Gophers on Saturday. And after we beat Minnesota, look out! I think we'll run the table and win the rest of them."

Jeff was right. MSU pounded Minnesota in East Lansing, winning 31–8. The next game was against Purdue also at home. Cousins injured his ankle once again, and the team was struggling. The Spartans were getting clobbered, even though the huge crowd was urging them to somehow pull out a victory.

"Go Green!" one side of the stadium yelled urgently.

"Go White!" was the response from across the field.

The chant went back and forth, but by the fourth quarter it was 28–13 Purdue. Yet Cousins was up to his old tricks, walking behind the bench, getting more and more agitated, just like at the Northwestern game.

Cousins leaned over and said something to one of the behemoth linemen, and the lineman growled. Then again to another lineman. When the final quarter started, the offensive line came alive. Cousins, bad ankle, and all, threw for three touchdowns with no interceptions, reaching an astonishing quarterback rating of 159.7. Freshman Denicos Allen blocked a punt near the end of the game and somehow the Spartans won 35–31. In the locker room after the win, the team counted out thirty-five and sang the Spartan fight song. We all knew that with one more win, MSU would get our Big Ten championship—and, hopefully, a shot at going to the Rose Bowl.

Between us and that goal stood Happy Valley, home of Penn State football. As the last week of practice for the regular season started, three teams in the Big Ten had a 10–1 record: MSU, Ohio State, and Wisconsin. We would have to win by a very big margin at Penn State to have any chance to jump over OSU and Wisconsin in the national polls—we had dropped from fifth to ninth in the rankings after the loss at Iowa and the close call with Purdue. If the Buckeyes and the Badgers each won their last game to create a tie in the league standings, we might not be the top-ranked team from the Big Ten. No matter what, it came down to winning at Penn State to at least get a portion of that Big Ten championship and have any chance for the Rose Bowl.

The practices were focused and the team seemed ready. The players also understood the opportunity to make history. Coach D., in his typical Thursday postpractice, on-the-field discussion with the team, said it all.

"We can do this," he said. "We should win at Happy Valley. Spartans have done it before, and we are ready."

My confidence was growing until Father Jake leaned over to get my head on right.

"Yes, we have beaten the Lions at Penn State before," he whispered, "but the last time was literally prior to the Vietnam War. Of course, I hadn't been born yet, but you must have just had your bar mitzvah, and look how old you are now. Better bring your prayer shawl with you to Happy Valley, Dave. We are going to need it."

With that less-that-optimistic statement from my usually upbeat road roommate, we were off to Penn State the next day.

There was reason for hope. Penn State was having (for the Nittany Lions) a tough year under Joe Paterno, who was in his forty-fifth year as head coach. Joe Pa had already accumulated a stunning 401 wins. MSU would also need to face the fact that Penn State was celebrating Senior Day. Coach Paterno always favored his seniors in the battle for playing time, and the seniors always responded for him.

As Father Jake and I made it through the check-in line at the airport, he again blessed me with some news.

"You know, Dave," he said, "Penn State has lost exactly once in the last twenty Senior Days over there. By the way, did you bring your prayer shawl?"

With that unhappy exchange, we both boarded the plane. Father Jake took his usual window seat in the next to the last row and I, of course, was placed right behind him. Even before taking off, Father Jake put his seat all the way back after the safety check by the flight attendants was done. There I was once again claustrophobic, nervous as hell, and with Father Jake's seat already in my face. I leaned over the chair as we taxied down the runway and asked the priest, "More penance?"

"No," he replied. "Retribution. You made me pay for the Scotch last time we were on the road at Iowa. Now let me relax, so I can pray our way to a win."

After arriving at State College, we immediately bused to Beaver Stadium. From the outside, the stadium looked more like a giant Erector Set than a college football stadium. Parts of it dated to 1909, but it had been moved six times before it reached its final location. In its current iteration, the stadium had an official seating capacity of 106,572, making it one of the largest in the world. It is also known to be a very difficult place to play; two years earlier, Kirk Herbstreit of ESPN declared that it had the best student section in America.

After learning about all the stadium moves, renovations, and expansions, I did feel a little nauseated inside the thing. The visiting locker room was located under the fragile-looking stands and had the appearance of a double-wide mobile home. There was a small but adequate athletic training room, the coaches' area, and two larger rooms, one for the offense and one for the defense.

After the typical Friday walk-through, we drove the buses through the town of State College itself. I found it charming. It was one of those iconic university towns that exist almost totally to support their university.

For the traditional pregame medical staff meal, everyone insisted we go to the Tavern, a beautiful steak and ale house owned by one of Duffy Daugherty's relatives. The meal was exquisite, and we were well-treated by the owner, who was still loyal to Spartan medical staff and alumni. Best of all, Mike again picked up the bar tab and paid for the meal to assure us all that good times were coming.

# CHAPTER NINETEEN
## *The Big Uglies*

At seven-thirty in the morning on November 27, 2010, State College was chilly and windy and already overrun by a crush of people from all over Pennsylvania. They came from Palmyra, Hersey, Harrisburg, Pittsburg, and Philadelphia to support their Nittany Lions.

After breakfast, the doctors went down to the training room to be sure there were no last-minute medical issues we could assist with. Jeff and Sally already had a lineup of players getting their issues attended to prior to the noon game. I had learned during the season that football is a game of attrition. By game twelve, everybody who was still capable of playing was nicked up in some fashion.

We always kept the injuries quiet. There was no need to let the opponent know which cornerback had a turf toe and was now a step slower, or which lineman had a bad shoulder. But no matter how bad the hurt, if they were not disqualified by the athletic trainers or team doctors, players played.

On game day, an injured shoulder that required a sling all week was just considered an inconvenience by a player. Once it was concluded no more harm could be done with playing, and even if a surgery after the season was being considered, that player played. If the student-athlete had a swollen knee that had been drained three days earlier, but the MRI and exam showed no significant structural damage, that player played.

After kickoff, it became clear the Spartans were determined to win. Less than five minutes in, MSU scored a touchdown. Penn State replied with a field goal and the quarter ended 7–3. In the second period , Coach D. reached into his bag of tricks and called for a double reverse at the Nittany Lions' forty-nine-yard line. Cousins headed left and handed the ball off on a reverse to Keith Nichol, who ran full speed to his right with multiple defenders in hot pursuit. At the hash mark, Nichol found Keshawn Martin, who took the lateral and headed back to the left.

The confused Penn State defensive squad were virtually all on the wrong side of the field by now. Martin flew thirty-five yards downfield to the fourteen-yard line. Then on a play-action pass, Cousins threw for the touchdown on what looked like a backyard postbarbeque toss—Laurie could have caught it. Even Coach Mannie was smiling.

On the ensuing kickoff, one of our players came off the field shaking his head. He looked normal enough, but after Randy's examination, it was not clear if the player had an mTBI or not. Randy asked me to get a look at him, and I began my typical in-depth neuro-ophthalmologic exam looking for a concussion.

This included a variety of advanced ocular motility tests called the VOMS. In one of those tasks, I asked the player to put their thumb out in front of them and while staring at it slowly and then more quickly move their head to the left and then to the right. If this evoked dizziness or a headache it implied they had a concussion.

I then had them cover one eye and look at my nose as I rapidly flashed one, two, or five fingers in various parts of their visual field to make sure there was no disruption of their sight. I followed this with a "tandem" Romberg test, where they had one foot in front of the other with their hands on their hips and eyes closed. They had to maintain this posture for at least ten seconds before I would declare their balance as normal.

I did this "tandem" Romberg to uncover any hidden imbalance that would imply a subtle concussion had occurred. It is a fairly sensitive part of an advanced neurologic exam, looking for any dysfunction in the vestibular-cerebellar (inner ear and brainstem) system that helps control balance. While the player was balancing, I heard a voice from the stands, about fifteen feet away.

"You call that a correctly performed Romberg?" the voice heckled. "That was as bad as the way you tested that poor guy's saccadic eye movements and his visual fields. What kind of neurologist are you?"

I was surprised to be heckled—who heckles the doctor?—but I was more surprised at being criticized in an academically meaningful way. I turned around to see who was heckling me, and I noticed three very large and ugly-looking people, all wearing the same mask, which made them look like beaten-up football players: a bad black eye or two, missing teeth, and broken noses. There was a fourth person behind them wearing a comically large nose and black horn-rim glasses with bushy eyebrows along with a light wind breaker. He bore a striking similarity to Joe Paterno.

I actually recognized these "super fans" from numerous national TV cut-away shots during Penn State football games. I also recalled a *Sports Illustrated* feature story about the four of them. The three in football uniforms were called Penn State University's "Big Uglies." The fourth was a diminutive "Joe Pa" look-alike.

On the one hand, I felt honored to be given a hard time by such famous fans. On the other hand, how did they know what I was doing, and how on Earth did they know the correct name of this advanced neurologic test?

I turned back to my student-athlete; it was obvious he had a positive Romberg and had to be disqualified. His balance was off, and I told Sally as much. I could still hear the taunting from the Big Uglies even after I had finished. I felt compelled to walk over to the stands and looked up to where they were standing about five feet above me. One of them in particular was still letting me know my neurologic examination was "sadly lacking."

"Okay," I responded. "What gives? Who is the ringer among you that actually thinks he knows something about neurology?"

"Me," came the reply. "I am Dr. John Duda. These are my two brothers and some guy who thinks he is Joe Paterno. And, frankly, your exam was lacking."

"Dr. Duda," I said, "explain yourself. What in the world are you doing here?"

Duda revealed that he was actually a neurologist at the University of Pennsylvania, specializing in movement disorders at one of that university's prestigious hospitals in Philadelphia. He quickly let me know he was also a Penn State alum (class of 1987). He and his two brothers were sons of a Penn State physics professor and had been at almost every Penn State game for over three decades.

I then recalled the *Sports Illustrated* article describing how the "Big Uglies and Joe Pa" had become so effective they were allowed to roam the stadium stands at will to stir up the crowd. The article also revealed they took great pride in being a major distraction to the visiting team.

"Dr. Duda," I countered, "your team is playing like they are in deep need of your neurologic expertise and skills. I suggest urgent testing for a neurologic disorder like rabies, especially in your quarterback."

"Wait until the fourth quarter," he retorted. "That's been where we have turned it on all year. You'll see."

"Duda, that could be, but we'll see who wins." I countered. "By the way, would you come to Michigan State to give neurology grand rounds next year when Penn State comes to East Lansing?"

His two brothers, still in character, silently nodded, pointed right at me, and shook their right arms up and down, then side to side, finally ending with a thumbs up. "Don't worry, neurology boy, we'll get our brother to MSU next year." Dr .Duda and the other Big Uglies then moved on to heckle others on the MSU sideline.

The half ended with the Spartans still up 14–3. There were virtually no injuries to care for except that one concussion. Coach D. kept it simple for his halftime theme, and then out the guys went, with a championship on the line.

The defenses dominated most of the third quarter until Cousins hit B. J. Cunningham with a twenty-nine-yard spiral to make it 21–3. Eighteen points! *Our defense is doing great*, I thought, *we are going to do this!* Then, right on cue, Penn State scored a touchdown.

Coach D.'s trickery at key moments had already been well documented. After Penn State had just scored, Keith Nichol was inserted into the game as a quarterback. Keshawn Martin, lined up at the flanker position, took two steps back after the ball was hiked. Nichol threw a backward pitch out to Keshawn who held the ball long enough to suck in virtually all of the Penn State defenders. Just as Keshawn was about to be crushed he completed a pass to Nichol down to the Penn State five-yard line.

The Spartans ran up to the line of scrimmage and Nichol then threw a laser shot through a hole about the size of a shoebox in the confused defense; it was caught in the end zone to make the score 28–10. Euphoria broke out on the Spartan bench, and everyone was hugging each other. *Game over*, I thought. Victory was there to grab! Up by eighteen points, all we needed was to run out the clock. But for some reason, that was not what we did. With just over two minutes to go, MSU fumbled, Penn State recovered and quickly scored six points. Then, Cousins inexplicably threw a pass, despite being ahead by twelve points with less than two minutes left. Penn State intercepted, and all of a sudden we were defending on our own three-yard line.

On the next play, Trenton Robinson, MSU's truly outstanding defensive back, intercepted the ball in the end zone. If Trent had simply taken a knee, a touchback would have been called, and the Spartans could have run out the clock from our twenty-yard line. No such luck. Robinson began running.

The entire bench yelled, "Nooooooo!"

Robinson was mauled by half the Penn State team, the ball popped out and was recovered by the Nittany Lions, and we were back defending at our own four-yard line. Three MSU turnovers in less than three minutes! Robinson did not bother to come to the bench. He just stood at the four-yard line shaking his head. It took the Lions exactly one play to score. They failed for the second time to complete a two-point conversion, so the score was now 28–22 with a minute and one second to play. I wanted to die. No one on the Spartan bench spoke.

The stadium was rocking as the Lions had come within sight of a miracle win on Senior Day over a top-ten MSU team. It seemed like fate had cast a shadow over the game. Mark Dantonio went to throw a blanket of calm over everybody. He called for the "hands team" to gather around him.

The "hands team" are football players blessed with "soft" hands and courageous hearts. Their job is to be the receiving team on an onside kick. The players train to catch a twisting, bouncing football while enduring the onslaught of opponents running at them like locomotives from ten yards away. They needed to be tough enough to ignore the impending collision yet calm enough to recover a bouncing football.

When I looked at our "hands team" what I saw were just eleven young kids. As a neurologist, I always hated onside kicks. They are among the most dangerous plays in all of sport. Everyone is jammed in tight, with eighteen to twenty people all within ten or twelve yards before they run full-tilt into each other. Hence the horrific collisions that occur.

Even from the upper deck, I thought football needed rule changes to make this play less dangerous. From the sideline, it was far worse than I imagined.

That little ten-yard kick, when correctly executed, takes a high, unpredictable bounce, allowing the kicking team a running start to collide with the receiving team, who are standing motionless. The player getting ready to catch the ball usually has to stand upright to grab it, making his entire body an easy target. Sadly, the MSU player attempting to catch the ball will get absolutely plastered causing an aggravated chest or abdominal blow, a concussion, or worse.

The "hands team" players were all tightening their helmet straps, getting ready for the collisions to come. I held my breath, then shut my eyes as the kicker approached the ball. The reaction of the Penn State fans would tell me the outcome.

There was a simple muffled roar followed by stone silence. I couldn't interpret what that meant.

When I looked up, I saw ten men in green hugging MSU's Brian Linthicum, who was holding the ball high over his head in triumph. Cousins knelt down twice to end the game. A confetti-filled Gatorade keg was upended over Coach D.'s head (the traditional Gatorade bath was nixed by Sally, given Coach D.'s previous heart attack). MSU was Big Ten champion. After twenty years, the wait was over.

# CHAPTER TWENTY

# *Agony and Then Wisdom*

Following the postgame prayer on the field, everyone was so excited, so happy. There were hugs all around. Coach D. said to the TV cameras, "Spartan Nation, we are Big Ten champs! We are Big Ten champs!"

Jeff turned to me and said, "Tough to tolerate this. Even with eleven wins, I don't think it's our year for the Rose Bowl. Oh, well."

That really hurt. After beating Penn State, and at State College, I had assumed MSU, at 11–1, would go up dramatically in the polls. Surely, people would recognize MSU had to leap over Wisconsin, a team we had beaten, right? We might be tied with Ohio State, but they had lost to the Badgers, so how could we be below them? It made perfect sense to me.

I wondered aloud: Wouldn't the Big Ten have to realize the Spartans deserved this? That we had not been to the Rose Bowl in twenty-three years? That MSU's eleven wins were the most ever recorded by a Spartan squad since we started varsity football in 1896? That we had a nationally ranked, top-five defense, an inspirational quarterback, and a truly spiritual coach with a flair for the dramatic? As Big Ten co-champs, MSU simply had to be allowed to go to Pasadena, didn't we?

Sally let me know the reality right away.

"Dave, Wisconsin at eleven and one will probably be selected instead of MSU, and even Ohio State. That is the way it is going to be."

I reminded her she was talking about the same Badger squad we had beaten only a few weeks before! I didn't get it.

Jeff added, "Dave, MSU at eleven and one is going to be ranked about eighth or ninth in the final BCS standings. The Bucks will be ranked higher than us since they're also eleven and one, and the Badgers are going to the Rose Bowl."

"Jeff," I said, "how can that be?"

"Well, Dave, you may know a lot about neurology—you may actually one day learn one or two things about sports neurology if you stay with the team long enough—but you still do not get college football. Ohio State will be ranked higher because of their reputation and tradition. Right now, the Spartans are new to the party. The Bucks are there year after year, and for decades. So they are also going to be ranked higher by voters, despite the same record. I suspect Wisconsin will get the nod, since they beat Ohio State and the Bucks will be selected for the Sugar Bowl.

"What about MSU? What BCS Bowl will we go to?"

Jeff stared at me for just a second. "Well, that's the irony. If Wisconsin and Ohio State both go to BCS bowls, the Spartans will be excluded from any of the four major bowls. That's because of the three-team rule. Three teams from the same conference can't all go to a BCS bowl game. So, for us, it's not going to be the Roses or the Sugar or any BCS bowl. Oh, well."

As the party all around us was warming up, I was heartbroken.

On the plane, Father Jake as usual leaned his chair all the way back after takeoff. "Dave, why are you so grumpy?" he asked, turning to where I sat. "Is it that silly thing where you thought we were maybe going to the Rose Bowl Game in your first year on the team? Relax, you're pretty young for an old guy. You'll get there one day. Maybe. If you slow down a little. Maybe you got another decade or so of life, although don't count on that. Calm down. This coach will get you there. I am sure of it. My issue is, I just don't know if I have already seen my last Rose Bowl."

There was a long silence as we both thought about what he had just said. Then he flashed a cheek-to-cheek smile that means he knew something I didn't.

"By the way," he said, "do you want my Dove Bar?"

"Father Jake," I managed, "I get what you just taught me, and I thank you. I guess another Dove Bar would really help. That would be a nice thing."

"Well, that's too bad, Dave. I ain't giving it up to you. Nothing tastes as sweet as a road victory over Penn State. We have not done that since the Duffy era back in sixty-five. It's been forty-five years. I was there then, and I was there for this one now. We are Big Ten champions and it's been twenty years for that one. But I got to see that again, too."

He continued, "You just haven't suffered enough to fully understand how special today is. I need to savor this moment. And so should you. I also need to savor my Dove Bar. Steal Mike Shingle's ice cream. While you're at it, learn to love every victory, let alone every championship. Learn to savor what you and I got to see and feel today. Savor every single day. Dave, do that for me, please?"

After we landed, I got home very late Saturday night. I said, "Laurie, what a day, what a win! But why do you look so sad?"

Laurie answered, "It's not me. The rankings are coming out. Everyone on TV said that since Wisconsin is listed ahead of MSU in the BCS polls, we aren't going to the Rose Bowl. Dave, you came so close to your dream, but now it's gone. I am so sorry! It just isn't right. What a tragedy."

I offered up a smile to the person who had given me the most during my life. "Laurie, it's okay. If I hadn't gotten to see all of this up close, now that would have been a tragedy."

She gave me a hug. "Honey" I whispered, "I learned enough about broken necks to get me worried on every punt and kickoff. I saw enough to wish Josh Rouse could have completed his senior season. I watched our coach, a good and honorable man, suffer a heart attack and maybe die, if not for his wife, Jeff, Sally, and Randy Pearson. I learned enough to realize the toll football takes on its players and coaches. I learned enough to understand you really never know when you are playing your last game, in football or in life."

We sat down and I became just a little weepy. "Laurie, football can be so beautiful as to take your breath away. It taught me that if you summon the will to try, you can do some amazing things. When that same feeling is shared by a committed team, you can summon the will to win.

"Maybe most important during this last year, I learned we all have to find a way to make football safer without making it unrecognizable. It's too special not to try to do that. As for my dream of one day going back for one last Rose Bowl, Coach D. will find some type of way to get us there. I am sure of it."

Laurie answered, simply, "Okay. I understand. Live every day as our last, but let's still shoot for a Rose Bowl, in our lifetime."

# CHAPTER TWENTY-ONE

# *"You Will Be the Ones"*

A t the end of the 2010 season, the Spartans were invited to the "second tier" Capital One Bowl in Orlando. It was a trip nobody wanted to take. MSU was demolished by Alabama. The Spartans had won eleven games in the 2010 season, mostly through grit. They had only two players drafted into the NFL (Greg Jones and Chris L. Rucker), and both were taken in the sixth round.

As the 2011 season started, I felt right at home on the field. No more panic. No more getting lost in the swirl of action around me. Things had slowed down to the point where I felt more in control and better understood what my role was. I became, in a word, confident. The Spartans were as good as in 2010, maybe even better. We beat Ohio State, Michigan, and Wisconsin on successive weekends.

Wisconsin was unbeaten and ranked fourth in the nation at the time. In front of a truly raucous crowd, the Spartans blocked two kicks, including a punt right before halftime for a touchdown. In the second half, Keith Nichol caught a forty-four-yard Hail Mary from Kirk Cousins on the game's final play for a 37–31 victory. I had never heard it louder in Spartan Stadium. Afterward, Coach Dantonio dubbed the winning play "Rocket."

MSU faced Wisconsin again in the very first Big Ten Championship game. The Spartans lost a heartbreaker 42–39. Gone for the second year in a row was a trip to the Rose Bowl.

The Football Bust, the annual end-of-the-year celebration of the football team, held the day after the game, was attended by eight hundred players, coaches, parents, and fans. It reminded me of a wake. Kirk Cousins was near tears as he addressed the crowd. What lingered in my memory was the forlorn look on Cousin's face and the emotion in his voice when he apologized for not bringing the Big Ten Championship home to send Spartan Nation to the Rose Bowl.

In his very last game as a Spartan, Cousins willed Michigan State to rally from sixteen points behind and win the Outback Bowl 33–30 in three overtimes against Georgia.

The Spartans ended the 2011 season 11–3 and were ranked tenth in the polls. After the game, I asked Cousins what it was like to come from sixteen points down to beat the Bulldogs. His reply was simple: "Dr. Kaufman, it was a measure of redemption. But the circle will not be complete until MSU makes it to the Rose Bowl. No matter where I am when that happens, I will be there—if not in person, then in spirit."

After we shook hands, I watched Kirk Cousins leave the locker room, assuming that would be the last conversation I would ever have with him. In the NFL draft, Kirk Cousins, Trenton Robinson, Jerel Worthy, Keshawn Martin, Edwin Baker, and B. J. Cunningham were all selected. That left the MSU team in a rebuilding mode.

Michigan State's 2012 campaign was a significant letdown from the previous season. The team only scored twenty-five touchdowns for the entire year. On the defensive side of the ball, led by Max Bullough, Darqueze Dennard, Denicos Allen, and so many others, the Spartans were ferocious. They led the Big Ten, giving up only 273.3 yards and 16.3 points per game. Still, the 2012 season was forgettable.

The Spartans' 2012 season ended 7–6, capped by a come-from-behind victory over Texas Christian University in the Buffalo Wild Wings Bowl.

At the traditional Football Bust, Coach Dantonio got up at the end to give his closing address. After briefly discussing the somewhat disappointing year, he stopped talking for a short moment and looked down at the podium. Then, with his voice barely above a whisper, Dantonio looked up and then pointed at all his underclassmen. He slowly said, "You will be the ones."

He shook his head yes and then repeated it again this time even slower and louder. "YOU . . . WILL . . . BE . . . THE . . . ONES!"

Laurie turned to me and asked, "What in the world is he trying to say to the team, Dave?"

Before I could answer, the team stood and started to yell and shout. All eight hundred of us stood up and applauded.

Laurie turned to me and said, "Okay. I get it now! He just let the team members know that 2013 will be the year Spartan Nation gets back to the Rose Bowl."

A month or so after the banquet, deep into winter, Jeff Monroe came over the house with his wonderful fiancée, Joyce deJong. I thought Jeff was trying to simply score some more fine Scotch at my expense. But I was wrong.

"I'm hanging them up, Dave," he said.

"What are you talking about? Why would you do that?"

"Too many sixteen-hour days. Too many heartbreaking injuries. Too many road trips. Too much time away from family."

I countered, "Jeff, we both know we should have a great year in 2013. Why would you leave now? Besides, who will give me crap on the sidelines? Who will remind me how little I know about sports medicine? Who is going to take care of these guys?"

Jeff slowly swirled the Scotch around in the glass while looking down at the floor. I could tell by his slumped shoulders and heavy sighs, Jeff was going to hang it up, no matter what I had to say to my mentor. He then looked at me with the tired eyes of a soldier who had had enough.

"Dave, I have been at it thirty years here at MSU. I've seen enough. Sally's big enough to do it all on her own. She'll find someone to help out. This game gives you a lot, but it takes away a lot. I have had enough. It's my time."

With that, Jeff took one last drink, gave me a fist bump, and walked out my door.

# CHAPTER TWENTY-TWO

## *2013*

**M**SU's 2013 football team was indeed terrific. The coaches, after a controversial 17–13 loss to Notre Dame, eventually decided to give a sophomore, Connor Cook, the start at quarterback over senior Andrew Maxwell. Following that decision, the Spartans seemed unbeatable. I actually saw the direct aftermath of that fateful decision.

I was outside of Coach D.'s office at the invitation of my good friend Sam Freedman, a noted author and journalism professor at Columbia University. Sam was invited by the College of Education at MSU to give a series of lectures. Ever since he and I worked together on the *Daily Cardinal* in the 1970s, we had remained close.

While on campus, Freedman asked for an interview with Coach D. to learn more about MSU's role in integrating college football in the 1950s and 1960s. Sam invited me along to be part of the discussion. I was reluctant, as I was still a bit intimidated by Coach D., but I was genuinely intrigued to learn more about MSU's role.

Andrew Maxwell, who had started the season at quarterback before being relegated to a relief role in the loss at Notre Dame, came out of the coach's offices while Sam and I were in the reception area. "Max" had a very sad look on his face and slumped shoulders; it was the body language of a man that had just received some unpleasant news.

I gave Max a simple fist bump and he looked up and flashed me a bright smile on his way down the steps and out of the football office. I really did not understand what had just occurred in the coach's office. Sam and I then had an amazing and insightful exchange with

Coach D. about how MSU helped Big Ten sports move toward diversity. The next day, the papers reported Connor Cook was named MSU's permanent starter.

From that point forward, the Spartans were relentless in their quest to win the Big Ten and go on to the Rose Bowl. During the ensuing Spartan win streak, Jeff Monroe was asked to come back and give a speech at a team meal in his honor. On October 12, 2013, just before the game against Indiana and two days before Columbus Day, Jeff was formally recognized as an important member of this team and for so many other teams throughout the years by Coach D. I was so happy for Jeff.

Jeff's speech was just like the way he lived his life, down home and very effective. At the end of it he looked up at the team and predicted, "Guys, like Columbus, you are headed into uncharted territory. But I know, like Columbus, you will return home at the end of this season's journey in glory."

Jeff was remarkably accurate. The Spartans beat Indiana 42–28, cruised past Purdue and Illinois, and then at home on November 2 crushed Michigan 29–6. We won the rest of our regular season games and were ranked tenth nationally at the end of the regular season. MSU would represent the Big Ten's Legends Division in the league championship game, played in Indianapolis, against undefeated Ohio State. The Buckeyes, ranked second, had won twenty-four straight games.

The 2013 Big Ten Championship game was in reality a three-act play. The Spartans won the first act 17–0 and the defense was worthy of its number-one national rating. In the middle act, OSU could not be stopped. Everything the Buckeyes tried worked, as they scored twenty-four straight points.

In between the Ohio State's barrage of touchdowns, at halftime, Coach Dantonio spoke to his team.

At first, from the softer words and tone he was using, I wondered if he and his team thought they might be outmatched by the remarkable talent of the Buckeyes. Then, suddenly, like a tornado forming without warning, Coach D. abruptly turned stern, and his voice rose to a volume and urgency I had never heard him use before. It was like he was once again the Oracle, able to see all and predicting in detail what would happen after halftime. Like so many other times, we believed him.

With clenched fists and a face to match, he told his players if they endured the coming third-quarter onslaught from the Buckeyes, MSU would no doubt achieve victory by outfighting the Buckeyes in the fourth quarter. OSU might have the better personnel, he conceded, but the Spartans would be the better team at the end. Once OSU was done scoring, he said the team would overcome them.

"Men, we are going to go down swinging!" he declared. "Got that? Lay it all on the line! Give everything inside of you! No matter what they throw at you, if you do it into the last quarter, you will achieve victory."

Coach D. then turned and looked directly at Darqueze Dennard, the Spartans unanimous All-American cornerback and winner of the Jim Thorpe Award as the nation's best defensive back. Dennard was sitting about ten feet away. Dantonio took four or five steps toward Dennard.

The All-American rose to his feet as Coach D. was walking over to him. Although Max Bullough at middle linebacker always led with his words and his play, Dennard was in my view, the best athlete on the team. He was a strong but silent leader who demonstrated what needed to be done, but only with his actions and rarely with his voice. The team had no more effective leader when it really counted.

Coach D. was nearly yelling now as he walked even closer to Dennard. He asked his All-American cornerback, "Darqueze! Darqueze! I am asking you. Are you going to be there? If I call for the mayhem play, will you get the ball?"

Coach D. was now yelling at the top of his voice, staring directly at his prized corner-back. He again asked slowly, "Darqueze, are . . . you . . . going . . . to . . . get . . . it . . . done?"

Dennard was from Dry Branch, a small town in Georgia. He was quiet and almost painfully shy by nature. As he crossed his arms, his face quickly revealed what he was thinking. I had personally never heard him say more than two or three words in the four years I had been with the team. He stood straight up, looked right back at his coach tough and fierce. Then he looked around at all his teammates. He yelled to Dantonio, "Coach! We will be there! We will get it done! All of us, every one of us, we will all be there!"

With that, the rest of the team rose as one, shouting, swearing, yelling. I could only describe it as an act of mass defiance against the juggernaut that was the undefeated Ohio State football team. Defiance against the Buckeyes' star athletes, their stature, their publicity machine, and everything else the undefeated, second-ranked Buckeyes brought to the field that day.

As everyone moved toward the center of the locker room in a tight huddle, they shouted, "Ready? Who wins?" The response: "We win!" A phrase I had not heard since 2010.

As everyone then turned toward the exit, I felt not only anxiety but also the very real urgency of the team. I had a sense of excitement and maybe even bravado I could not overcome. My arms, my shoulders, my body began to shake. Yet I was also rational enough to wonder: How could this team, my team, overcome the mammoth that was Ohio State?

After halftime, the relentless Buckeyes indeed scored two touchdowns to go up 24–17. At that point, Coach Narduzzi uncharacteristically left the press box, where he had been calling the Spartan defense, and came down to field level much earlier than was usual; his typical entrance onto the field was in the middle of the fourth quarter.

He did not stop shouting, encouraging, pleading, scolding, hugging, begging, and otherwise coaching his defense for the rest of the game while walking among them shoulder to shoulder. After Narduzzi showed up, somehow MSU's defense started to rally. I am not saying it was Coach Narduzzi's early appearance that turned the tide. Yet even though I was there watching every move, I could not explain any other way the MSU rally began against the undefeated Buckeyes, except maybe the collective will that championship squads can summon when they inspire one another.

As the game went into its final stages, Max Bullough now served as the on-field Leonidas guiding his Spartans at Thermopylae. He diagnosed play after play and positioned his defensive teammates in just the right way prior to the Buckeye snap of the ball. Denicos Allen, Tyler Hoover, Marcus Rush, Micajah Reynolds, and Darqueze Dennard were all outstanding warriors for the defense and, as predicted by Dantonio, the team somehow endured and then stopped the Ohio State onslaught cold.

Then, as the third act started, it was MSU's time to impose its will on the Buckeyes. The Spartans scored seventeen straight points. It was a forty-four-yard field goal by Michael Geiger with two minutes and twenty-nine seconds left in the third quarter that broke the Buckeyes' scoring streak. In the fourth quarter, a relentless, meat-grinder drive whipped the Spartan fans into hysteria. As Ohio State gave up a touchdown on a nine-yard pass from Cook to Josiah Price, MSU took the lead 27–24. It struck me at that moment that Ohio State may have punched itself out in the earlier parts of the game; it simply was no longer able to respond to the physicality of the Spartans.

Near the end of the game, Ohio State was only down by a field goal. But a critical stop of the Buckeyes' quarterback by Denicos Allen on fourth and short seemed to break the Buckeyes' will. A simple running play by Jeremy Langford near the end of the fourth quarter sliced through the entire exhausted Buckeye secondary for a touchdown to make the final score 34–24, Michigan State.

Ohio State ended the game with a whimper; the Buckeyes could not mount any response. As the game ended, there was pandemonium in the stands and singing and dancing in the East Lansing streets.

The victory over Ohio State assured the Spartans a trip to the 100th Rose Bowl. No Big Ten Office shenanigans. No back door. No need to wait for some poll to break Spartan Nation's heart. We had won, and we were in!

The locker room held a euphoria I had never experienced. I had given my heart and soul to sports teams in the past, but only as a fan. Here, I was an accepted member of the medical team, fully embedded within this championship squad.

Both Laurie from East Lansing and my daughter Sarah from St. Louis had made the trip to Indianapolis to experience the game. We eventually found each other outside the team hotel. When we walked through the doors to enter the spontaneous after party, I witnessed a gathering like none I had ever experienced before. The lobby was filled to overflowing with players, parents, girl-friends, alumni, cheerleaders, administrators, coaches, fans, and physicians. Everyone was ecstatic over the triumph they had just witnessed.

University administers hugged players. Players hugged alumni. Cheerleaders hugged everyone. Coaches hugged the medical team, players' families hugged the team neurologist, and on and on. It was like Christmas had come early, and New Year's was about to happen. I also noted a fair amount of alcohol being purchased from the hotel bar and shared with whomever was standing next to you, old friend or new.

Around two in the morning, I looked up from the truly spectacular partying going on and spotted Coach Dantonio. He was standing by himself on the second floor of the atrium, looking over the celebratory action fifteen feet below in the hotel lobby. Feeling the alcohol-induced bravado, I made my way up the escalator to try and have a word with him, if I could. I found him silently enjoying the scene down below. He greeted me with a warm smile and we shook hands. I said, "Coach, you did it! Rose Bowl! And in my lifetime!"

Coach D. looked down at the spectacle going on below.

"Dr. Kaufman, they did it," He said. A few seconds later, he continued, "You did it, we all did it, and, best of all, we did it as a team."

"It really meant a lot to me, Coach. It is hard to describe what it was like being part of something far bigger than myself. Thanks for allowing that."

He had a quizzical look on his face for just a moment. "Well, Dr. Kaufman, thanks for joining our medical team. You've helped us. Besides, we all have a lot more fun still ahead. Get ready."

With that, he shook my hand again, looked down below one more time, smiled a secret smile and turned toward the elevators.

I made my way back down to the party, which was still going strong. Eventually, I had to bid Sarah good night so she could make her way back to her medical school and laboratory work at Washington University in St. Louis the next day. Laurie, who had traveled to the game with our close friends, the Leahys, told me they all had to head back to their hotel.

As my family and friends left, I went and found Father Jake, and we decided to see what Mike Shingles was up to. We found him in his room and convinced him to bring down his two young sons and pillowcases full of minibar treats. It was now well past three o'clock in the morning, and the hotel bar had closed. That made Dr. Shingles with his pillowcase filled with goodies quite popular.

By four o'clock, things started to get even a bit rowdier, and security came to shut us down. I watched all six feet and seven inches of 290-pound Tyler Hoover have a very polite and eloquent discussion with the three security officers.

"Boys," said Hoover to the officers, "if anybody or anything gets out of hand, I will personally take care of it. " The team neurologist and orthopedic surgeon assured the officers that Tyler Hoover was a man of his word. They believed us.

The last thing I remember about the party was it being five o'clock in the morning and Mike mentioning maybe it was time for him and his two young sons to leave so they could go upstairs to get some sleep. I would not let that happen. I made my way up to his room and all of us continued to go over game details, not wanting to forget a single thing about what we had just seen.

Without stopping to sleep, I eventually found Father Jake. We packed up our things, went downstairs, and had a cup of coffee. As we waited patiently in the dark for the victorious police escort to the Indianapolis airport we were both silent. On the plane our smiles said it all.

"I always knew I had one last Rose Bowl in me," said the priest right after takeoff. As he reclined his seat all the way back he added, "I just didn't know I would be on earth to see it."

He turned, gave me a fist bump and a smile. I watched him turn and look out the window at the stars guiding us home.

# CHAPTER TWENTY THREE

# *Christmas Bomb Shell*

The next three weeks were devoted to getting ready for the Rose Bowl. Although now ranked fourth, MSU was still considered underdogs against fifth-ranked Stanford. The Cardinal had won the Rose Bowl the year before, beating mighty Wisconsin. They were 11–2 and were Pac-12 champions. They had tremendous momentum going into the New Year's Day game, and we all knew that Vegas oddsmakers thought the MSU win over Ohio State was simply a fluke.

By Christmas Eve, most of the on-campus preparations at MSU for the trip west were concluded. As was the bowl tradition, the coaches, players, support people, the medical team, spouses, and even their school-aged children would all climb aboard a Boeing 747. The plan was to leave on Christmas afternoon and set up camp outside of Pasadena for seven days in Southern California. What could be better than a plane filled with the entire Spartan football family being given the gift of a holiday week in the warm, West Coast weather?

Then, on Christmas Day, the bombshell hit. Max Bullough, our All-American linebacker, two-time captain, and celebrated leader of the team, was suspended by Coach Dantonio for a violation of team rules. Bullough had always called the Rose Bowl "the promised land." He was a gigantic force for good; a true inspiration to his fellow teammates this entire exhausting Big Ten Championship year. But now he had lost the opportunity to experience that ultimate experience with his teammates.

A profound sadness descended over the entire campus as we all realized Max was victimized by a self-inflicted wound. Furthermore, there was no doubt we were going to lose the Rose Bowl as a result. I needed insight, and so I called up my old sports medicine mentor and coach, Jeff Monroe.

"Yep, it's bad, Dave. Like you and everyone else, I feel for Max," came his familiar, slightly accented voice. "But something like this sometimes can bring a team even closer together. They'll probably move Kyler Ellsworth up to take Max's spot. I've known Kyler and have watched him for years. We'll be all right. Kyler's got this."

When we left Lansing, it was thirteen degrees on a dreary overcast winter day. The mood was correspondingly bleak. As was the custom, the spouses and children of the "official travel party" were also transported by MSU to the bowl game. Laurie and I were given two outstanding seats, with a window on one side and the aisle on the other, halfway down the length of the enormous airplane. What a treat! No dealing with boxed-in claustrophobia for hours. No panic, and no shortness of breath.

"Dave, why were you always complaining about the travel arrangements?" Laurie asked. "These are great seats!"

I summoned a halfhearted smile and held back on my whimpering. I decided to not explain the reality of being the least valuable person on this football team. Nor did I review with Laurie the usual seat I was typically provided for every other trip I had taken with the team these past four years.

As the five-hour ride went on, whenever the subject of Max came up among team members, the invariable response from everyone was the same. "Tough one for Max. But we have to move on. We have to look forward. Next man up. He would want that, and he told all of us as much."

As the flight got closer to California, everyone began to smile a bit more as they thought about the opportunity in front of them.

When the plane doors opened in Los Angeles, it was sunny and seventy-three degrees and the team had somehow moved on from the Christmas bombshell.

On the bus ride to the hotel, all we saw were palm trees and sunshine. The promised land, indeed!

Trips to Disneyland, the Lawry's Beef Bowl (a head-to-head Cardinal versus Spartan event to see who could eat the most roast beef), the Hall of Fame ceremony, the Kickoff Luncheon, and the beach were all part of the week. The downtown pep rallies were stirring, complete with Magic Johnson — a Hall of Fame point guard for the Los Angeles Lakers and Michigan State alum — making every Spartan feel like LA was their West Coast home.

The Spartan practices at the LA Galaxy's soccer facility were ferocious, smashmouth, and brutal. A few days before the game, things were particularly intense. The team ran one-versus-one drills again and again. People were working hard in the heat, and a sense of exhaustion seemed to sweep over the team. In the middle of practice, our nose guard, Micajah Reynolds, all 330 pounds of him, came off the field, sweating hard, angry, and beyond frustrated. He bitterly complained, "Sally! What up with this practice! Just a few days before the Rose Bowl? Coach must have gone crazy!"

I found myself walking over to them, though I knew I shouldn't. As I gently offered the gigantic nose guard a bottle of Gatorade, I said, "Stanford's tough as hell, Micajah. Coach and everyone else is just getting ready for the coming fight. That's all that's up, big man."

Sally offered Reynolds an ice pack, but he just stared at me for a very long time. Uh-oh, I thought. I might die right here and right now.

Then, after what seemed like an eternity, he cocked his head to one side, took a sip from the bottle, looked at me again, nodded and said, "I feel you, Doc."

He took a big breath, walked over to Coach Narduzzi, and let him know he was ready to go back out. Narduzzi pointed to the field, and with that, Micajah trotted out into the Southern California heat. I also took a big breath in relief, while Sally just shook her head at me and laughed right out loud.

Fifteen minutes after that, near the end of this last practice, Darqueze Dennard went down. Everything and everybody stopped what they were doing. An eerie silence descended onto the field.

Sally had seen him go down and ran to get to him. She and one of her assistant trainers talked to Dennard for a long time as he lay on the field. They were eventually able to coax him to his feet, but they had to help him off the field, half dragging him to the training table. It seemed like an ankle or maybe fatigue or maybe something else. Not good for a defensive back to have a leg injury with less than two days before game time.

As all five of us surrounded the treatment table. Pearson looked at him and said, "Was it the heat?"

Mike looked at Dennard's leg and ankle carefully and then gave a thin-lipped, quizzical glance at Sally. The ankle was stable. Maybe it was a first-degree sprain. Maybe something less or something more. I called for the transport cart, but Sally said, "No. Don't do that, Dave. We need to wait to the end of practice. Then we'll load it up with a bunch of players for the trip up the hill to the locker room."

"Sally," I asked, "why wait? Why load up the cart with a bunch of people?"

Sally gave me her best football-motherly smile and said, "Dave, think. Sure as we are talking, Stanford has people stationed outside this practice field. If it's only Dennard on a cart and we take him up the hill to the locker room, Stanford will see he is injured. Why let them know that? We put a bunch of people on the cart, and then Stanford will have no clue who is so banged up they can't walk."

After such a tough practice, the locker room was like a morgue. Everyone seemed exhausted. In the training room, Mike and everyone else was again examining Dennard. The All-American just sat on the training table, limp, almost lifeless, with a cold towel over his head. Not a word was said by him or any of us. Then unexpectedly, Coach D. came into the training room. He went right by us and just locked at Dennard's face.

"Darqueze, let me have a word, over in that other room," Coach D. said quietly.

Dennard pulled himself off the training table and the two walked very slowly over to the adjoining whirlpool room. Coach D. shut the clear glass door. We all remained silent and watched through the window as the All-American and his coach talked. It was impossible to hear what was being said, and I thought to myself, "Max is gone. If we lose Dennard, we're dead."

After about ten minutes the door opened, and Dennard slowly walked out. He went through the training room area back to the locker room without saying a word. Coach D. watched him leave and then eventually came over to where we were all standing in a semicircle. We inched closer to one another, maybe actually afraid to hear what Coach had to say. "Darqueze will be fine," he informed us. "He is going to play, and I am telling all of you right now, he is going to play great."

With that, Dantonio turned and walked out the room as we all looked at one another. I wondered what had been said between the coach and his star defensive back. Sally got a twisted smile that broadened and then filled her entire face. She simply said, "Maybe it wasn't his ankle. Maybe it was something inside of Dennard that only Mark Dantonio could heal."

Father Jake turned to me and motioned with his finger to get closer to him. He then grabbed me by my shirt and whispered in my ear, "We are going to win!"

Michigan State had started off Christmas week a two-point underdog to Stanford. After it became known that Max Bullough was out, the point spread began to widen. The Cardinal had consistency: they had won eleven or more games for four years in a row. It was also a fact that the Big Ten had lost nine of the last ten Rose Bowls. In the end, Stanford was favored by more than a touchdown.

The Cardinal's reputation was earned. The Stanford defense was led by two phenomenal linebackers, Shayne Skov and Trent Murphy. On offense, Stanford had wide receiver Ty Montgomery, who averaged more than 160 yards and a touchdown every game. Even more impressive was running back Tyler Gaffney, who had twenty touchdowns and averaged over 125 yards a game. Stanford had also beaten Notre Dame 27–20, and the Irish were the only team that had defeated MSU all year.

Offensively, the Spartans had Connor Cook at quarterback, Jeremy Langford at running back, and a truly gifted group of receivers.

But everyone knew our true strength was defense. The Spartans led the Big Ten in all four major defensive categories: scoring, rushing, passing, and total defense. We also had an All-American at defensive end, Shilique Calhoun. If Darqueze Dennard could actually play, as predicted by Coach D., they also had the top cornerback in America. It was the defense, with or without Max Bullough, that would have to be the difference on New Year's Day.

On New Year's Eve, I was nervous as hell. Laurie and I returned from the hotel gala with our son, Matt, who had arrived a few days before. We celebrated New Year's at nine o'clock California time, which was midnight East Lansing time, so we could try and get some rest. Personally, I couldn't sleep. I yelled at Laurie for making too much noise as she turned her pillow over. She then pulled the covers over her head and told me to "cool it." The next morning, we got up at four o'clock, and I was still ornery.

As Laurie got ready to go to the Rose Parade, she was understanding as always but got right down to business.

"Okay, Dave, calm down. They are going to win or lose without you. I know you are nervous. All you need to do is make sure everyone's head is still attached at the end of the game. After four years of doing this, I think you can diagnose a detached head. So, please, just get up and get ready."

Next thing I knew, I was on one of the team buses with the physicians and auxiliary staff getting a police escort from downtown Los Angeles to Pasadena. Sally was in another bus up ahead with the offense. Not a word was said on the way to the stadium. The team had not been allowed to practice on the Rose Bowl field—or even look inside. Pictures outside the stadium were allowed, but there was no peeking inside the stadium.

Finally, we got off the buses and headed into the Rose Bowl locker room. It was among the largest I had ever been in. The walls were lined with artistic and beautifully framed photographs of every Rose Bowl ever played. Each player on MSU had his name and a special graphic attached to his assigned locker. The treatment room was also huge, and the entire facility was immaculate.

After the pregame warm-ups, I watched Father Jake talk with Connor Cook for a long time. After they hugged, I heard Coach

D. call the team together. As always, the team was shown a short inspirational video reminding them of the great Spartan plays from throughout the year. After some last-minute words from Coach D., we all moved through the locker room doors and into that two-story incredibly loud stone tunnel.

We all ran out onto the field just after the national anthem was over. Father Jake eventually came over to talk just after Kirk Cousins and I had finished talking.

"What do you think, Father Jake?" the NFL quarterback asked the aging priest.

"Kirk, I like our chances."

Cousins responded with a smile and a fist bump to both of us. As he began to walk away, he smiled, and shouted above the crowd noise, "Time for us all to go to work. Let's complete the circle."

I waved, as Father Jake and I took our place with the medical team at the twenty-yard line and waited for the kickoff. Right then, inexplicably, a strange all-encompassing calm came over me, like none I had ever felt before. In the midst of this surreal inner serenity, I looked around at the ninety-five thousand people jammed into this iconic setting, with the San Gabriel Mountains in the distance. I smiled, thinking how strange it was that fate had brought me to this moment, on this field, and, in my own way, helping a team I had loved for so many years.

I took a deep breath and realized all I needed to do was my job and only if and when called upon. Nothing more, but nothing less. I was more focused and calmer than at any other time that I could recall. As MSU kicked off, I took another deep breath, watched, and waited.

# CHAPTER TWENTY FOUR

# *January 1, 2014, and the 100th Rose Bowl*

t was evident from its first series that Stanford had come to play. The Cardinal took a 7–0 lead on Gaffney's sixteen-yard run and added three more points to make it 10–0 at the end of the first quarter. I did not flinch. Despite falling behind, I had uncharacteristically not said a word to anyone. As the second period started, MSU's offense came alive and Langford scored at the end of a seventy-five-yard drive to make it 10–7.

Then both defenses took over. The smashmouth aspect of the game was frightening up close. It reminded me of a heavyweight fight, except with twenty-two people in the ring duking it out. Nobody could move the ball. After punt exchanges on both sides, MSU's defense rallied around its replacement middle linebacker, Kyler Ellsworth, and forced Stanford into a fourth-down situation, close to the Cardinal end zone.

After a spectacular Cardinal punt, the Spartans started from their own forty-one-yard line with just over three minutes left in the half. On second down, the game turned ugly for the Spartans. On a planned screen pass, Langford, unseen by the refs, was held by a Stanford player. Connor Cook, while being hit, threw a pass blindly in anticipation of where his running back normally would have been. The ball was easily intercepted by Kevin Anderson, who went forty yards untouched to make it 17–7 Stanford.

I still did not flinch a muscle and felt surprisingly confident even after that disaster. I watched Cook come over to the sidelines without much emotion on his face. Coach D. asked him softly, "You good?"

The sophomore quarterback's response was immediate. "I'm good."

After the Stanford kickoff, with just over two minutes remaining, Cook calmly ran out onto the field for arguably the most important series of offensive plays the Spartans had in the last twenty-six years. Without hesitation, he hit Tony Lippett for a twenty-four-yard catch-and-run to the fifty-yard line. Langford caught another pass for a first down. Then that old timer from Detroit Country Day School, senior Bennie Fowler, caught a rainbow heave from Cook. Bennie was leaning to his left, away from the defensive back at the Stanford three-yard line, and somehow made the grab.

With seconds remaining in the half, Cook, scrambling to his right, found his blocking back Trevon Pendleton, for a touchdown. It was one of Pendleton's few catches of the entire year to make it 17–14. When Pendleton caught that touchdown, I immediately thought back to Josh Rouse's score against Michigan six years earlier. Then I thought of Rouse's last game when he broke his neck in 2010. I knew he would be watching, and I wondered what he might be thinking at this moment, as Pendleton ran to the Spartan bench, triumphant.

A comeback score right before halftime is like no other momentum accelerant. After the extra point was successful, Pendleton was surrounded by his linemen, and they all hugged in celebration, except for our huge center, Jack Allen. Jack uncharacteristically had walked over to get a glass of Gatorade and calmly watched as everyone else congratulated Pendleton.

I thought that was just a bit odd but did not make much of it. Stanford received the kickoff with only a few seconds left before halftime and decided to run out the clock. As both teams started to trot off the field, I was stunned to hear Coach D. yell out, "Where's Kaufman? Kaufman, look at Jack Allen, and make sure he's alright."

My heart went from a calm sixty-five beats per minute to buzzsaw speed with those twelve words. Father Jake was running off the field right next to me and said, "Time to go to work, Dave."

Inside that enormous Rose Bowl locker room, Randy and I steered Jack Allen into the training room. Jack had taken off his jersey and shoulder pads and was wearing a tee shirt slightly stained from what appeared to be misplaced pizza sauce. He leaned on a training table with his left arm on his hip while drinking a cup of Gatorade. As we started our evaluation, Randy was his usual calm understated self. I was not.

When Jack saw us he smiled and, using his sarcastic voice, said, "Hello, boys. How are you two doin'? Exciting game, isn't it?"

Randy and I looked at each other. We knew Jack was famous for clowning around when things looked their darkest. However, this was halftime at the Rose Bowl. Coach D. was deeply worried about his All-American center, and he'd called out loud for the brain doctor, who happened to be me. And here was Jack Allen, the key to the offensive line, greeting us like we were walking into his house party.

"Hey, Big Man," I said, "take a seat and please let the doctors do the jokes."

With that, Jack laughed, plopped himself down on the black-covered training table, and took another drink of his Gatorade. Randy went into doctor-mode immediately. He asked Jack why coach was so worried. What did he remember about the last series of plays, and did he have any issues with memory or headache? Jack gave some vague, halfhearted answers.

Then Randy conducted the standard concussion exam, as he had done for hundreds of student-athletes over the previous two decades. I simply looked on.

"Jack, I am going to give you three things to remember," Randy explained. "Apples, paper clips, and automobiles. Got it?"

Randy then checked Jack's brain physiology. He evaluated the big lineman's ocular motility, visual fields, cranial nerves, cognition, naming tasks, motor strength, and balance using the standard SCAT protocol. They all looked normal.

Randy looked at me, and I raised my eyebrows. I really did not understand what Coach D. had seen or heard; his center looked fine. Randy concluded his exam with the Romberg test of balance and position sense. Pearson then turned to me and said, "You're up."

Using fairly advanced techniques, I looked carefully at Jack's vestibular-ocular motor system and other neuro-ophthalmologic functions to find any change implying he had a concussion. He still looked fine to me. I asked the 300-pound lineman to do the tandem Romberg and then a tandem gait to stress-test his balance even more. He did it perfectly, both forward and backward.

As the smile ran away from his lips, Jack then said, "Okay. Play time is over. Can I go now? We have a Rose Bowl to win."

Randy responded, "In a minute or two, Jack. What were the three things we asked you to remember?

Jack flashed a smile but just for a second. Then he said nothing for what seemed like an eternity. That's when I really got worried.

"Well, let's see." Jack was stalling. "'There was a fruit. Apples, I think you said. Yep, you did. Apples, no doubt. Then there was cars. Except you said automobiles." Jack shook his head up and down. "Yep, it was automobiles."

Then came the smile again, and a very, very long pause. Seconds passed like days.

"Jack, what was the third thing?" Randy finally asked.

As the seconds multiplied, my heart was in my throat. Jack Allen was an amazing athlete. He was the Illinois state champion heavyweight wrestler when he was at Hinsdale Central High School. Scholastically, he was brilliant and was also an academic All-American. Even though he was a sophomore, as the center of the MSU offensive line, he was arguably the most important part of that essential offensive weapon and also was talked about as a potential All-American by multiple polls. He had everyone's respect, and, above all, he was a clutch football player. Yet here he was, hesitating on the memory part of the exam. I took a deep breath and then I hung my head.

When I looked up, Jack was laughing. "Don't worry, Dr. Kaufman, I know the answer was paper clips. I just wanted to see if I could make you nervous. You got pretty nervous there! It's apples, paper clips, and automobiles. It is always apples, paper clips, and automobiles. Every time you, or even Dr. Pearson, asked me to remember three things, it is always the same. Apples, paper clips, and automobiles.

"Now, both of you, listen. My memory is excellent. Trevor scored our last touchdown after Bennie made that diving catch at the three-yard line. My memory is fine. We closed the half strong, and I'd like to get back with my guys so we can win the Rose Bowl. Okay with you two gents?"

With that, as Jack Allen walked past us into the locker room, he gave me a playful forearm to my shoulder. Randy and I looked at each other and started to laugh. In the middle of the Rose Bowl, at halftime, who on earth pretends to have a concussion and makes goofs out of two doctors?

Offensive line coach Mark Staten came over and asked, "Is he okay to play?

Randy and I looked at each other again and then Randy said, "Other than being just a little crazy, we think he is okay."

Staten replied, "Jack acting crazy? Great! That means he is stone-cold normal, at least for him! Thanks, guys."

Randy and I chatted a bit with Sally, who was concluding a lower back manipulation on Micajah Reynolds. Reynolds along with Tyler Hoover, Marcus Rush, Shilique Calhoun, and Mark Scarpinato had been tasked with battling the amazing Stanford offensive line and were playing them to a draw. Mike was concluding the examination of a knee on another player and seemed quite pleased it felt stable. They got a black elastic wrap over the knee and after two oral Motrin, the linebacker was deemed ready to go. Then Sally asked, "Dave, you sure about Jack?"

I said, "Well, yes. He checked out fine to me."

The Spartans were going to get the ball to start the third quarter. The locker room was alive with activity and shouting from every part of the room. The team had just scored to end the first half. No one gave a thought to the pick-six thrown just seconds before that by Connor. Another lesson in momentum. The last score of the half in a close game can make all the difference. Everyone was talking it up, and all I could feel was confidence radiating from every corner of that huge Rose Bowl locker room.

As I began to walk through the locker room. I found a seat next to Father Jake, who had just concluded a talk with Jack Allen. Jack had just turned away as I sat down and was listening to his line coach.

Still wondering about Jack; I asked Father Jake, "Did you just have a talk with Jack Allen? How did he seem?"

"Dave," he said, "now I have to do your work for you, too? He told me you and Randy thought he was fine. He is itching to play. He seemed like himself. Let me do the worrying, okay?"

Coach D. called everyone up to the front to get them ready for the last half of the game.

"We are right there to get this done," he said. "We are where we need to be. We get the ball. If it's open, we are going to take a deep shot on them right away. But for this last half, I need the defense to play its best game. Now let's get ready."

Then everyone lined up. There was no screaming or yelling like at the start of the game. After the quiet passed, an almost religious, spiritual half-hum, half-chant began to fill the air. It was like something you might hear in church as part of a hymn, but without any words. It spread slowly among the players as we exited the locker room.

That unique softly persistent murmuring hum accompanied us as we all walked through the locker room door and into that stone tunnel. It was like the players knew what was in front of them and what they had to do. They were not going to be denied, and they certainly were unafraid. That haunting spiritual humming continued as everyone waited. Then came the signal to run out onto the field and into that wall of noise to start the second half.

The Spartans received the second-half kickoff and Coach D., true to his word, called for the bomb on the second play from scrimmage. Cook found Bennie Fowler wide open and hit him in stride with a bullet. Jeff had always said, "Ol' Bennie, once he gets movin,' he is a hard man to bring down."

Fowler proved worthy of the compliment. After the catch, Bennie did not turtle up to absorb a cornerback's hit. He just started to run. For the next forty yards, he straight-armed multiple Stanford players and lugged the ball inside the Stanford fifteen-yard line until he was wrestled to the ground.

The Cardinal defense, however, stiffened. Michael Geiger came on and chipped a short field goal to tie the game 17–17. Although MSU had to settle for the three points, it was obvious we had come out of the locker room to win the Rose Bowl.

Stanford had the same idea. When the Cardinal got the ball, they also tried for a quick score. Kevin Hogan's long pass downfield was intercepted by MSU cornerback Trae Waynes. After the Spartans were unable to move the ball, a gigantic Mike Sadler punt backed up the Cardinal. However, Hogan again went deep. This time he hit his tight end for a fifty-one-yard gain. Then it was the MSU defense that needed to shine. We forced a fourth down and short. Tyler Gaffney, one of the country's best running backs, was given the ball. Denicos Allen, in yet another clutch play from his linebacker position, somehow dropped Gaffney for a loss, ending Stanford's gamble.

MSU was energized. The Spartans started to move down the field for the go-ahead score, using Langford over and over again. The junior running back plowed through a Stanford defensive line that had sustained body blow after body blow from the inspired MSU offensive line led by Jack Allen. Langford was given the ball four straight times and gained thirty yards.

As Stanford tried to adjust, Cook hit two passes for another first down inside the Cardinal red zone. Then, tragically, Langford fumbled while fighting for extra yardage at the Stanford eight-yard line. He came off the field heartbroken. I watched him take a deep breath and gather himself. He then went over to talk to each of his offensive linemen to apologize. They each responded with a hug or a handshake and a knowing smile for him.

It struck me that if we had scored right then, maybe the Stanford players would begin to doubt themselves. In the old days, back in the upper deck, I would have been disappointed or even mad at the change in fortune. But I had such faith in this team and this coach I did not doubt. I was still enveloped by that cloak of serenity, knowing this was all going to turn out just fine. My only thought was, "Too bad. The final score will look closer than it actually was when folks read about the MSU win in the paper."

I was totally convinced there was no way the Spartans could lose, not after all they had done this amazing year. Sure enough, the defense rose up off the bench as one and ran out onto the field knowing what had to be done. They were ferocious. As the fourth quarter started, tied at 17–17, Stanford could not move the ball at all after the fumble. They were forced to punt from their own ten-yard line.

A nice return by Macgarrett Kings Jr. after a poor Stanford punt gave MSU the ball at the Cardinal twenty-seven-yard line. On third and eight, Cook found Tony Lippett on a post pattern for the go-ahead touchdown, making it 24–17.

After another exchange of punts, Stanford found itself with the football at its twenty-eight-yard line, down by seven but determined not to go quietly. After its drive stalled in Spartan territory, a botched hold on a field goal appeared to end in a miracle play for Stanford, with linebacker Trent Murphy catching a desperation pass for a first down. Fortunately, a penalty for an illegal man downfield was called instead. The Cardinal successfully retried the field goal, making it 24–20 with about four minutes remaining in the game.

Michigan State got the ball back and tried to run out the clock. They were thwarted by a tenacious Stanford defense, and the Spartans had to punt to the Cardinal with just over three minutes remaining. With the ball at the Stanford twenty-five-yard line, I walked over to Father Jake during the TV time-out and asked him what he thought.

"What do I think?" he said, "I'll tell you what I think, Dave. Try not to get arrested tonight during the celebration after we win this game. Make sure you tell Laurie and your kids you love them. Then call your daughter, Sarah, and tell her and all of them you realize that forever more you lived to see your team on this day fulfill a dream a quarter of a century in the making. Try to absorb every nuance of these next three minutes, Dave. You never know when you have seen your last Rose Bowl."

"Father Jake, how can you be so sure about a win?"

He smiled slyly and said, "I've got a guy on the inside, living upstairs. He let me know we are going to do it. Now let's finish strong. And just do your job."

At its own twenty-five-yard line, Stanford began its quest to pull out a last-second win. Three minutes and six seconds, essentially an eternity, remained.

After three plays netted the Cardinal just nine yards, the clock had ticked down to a minute and forty-six seconds. Stanford called its last time-out to plot a fourth-and-one strategy. The Cardinal decided to put their "jumbo" package on the field. Truly enormous men were placed throughout their backfield, across their line and at the tight end positions to help with blocking. Everyone on MSU's side prepared for a mano a mano fight to prevent a lousy thirty-six-inch gain.

I heard Coach D. yell something over to Coach Narduzzi. They looked at each other, and then Dantonio called a time-out. The key was to figure out which personnel and what defensive play to run to counter the Cardinal's jumbo offensive lineup. It was clear there was about to be a brawl between twenty-two men, a dozen or more of them weighing over three hundred pounds. Everyone would be lined up within inches of each other to fight over one yard of grass. Whoever wanted it the most would win this play—and maybe the day itself, if MSU held.

The ref called the players back onto the field. As Coach Narduzzi was having a last word with Kyler Elsworth, I tried to read the coach's lips. It appeared that he told the linebacker, referring to the timing of the snap and the play that will follow, "Anticipate run, but don't guess."

After a long count, an attempt to draw the Spartans offside, the ball was snapped, and the two lines collided with an audible thud. I could clearly hear the groans from multiple head-on collisions. The neurologist in me winced, while the fan in me was enthralled by the courage of the people who played this game.

Stanford quarterback Kevin Hogan handed the ball to up-back Ryan Hewitt, who moved forward almost in slow motion. Nose tackles Tyler Hoover and Micajah Reynolds somehow had completely collapsed the center of the Stanford offensive line. There was essentially no push forward by the Cardinal. As Hewitt tried to move the ball over the humanity in front of him, he had to leap. The bodies that used to make up the Cardinal and Spartan lines were now all intertwined with each other and sprawled in bizarre clumps on the ground.

The soul of the Spartan defense, middle linebacker Max Bullough, was missing. But the next man up, Kyler Ellsworth, was exactly where he needed to be and knew exactly what needed to be done at the moment of truth. He and Darien Harris both did a rainbow dive over the fallen men in front of them and met the leaping Cardinal ball carrier in mid-air helmet-to-helmet. The two linebackers struck Hewitt dead-on and overwhelmed him.

In a play that Spartan fans will long remember, all three of these men fell to the ground in a heap. Multiple referees looked on, blew their whistles, and eventually let the stadium know there was no gain. "First down, Michigan State" was the call by the head referee.

A scream of heavenly joy erupted from the stands behind the Spartan bench as victory on this day would belong to the Green and White. I said nothing and did not move. I simply continued to watch the lines untangle, realizing the force generated by those multiple head-on collisions. Overlooked on that play by many was the sacrifice of both Tyler Hoover and Micajah Reynolds. They, along with defensive ends Mark Scarpinato and Shilique Calhoun, had held the entire Stanford offensive jumbos to a draw.

That allowed the two Spartan linebackers to make the game-saving play. Kyler was correctly seen by the TV announcers as the main weapon that allowed victory. Yet the ever-modest Darien Harris was also right there to make that stop. Shilique Calhoun assisted to their right, leaving Hewitt with nowhere to go except down.

As the hugging and excitement on the Spartan sideline erupted, I was still just doing my job. As all of these fallen bodies began to untangle, it was immediately apparent even from twenty-five yards away, Micajah Reynolds was concussed. Although conscious, he was obviously stunned and not moving at all. He was down on his knees, unable to get up. I had no doubt he had suffered a significant mTBI on the play.

While everyone on the sidelines were waving huge white towels, celebrating, and dancing, only Sally Nogle and I noticed Micajah. We both understood the consequences of what he had just done and I felt compelled to break Jeff Monroe's number-one rule: "Do not, under any circumstances, go onto the field."

So, despite the Spartan players dancing around on the field, I walked onto the turf to try and help Micajah Reynolds get to his feet. Once standing, it was obvious, he was dazed and unable to move on his own. He simply hugged me as he struggled to regain his balance so he wouldn't fall.

I thought Sally would tear into me; I had broken the number-one rule. Instead, she grabbed him, and together we guided the three-hundred-plus-pound nose guard off the field. Using her mom voice, Sally said, "Dave, quite a play. What a game. Thanks for helping Micajah. And thanks for helping me get him off the field. He got it done for us."

On the sidelines, Reynolds' mTBI was painfully obvious. Initially, he was unable to speak, could not stand without assistance and was totally confused with that glassy eye appearance. That got me really worried. Then the concussion began clearing quickly and within a few minutes he became more aware and was able to stand on his own.

I took a deep breath as I realized we would not need a trip to the emergency room, at least not yet. I was worried enough to promise myself I would personally check him multiple times before we left the stadium and then again later that night to be sure there was no intracranial bleeding.

Behind us the celebration grew on the sideline and into the stands. Once the TV time-out was finished, and the field was cleared of dancing green and white players, MSU's offense came on and went in "victory formation." Their job was simply to run out the last minute and forty-three seconds with three easy kneel-downs. But on the last play of the game Coach D. did one more thing to cement his legacy as a kind and trusted leader.

He chose to insert former starting quarterback Andrew Maxwell to take the last snap in Michigan State University's most important football game in the last quarter of a century. It was Mark Dantonio and all of us paying homage to "Max," a quiet but intense competitor who dealt with his situation as a backup quarterback with enormous poise and dignity. After Maxwell took that last snap, MSU had its first thirteen-win season ever and its first Rose Bowl win since 1988.

As the formal on-field celebration got organized, I turned and looked for Laurie and Matt in the stands, a dozen rows behind the Spartan bench. They waved back and had such joy on their faces. Maybe it would have been better for me to be sitting with them, watching all of this together, rather than doing my job on the field. I reflected on the conflicted emotions: pride for what I was part of and sadness of not being with my family. It was one of the most gratifying but surprisingly lonely moments I ever had.

The Rose Bowl committee recognized Connor Cook and Kyler Ellsworth as the offensive and defensive players of the game. Coach D. was then given the 100th Rose Bowl Game trophy and the microphone to address the triumphant Spartan crowd. When asked by the commentator, "What does this win mean to you?" Mark Dantonio's response was simple: "Completion."

During the applause from the MSU crowd that followed that simple statement, I immediately thought of Kirk Cousins, and his statement about "completing your circles." His Spartans had been denied a trip to the Rose Bowl in 2010, then lost the 2011 Big Ten championship game on a penalty at the worst possible time. I remember Kirk telling me that whenever it happened, he would find some type of way to be at the Rose Bowl to support MSU. He had kept his word, and the MSU football team had won a thrilling game. I was so proud of all of them and my university.

Dantonio was next asked by the TV commentator, "What does this win mean to Spartan Nation?"

"What it means," Coach D. responded, "is you are going to be able to see Michigan State's name up there as a Rose Bowl winner on a plaque outside the Rose Bowl fifty years from now with your grandchildren."

As I listened to him, I suddenly realized this might well be my last Rose Bowl. For once, I was totally in the moment, with a serenity I had never felt before.

In the locker room after the game, Randy and I found Micajah Reynolds by his locker. His cognition and memory were improving by the minute. I found it encouraging Reynolds was using his well-worn iPad to communicate with family and friends. What was incredible was the broken, cobwebbed shattered screen on the big lineman's iPad.

"Big man," I asked, "why do you use that broken iPad. Why didn't you get another?"

"Doc, I can't afford another iPad. Man, where would I get the money to buy such a thing? Besides this one still works just fine."

The scene of a university student-athlete and newly created football hero using a well-worn and nearly broken iPad was incongruous when thinking about what he had just sacrificed minutes before. I briefly thought about the fairness of big-time college football generating multi-million dollar opportunities for television sponsorships without some measure of adequate compensation to the players who make this sport possible. I looked forward to the day that might change.

I also noted that Reynolds' strength, thinking, and memory were clearing and headed back toward normal. He had an aggressive mTBI, but I was now far less worried about intracranial bleeding. We'd still watch him carefully over the next several days, but I suspected he would be fine.

After the laughing and screaming calmed down just a bit, the room was called to order by Coach D. He let everyone know this would be a memory that would last inside each of us for our lifetimes. We all knew he was right. When he was done, as was the tradition, he called upon the players to count out the victorious twenty-four points and sing the MSU fight song.

They did that along with two hundred others who were assembled in that locker room, including the student-athletes, a dozen athletic trainers, the press, numerous videographers, the on-field communication staff, Mr. Nick and his equipment people, Glen Edgett and his team that always transported the heavier football equipment by truck from East Lansing, the dozen equipment personnel, the cheer team, MSU administrators, the sports information directors, and the five members of the medical staff that made up the 2013 MSU football family.

Once that was done, the hip-hop music, featuring "Type of Way," was started up extra loud. Rich Homie Quan (from Darqueze Dennard's home state of Georgia) somehow found his way into the locker room to help sing his hit that had become an anthem for this 2013 Spartan football team. Jack Allen got two Tylenol from an athletic training student, drank some Gatorade, turned back my way, gave me a fist bump, then walked over to the president of Michigan State University, Lou Anna K. Simon. I could only shake my head.

Allen and others started working on her and the MSU athletic director Mark Hollis to get in the middle of the celebration that was just starting. Dr. Simon did indeed (more or less) dance along with everyone else, including coaches, athletic trainers, administrators, a catholic priest, and an orthopedic surgeon included. Despite urging, I pointed out that neurologists do not dance.

After twenty or thirty minutes of raucous celebration, the players drifted in and out of the showers and got back into street clothes. We all boarded the buses and traveled to the hotel. I was on the first bus to arrive.

There I found the hotel atrium on the floor below us was already jammed with more than two thousand family, friends, alumni, and undergrads. The yelling and screaming started just as the players and staff on the first bus (including me) filtered down the escalator into the total mad house. I found Matt and Laurie just as the party started to amp up. It made the Big Ten playoff celebration three weeks before "look like church," according to one of our receivers.

The next morning, after every one of the injured, including our concussion case, was checked, and improving, we all made it onto the 747 for the ride home. Laurie and I took our place in the luxury of that two-seat row by the window. She turned to me after takeoff and asked, "Dave, we won! What do you have to say for yourself?"

I looked up at the ceiling of the plane and said, "What a game. What an opportunity these last four years to see it all up close. Laurie, I saw what it was like for a coach to inspire highly disciplined but violent young men playing a collision sport and keep the 'lion in the cage' until it was time to let it out.

"I learned what football truly means to the culture of a community. I learned to have the utmost respect for athletic trainers and the medical team that helps these young men compete in a game that twists and turns on injuries. I learned, even at my age, I could fulfill my lifelong ambition to help a college football team. I learned to be in the minute and never take anything in life for granted. Maybe that was the most important of all the lessons.

"As to football itself, Honey, it is simply not going away. It is too engrained into American culture, despite its danger. If folks took the time to look closer, beyond the players and coaches, I think people would love it even more. The equipment and communications people, the ushers, the alumni, the students, the emergency medical transport folks, and all the other people that surround a team are also huge contributors, especially those athletic trainers."

At the end of my five-minute speech, I finally turned toward Laurie and realized she was fast asleep with her head leaning against a pillow positioned on the plane's window. She had probably not heard a thing. I just shook my head, laughed to myself, and quietly got up from my aisle seat. As I looked around, almost everyone had dozed off or was trying to recover from the last night's celebration.

I worked my way past sleeping players with ice packs on shoulders and ribs, a group of student athletic trainers, half awake and half asleep, and coaches still analyzing the game. I walked past my fellow doctors, their spouses, and children. I found myself walking to the very back of that vast 747. I thought about all that I had seen the previous day at the Rose Bowl and every day I had been with this MSU football team for the past four years.

I noticed the last row was completely empty. I smiled and couldn't help but sit down and then slide from the aisle over to the end of the row, where there was as always, no window. The seat in front of it was leaning all the way back and I had to somehow worm my way into that airtight space. I did not bother looking at the person who decided he had to have his seat all the way back. Instead, after easing into my customary seat at the back corner of the plane, all I noticed was that an aging, incredibly skinny and wrinkled hand squeezed tight into a ball was coming over the top of that chair. It was the doctor of soul seeking one more fist bump from his college-football road roommate. I obliged, and it felt like home.

# CHAPTER TWENTY FIVE

# Epilogue; Where Are They Now?

## Kirk Cousins

Kirk became well known as an outstanding leader within the NFL. He retained his college nickname "Captain Kirk" (after the *Star Trek* character). And Sally Nogle was right: He has also become a very wealthy man. He did end up playing on Sundays, first for the Washington Football Team, later for the Minnesota Vikings and in 2024 received a handsome contract to play for the Atlanta Falcons.

At the time of this writing, after a dozen years in the NFL, he has played in 150 games with a completion rate above 66 percent. Kirk has so far thrown for 39,471 total yards with 270 touchdowns. His QB rating is hovering just around 100. Following his ninth year after graduating from MSU, he was the most coveted free agent in the NFL. According to NFL data, Cousins signed a two-year, $66 million contract with the Minnesota Vikings, including a $30 million signing bonus. In 2024 he received a four-year contract for $180 million with $100 million guaranteed to move to the Atlanta Falcons. Kirk has been invited to four Pro Bowl games.

Kirk Cousins still visits MSU periodically. Somehow, he always found time to visit with Sally in the Duffy Daugherty Football Building after finding Coach D. Occasionally, I might run into him during his campus visits. Last time I saw him was 2019, the year prior to Coach Dantonio's retirement, during a late summer indoor practice.

Kirk still recognized and greeted people from his college days, displaying his uncanny memory for faces and names. He addressed me as he always did: "Dr. Kaufman, good to see you. Thank you for all the things you did to help us out as a neurologist." As we shook hands, I responded, "Kirk, you have an amazing memory. Thanks for always completing your circles."

## Josh Rouse

After Josh Rouse suffered his broken neck in the opening game of the 2010 season, he asked Coach Dantonio if there was an opening to explore coaching. Rouse was provided an opportunity to work with strength and conditioning coach Ken Mannie. By 2012, Rouse served as a graduate assistant coach on offense for MSU, where he worked with Mark Staten, MSU's offensive line coach. Josh eventually graduated from MSU with a major in human resources and then got a master's in kinesiology. He decided to leave coaching to work for Storage Solutions, in Westfield, Indiana. He served as their national account sales manager. He was also at the 2014 Rose Bowl to watch MSU win—and to complete his circle. When I was preparing this memoir, I called Josh to make sure it was okay to tell his story. His email response was beyond almost anything I had ever experienced in my time as a sports neurology doctor. He said in part, "My daughters and I are so thankful you were on the sideline that day."

Those moments helping him in the locker room during my first game on the field still haunt me to this day.

## Le'Veon Bell

Described as "The Great Hesitator" based on his very patient running style, he did very well financially and athletically. After ten years in the NFL, Le'Veon had 6,554 rushing yards and 3,289 receiving yards for fifty touchdowns. During his five celebrated years with the Pittsburgh Steelers, he scored forty-two touchdowns, had three seasons where he had more than 1,200 yards rushing and 600 yards receiving.

According to NFL data, in 2019, Bell signed a four-year, $52.5 million contract with $35 million guaranteed with the New York Jets. That made him the second-highest-paid running back in the NFL at the time. Le'Veon too was at the 2014 Rose Bowl, completing his circles. At the end of the game he tried to get on the field to help his Spartans celebrate. The on-field security denied that despite my pleading, "Don't you recognize him? It's Le'Veon Bell!"

Security's response was, "I know who he is. I'm not dumb. I want him on the field, too, but I'd lose my job!"

Le'Veon pulled another acrobatic move by finding an assistant coach who snuck him a field pass to join in the Spartan on field festivities. He sang the fight song in the locker room along with the rest of us, just one of the guys.

## Bennie Fowler

After Bennie's senior year at MSU, he played receiver and special teams for a variety of NFL squads for eight years. My favorite memory of him as a pro in the NFL was as a Denver Broncos player. On February 7, 2016, Fowler caught the great Peyton Manning's final career pass for a two-point conversion in Super Bowl 50. The Broncos beat the Carolina Panthers 24–10, earning Fowler and his teammates that coveted championship ring.

Later on, while still playing in the NFL, Bennie wrote a delightful book on how to achieve success. In part, he referenced his uncommon path to the football field, pointing out he had grown up among wealth and was mentored by his ultra-successful parents. Appropriately, he called his guide to success, "Silver Spoon." After his NFL playing days were over, Bennie returned often to the Spartan Stadium sidelines to watch a game or be honored. It's always joyous to speak with such a remarkable Spartan.

## Jack Allen

Jack was the unquestioned leader of the MSU offensive line during the Spartans' glory years. He received first team All-American honors from the Associated Press and other polls in 2014 and again in 2015. He was also a Rimington Award finalist twice as the country's best center. Of considerable interest (at least to Jack), he also scored a touchdown on a designed handoff that went nine yards in 2015 against Penn State. Jack was signed by the New Orleans Saints and played two years in the NFL. More importantly, he proved to be among the nicest and smartest football players I ever interacted with. He also won multiple academic awards.

Many years later, over a drink at a Spartan bowl game, he confided in me he did indeed suffer a concussion at the Rose Bowl but "faked my way through it." I asked him if he was serious, and he said, "Maybe yes and maybe no, but you need to buy the next round of Scotch just in case." Jack and his two brothers, Brian, and then Matt, played for MSU (mostly at center) for a total of twelve years. At Matt's last game for MSU (the Spartans' 2021 Peach Bowl victory over Coach Pat Narduzzi's Pitt Panthers) I asked Leslie and John Allen (the brothers' parents) when we could expect another Allen to play center for MSU. They both implied that Jack had better get busy creating that next player.

Jack Allen was incredibly helpful in inspiring me to write this narrative. He is an amazing leader, highly admired by the people he worked and played with during that special time at Michigan State University.

## Michael Shingles

Mike remains the go-to guy for anyone with a sports-related orthopedic issue in Michigan and well beyond. Calm and reasonable at the moment of truth when caring for student-athletes, he also proved to be a remarkable physician leader. He occasionally did point out to administration with gusto how to do things better while he was at MSU. There is no finer friend a man can have than Dr. Michael Shingles. That was true in 2010, and that is true today. Michael left the field in 2021. I miss him every time I see the Spartans run onto the turf at Spartan Stadium.

## Jeff Monroe

Jeff Monroe's absence for the 2013 Rose Bowl year was palpable because he had such an enormous locker room presence. But it proved every one of us is replaceable—even Jeff Monroe. Jeff continues to do well as of this writing. Instead of herding football players to do their best, Jeff now does carpentry and can occasionally be seen encouraging his flock of chickens to be more productive. He remains the executive director of the annual Big Sky Athletic Training Sports Medicine Conference. In addition, he builds ramps for the handicapped to help ease their life. He married Joyce deJong, DO (professor and founding chair of the Department of Pathology at the Western Michigan University Homer Stryker MD School of Medicine). Jeff and Joyce moved to Kalamazoo, Michigan, where he happily retired after thirty amazing years as an athletic trainer for MSU. In 2024, Joyce was recruited to serve as dean of the College of Osteopathic Medicine at Michigan State University. That now makes Jeff the MSU College of Osteopathic Medicine's "first man."

## Sally Nogle

Sally retired from MSU in 2023, having spent more than three and a half decades as a Spartan. She was inducted into the National Athletic Trainers' Association Hall of Fame years before she retired. In 2020–2021 her daughter, Tracy Nogle, DO, having completed medical school and a physical medicine and rehabilitation residency, returned to MSU to do a year of sports medicine fellowship with her mom as part of the curriculum faculty. It was heartwarming to see Tracy completing her circles by learning from her mom on the field. I am convinced Sally Nogle is among the most amazing humans I have ever encountered. I have plenty of company in that regard. Sally is without peer regarding her style and professionalism with student-athletes. MSU became a better place because of her presence. In 2023, MSU named the training room area for injured Spartan student-athletes within the Duffy building after Sally Nogle to appropriately honor her.

## Brian Kirkland, DO, and Joseph

Brian has survived many football seasons after his bone-marrow treatment for leukemia in 2010 and has been cancer-free for more than a decade. He and Joseph have attended numerous MSU–Notre Dame football games with Laurie and me over the years since the Little Giants game. They travel extensively, including annual pilgrimages to Notre Dame to light a candle at the Grotto. More recently, the two of them bought their third home, in South Bend, Indiana, about a mile from Notre Dame's football stadium.

## Jim Pignataro

Five years after Jim Pignataro provided Brian and Joseph those special seats for the Little Giants game, he also came down with cancer. Jim continued on heroically in his role as an associate athletic director for the next six years until, in 2021, he finally succumbed to the disease. I think about him often and the kindness he showed me in my attempts to help Brian achieve his wish of "attending at least one more Notre Dame football game." The wind blew just a little colder the day Jim passed away.

## Max Bullough

I still feel sadness realizing Max was not in that Rose Bowl tunnel with us in person, victimized by a self-inflicted violation of the strict team rules laid down by Coach D. However, his spirituality still had a profound effect on his team that day. He signed with the Houston Texans as an undrafted free agent in 2014 and went on to play for three years in the NFL. Max has done well financially and is still involved with football. He worked as a graduate assistant for the University of Alabama Crimson Tide football team under Coach Nick Saban. Bullough was engaged to his fiancée Bailee on Christmas Eve 2015, and they married in Traverse City, Michigan, on July 2, 2016. Bailee and Max now have three sons. Whenever on campus, Max is still easy to recognize, and he remains an all-time MSU favorite, among the very best to ever play the game for the Green and White. In 2024, he became the linebacker coach for Notre Dame.

# Will Gholston

On April 27, 2013, Will was drafted by the Tampa Bay Buccaneers in the fourth round as the 126th pick. So far he has played 11 seasons in the NFL, all with the Tampa Bay Buccaneers with a total of 169 regular season games (420 tackles) along with nine playoff games (eight tackles). His initial four-year deal was worth $2,560,544 (with a $400,544 signing bonus). By the next year, he became a starter and eventually signed a five-year, $27,500,000 contract, including $13,500,000 guaranteed (with $7,000,000 given at signing).

I once ran into Will in the Detroit airport. He was wearing a Tampa Bay Buccaneers letterman jacket. He walked right over and greeted me with a huge bear hug. We talked about some of the old days with the Spartans. He promised he would one day get a Super Bowl ring. Will accomplished that when Tampa Bay defeated Kansas City 31–9 to win Super Bowl 55 on February 7, 2021. He played great.

# Mike Sadler

Mike Sadler was one of the very few four-time Academic All-Americans. He also averaged 43.3 yards per punt as a sophomore in 2012, 42.5 as a junior in 2013, and just slightly less in 2014, his senior year. He was perhaps the most popular player among the fans and players during that 2013 Rose Bowl season. He had an uncanny ability to succeed with trick plays. His raw sense of humor and intellect made him seem more like a doctoral student than a football player every time we talked. That was until he put on that helmet to flip the field after one of his incredible punts. He truly embodied both halves of the term *student-athlete*.

Sadler died tragically in a car crash in Wisconsin on July 23, 2016, after attending a kicking camp to teach young players the art of punting. Only twenty-four years old, he was the first among those in that Rose Bowl tunnel on January 1, 2014, to pass away. In a remembrance, Coach Dantonio stated, "He gave us all so much in so little time. Our thoughts and prayers are with him and his family."

In a later statement, Coach D. added, "The world has lost a rising star who dreamed big and was accomplishing those dreams one after the other. He was one of those people that brightened your day. I always say to try and be a light and he was a light in this world."

Michigan State University was devastated. To honor the memory of Mike Sadler, a celebration of life was held at Spartan Stadium with approximately nine thousand people in attendance. It was officiated by Coach D. The eulogy was delivered by Father Jake Foglio. I noticed that every single member of the 2013 Rose Bowl Championship team who attended wore their Rose Bowl ring, including me.

The Big Ten Conference decreed that on September 28, 2016, all seven Big Ten Conference games would have officials and captains use a special commemorative coin for the opening coin flip to honor the lives of Sadler and Nebraska punter Sam Foltz, who was in the same car. The coin was developed collaboratively by representatives from the University of Nebraska, Michigan State, the Foltz and Sadler families, and the Big Ten Conference. According to the Big Ten's statement, "Both left an indelible mark on their teams and schools and positively impacted the lives of those around them."

## Mylan Hicks

Hicks was a Michigan All-State player at Detroit Renaissance High School and committed to Michigan State as part of the 2010 class. He redshirted that year and switched to safety the next season, battling injuries on and off until his senior season.

Mylan was a quiet but spiritual three-year letter winner for MSU, playing for the Green and White from 2012 through 2014. He had twenty-seven tackles in thirty-two career games. He suffered a broken arm against Nebraska in week five of his senior year, but rehabbed like crazy, amazing the sports medicine physicians and athletic trainers. He somehow suited up four weeks later and was outstanding for the rest of the year.

At the football banquet in 2014, he won the Biggie Munn Award for most inspirational player. He earned his bachelor's degree in psychology and lived his dream of playing professional football in the Canadian Football league in Calgary.

Two months after Mike Sadler's death, on Sept. 25, 2016, Hicks and teammates were at the Marquee Beer Market, a Calgary nightclub, celebrating the team's victory against Winnipeg. Suddenly, a fight started among the patrons of the bar. According to police reports, Mylan, ever the peacemaker, tried to break up the fight. Then someone pulled a gun and fired, hitting one person: Mylan Hicks. He died later that night—he was twenty-three years old. A Canadian judge found Nelson Lugela, twenty-one years old, guilty of second-degree murder. Coach D. and the team went to Detroit to support Mylan's parents at the service honoring his life. Mylan was the second Spartan who stood in that Rose Bowl Tunnel on January 1, 2014 to be lost.

## Randy Pearson

Randy continued on as the lead team physician for MSU football until 2023. He still maintains his active MSU clinical practice as a family physician. It is always a privilege to watch him work.

Well after MSU's 31–21 victory in the Peach Bowl on December 30, 2021 (defeating head coach Pat Narduzzi's Pittsburg Panthers), the now-retired Coach D. joined us for the traditional Randy Pearson postvictory Scotch celebration.

Coach D. looked at each of us while downing his Scotch and said, "Thanks Randy. Well, I didn't understand when I was coaching how nice things could sometimes be when you went to see the team doctors."

## Ken Mannie

As my years with the football team mounted, Coach Mannie was actually one of the nicest human beings I had ever met. I had grown very fond of Ken and his wife, Marianne. After the Rose Bowl victory, Ken told me he took the bonus money from such an important victory to buy his beloved wife a proper engagement ring.

The diamond ring was so huge my fear was Laurie would see it and demand something similar. In an attempt to protect myself from that fate, I bought Marianne some stylish dress gloves to "hide the ring" if she ever thought Laurie might be in the same room with her.

After twenty-five years as MSU's head strength and conditioning coach, Ken retired on February 13, 2020. He had been in coaching for a total of forty-five years. I have yet to meet a more fearsome motivator and loyal human being on any football field.

## Father Jake Foglio

Father Jake, revered by so many of us at MSU, was honored by his university in 2019 when Lou Anna K. Simon, MSU's president, announced the university had endowed the Father John (Jake) Foglio Chair in Spirituality to be within the College of Arts and Letters. Later that year, Father Jake and I saw little of each other, but we talked often on the phone as COVID started to rage.

He decided he could not travel with the team for the 2020 season, shortened for COVID. In true Father Jake style, whenever we talked by phone or when possible live, he always thanked me for taking time with him as I always thanked him for the same. In his last call to me, on September 13, 2020, he referred to himself as the "wounded warrior." I could tell his breathing was labored, but we had one of our best conversations ever.

Randy Pearson called me on a miserable, cold, and rainy October day in 2020 to let me know Father Jake had just died. Another deep blow in the world of COVID and during one of Michigan State University's darkest times. As much as anything else, Father Jake's passing signaled the end of a remarkable era for my university. It was his death and my sweet wife Laurie's inspiration that drove me to conclude I had to write down my early experiences as a sports neurologist for the Spartan football team. That led me to write this book.

When we lost Father Jake in October 2020, I knew it was the end of a special time. Yet in my mind, and through his named chair, Father Jake lives on here at his home within the walls of MSU. One year later, on the anniversary of his passing, there was a celebration of his life on campus. Six of us were called forward to describe to the hundreds gathered what made Father Jake so special. Two medical school professors and the dean of the MSU College of Arts and Letters spoke about Father Jake's academic life. One of his closest friends, a priest, reminded us of Father Jake's special relationship with the Lord.

Then I was asked to the podium. Wearing my 2014 100th Rose Bowl ring, I told some of my stories about what it was like rooming and working with Father Jake on travel days with the MSU football team. I felt it necessary to repeat the David and Goliath homily the ancient priest worked on all night prior to that U of M game. In addition, I did provide an example or two of his interactions with a variety of referees through the years.

Then Mark Dantonio came to the podium. He reiterated what a force for good Father Jake was for his football family. Coach D. talked about what Father Jake had done behind the scenes for his own family. I tried my best to contain my emotion as the coach spoke about how Father Jake helped him, his wife, Becky, and his two daughters during health issues within the family. I could not hold back the tears. Seeing my reaction, Laurie gave me a gentle hug.

## Mark Dantonio

Coach D. retired on February 4, 2020, after thirteen remarkable seasons at MSU. His record while with the Spartans was 114–57. That included six seasons with ten or more victories, eight of them against the Michigan Wolverines. During his time as head coach, MSU won three Big Ten Championships, including the 2013 thirteen-win season that ended with a victory in the 100th Rose Bowl. The 114 victories made him the winningest coach in MSU's 125-year history, eclipsing the previous record of 109–69–5, compiled by legendary Duffy Daugherty over eighteen seasons. He was inducted into the College Football Hall of Fame in January 2024.

Bennie Fowler said of his former coach, "There are so many great and wonderful things I can say about Coach D. First, he embodied the values of my parents, and, therefore, he quickly became an extension of my family when I arrived on campus in 2009. He pushed me past my comfort level and made me believe I could be a champion. When I became a senior, he entrusted in me the responsibility to pass on that work ethic to the underclassmen on the team. Finally,

Coach D. is a man of great faith. That influence will forever shape the missions in my life."

When Laurie and I first came to MSU after spending time within the Harvard Medical School system, it was so obvious that Spartans at all levels received little or no respect from U of M in anything: not in football, basketball, neuro-ophthalmology, physics, chemistry, neurology, concussion, or anything else. Stating that the development of a true rivalry in football between the schools was *the* switch in getting respect for MSU from U of M over the last two decades might strike some as too bold a claim.

But I am personally of the belief football did have something to do with the newfound respect from U of M and the rest of the Big Ten. Maybe only a few of the Michigan State faculty and staff would agree with that. But I think many—if not most—of MSU's more than 640,000 living alumni would surely concur. At the center of that shift for this generation of alumni must be Coach D. Not only because of what he said, but because of the way he said it and how he came through, time after time. Seven out of eight times during the glory years, he beat U of M. He took his team to twelve bowl games and won the Rose Bowl and the Cotton Bowl back-to-back. History will be very kind to Coach D.

Mark Dantonio brought respect to his university through a combination of dignity, grit, and ethics. He instilled the will to try in his teams and he helped his players find the will to win time after time. It may be "only football," but Coach D.'s attitude meant so much to so many of us sitting in the upper deck, or in the classroom, or in the medical school clinics and laboratories. Very few people get to be true difference makers in other people's lives. Mark Dantonio is surely one of those folks, and his influence extends well beyond football.

## Rule changes

During my early years with the team, people began to actively point out college football had become a game of attrition, just as is true in professional leagues. As a result, less violent practices began to come into play to prevent injury. That adjustment was wise for so many reasons. Some rule changes, such as the prohibition on "targeting" (using your helmet to strike an opponent's head) were implemented both in college and pro football, which helped lower the number of mTBI.

Slowly but surely, other rules, especially those associated with kickoffs and onside kicks, were implemented. Awareness of concussions and learning how to recognize them became more and more important among players, coaches and medical staff. The mTBI numbers, thankfully, have begun to decline.

## The College Football Playoff System

The College Football Playoff was launched in the 2014 college football season, the year after the 100th Rose Bowl Game was played on January 1, 2014. This new format meant that every third year a semifinal game for the national championship was played in Pasadena. The Rose Bowl's involvement in the BCS (after "The Last Rose Bowl") brought with it an enormous change in the symbolism of what it meant to Big Ten and PAC-12 loyalists. Yet for so many of us "old school" football fans, especially in the Midwest, there still is nothing quite like the Rose Bowl.

Starting the year after the "Last Rose Bowl" was played on January 1, 2014, the actual formal playoff system between the top four college teams was implemented. In addition, two more bowls were added (Peach and Cotton) to create the "New Year's Six." The top-rated twelve teams in the country were invited to participate in those six games. MSU, ranked second in the Big Ten, was invited to the Cotton Bowl on January 1, 2015. The Spartans defeated Baylor 42–41, scoring twenty-one points in the final quarter, the last on a pass from Cook to Keith Mumphery with seventeen seconds remaining. No Big Ten team played in the Rose Bowl that year.

The next change was that two semifinal national championship playoff games were rotated between those six bowls to select the final two teams to play for the national championship. The national championship game between the two winners of the playoff games was typically played ten days after the New Year's Six games were concluded.

The Spartans were one of four teams selected to participate in the College Football Playoff (also at the Cotton Bowl) on December 31, 2015. This was after winning the Big Ten playoff game against Iowa. The fact MSU had won the Big Ten and did not go to the Rose Bowl helped break the usual format of the best Big Ten team getting that very special trip to Pasadena. In the minds of many fans nationally, that made a trip to the Rose Bowl a "super-consolation game" for the team that did not win the Big Ten playoff game. An even larger playoff system, (up to twelve teams) is the next major change being enacted in college football.

## Division One College Football Changes

The 100th Rose Bowl also signaled an end, in so many ways, to the "innocence" of college football with the introduction of the College Playoffs. That event caused a reduction of what individual bowls meant to the teams and players that participated in them. Television revenue drove the need to crown a "true" national champion through a more organized playoff system. That event made essentially all postseason games except the playoffs seem like they were devoid of any true national relevance.

A few years after that, payments to players through the Name, Image, and Likeness (NIL) rulings came into being. Although appropriate, the NIL and other changes (like the ability to transfer schools without penalty through "the portal") lead to college football no longer being an amateur sport and more and more like a stepchild to professional (NFL) football. That was regrettable.

In the *Wall Street Journal* on January 10, 2022, Jason Gay wrote, "College football . . . remains a cultural behemoth, but it's finally shedding its pretense about amateurism . . . the sport has diminished its relevance and interest in [after season bowl] events."

Gay continued, "There's worry about participation (even in a Rose Bowl) as a small number of college players, concerned about getting hurt in a 'meaningless showcase,' have dared to opt out of games, choosing instead to prepare for the NFL draft."

In my view, despite all of this, the college game is still great if you take the time to truly look at it, at the people surrounding and

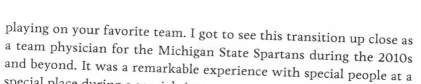

playing on your favorite team. I got to see this transition up close as a team physician for the Michigan State Spartans during the 2010s and beyond. It was a remarkable experience with special people at a special place during a special time.

I also lived to see probably my "Last Rose Bowl" on January 1, 2014, as a formal member of the MSU football team's medical staff, including getting a ring and my name on the plaque commemorating that game. That plaque still hangs on the west wall of Spartan Stadium in East Lansing, Michigan. It is one of the greatest honors I have received during my four decades at a great university.

## Laurie Kaufman

Laurie remains a tenured associate professor practicing endocrinology at MSU. She is now heavily invested in teaching medical students at MSU's College of Osteopathic Medicine and is a clear medical student favorite. She has won so many "Golden Apple" teaching awards these past several years we have both lost count.

Laurie also remains a remarkable football fan with incredible insights regarding performance and football strategy. However, her full-time job remains helping out our son, Matt Kaufman, BA, MA, and daughter, Sarah Kaufman, MD, PhD, whenever appropriate. Even harder, she does her best to keep me out of trouble.

## David Kaufman

This experience allowed me, on occasion, to change from being a rather stuffy academic neurology professor into a sports neurologist. It was not an easy journey. The experiences I enjoyed and sometimes endured forged that transformation. Along the way I diagnosed three significant neck injuries (one nearly fatal), 112 concussions, and so many "stingers" (temporary paralysis of an arm due to a brachial plexus nerve injury) I forgot the number. I also saw and treated several eye injuries, a Bell's palsy, a stroke in a twenty-year-old player, and two brain masses.

I also had to deal with a horrible loss to Wisconsin in the first Big Ten playoffs in December 2011, the truly obnoxious fans at the

University of Iowa and Penn State University heckling me from not more than a few feet from the bench, and I have endured the Notre Dame band. I also got to room on the road with a truly inspirational man, Father Jake Foglio.

I saw what it was like for Coach Dantonio, only a month removed from his heart attack to inspire men at halftime at Northwestern to keep a win streak going. I saw the same man during halftime at the 2013 Big Ten championship game literally will his team to victory, and finally, after seven years of trying, to earn the right to play in the 100th Rose Bowl. As a fan and as a neurologist, I got to see what this was all like during MSU football's modern glory years, up close on the field and as far away from the upper deck as you could get.

As a brain doctor at one of the country's great universities, I treated many patients with life-threatening brain diseases for many years before my time on the football field. Such practice had tempered my emotion so that, at the moment of truth for my nonfootball patients, I was poised and skilled enough to provide what was needed. But I really had no clue what football meant to the people that played it, coached it, or watched it until I had these on field experiences. Along with Randy Pearson I also walked off the field in 2023 and returned to the stands after thirteen years with the team.

I did not mean this book in any way to be a "tell-all" exposé about Spartan football, its players, coaches, and medical staff. Just the opposite. I have very rarely developed such respect for a group of people as I did during those days of growing into my role as a sports neurologist. Fulfilling that lifelong ambition to somehow help my university's football team, long after any rational possibility of doing that was gone, is without a doubt the most amazing thing that happened to me during my university tenure.

As for football itself, it is simply not going away. It is too engrained into American culture. Yes, there is danger to it, no doubt. There is danger, too, in riding in a car on a highway. The key is safety. One of the reasons I wrote this book was to implore us to seek even more safety in football. We need to make football safer because, as stated, it is not going away. It is too terrific for those that play it, coach it, work within in it, write about it, or watch it.

In addition, I urge you to take the time to look just a little closer at this sport beyond its players and coaches. The equipment and communication people that surround your favorite team are also huge contributors. Occasionally, you may also want to look over at the medical team on the sideline. Be sure to spot the athletic trainers because in my view they make the true difference for a player on game day.

If you do spot a fan yelling at the refs from the stands at Spartan Stadium that may well be me, wondering when my team will make it back to the Rose Bowl.

# ABOUT THE AUTHOR

Dr. David I. Kaufman has served as the on-field neurologist for the Michigan State University football team for over 13 years. He is a tenured Professor and is the Founding Chair of the Department of Neurology and Ophthalmology at Michigan State University. He was recently appointed as the Assistant Vice President of Clinical Affairs for the Office of Health Science at MSU.

Dr. Kaufman received his bachelor's degree from the University of Wisconsin and his medical degree from the Philadelphia College of Osteopathic Medicine. He then served as a Neurology resident and visual electrophysiology fellow at the University of Wisconsin. He was a Harvard Clinical Research Fellow while obtaining his neuro-ophthalmology training at Massachusetts General Hospital. He has been a practicing Neuro-Ophthalmologist at MSU for over 3 decades. Dr. Kaufman has helped train eighty post-doctoral students and clinical research fellows in Neuro-Ophthalmology at MSU during that time. He has won more than 25 MSU teaching awards over the years along with one from the University of Wisconsin.

Dr. Kaufman's research and clinical interest have included using the afferent visual system and visual electrophysiology to assess prognosis and early therapeutic strategies for brain disease such as multiple sclerosis and stroke. He has been cited in "Best Doctors" in Neurology multiple times over the last two decades. He has had multiple NIH funded grants and participated on the Executive Committee or the Data and Safety Monitoring Committee of multiple clinical trials for the National Eye Institute. He has more than 160 peer reviewed publications and book chapters. These publications and his abstracts have typically focused on Neuro-Ophthalmology including several publications on mild traumatic brain injury. Those manuscripts focused on sports concussion and fMRI radiographic biomarkers to assist with prognosis. He now has directed his research toward Thyroid Eye Disease.

Dr. Kaufman recognizes his greatest accomplishments as meeting and marrying his wife, Laurie Kaufman, M.D, and helping to raise their two children, Matt and Sarah, to become college graduates.

# ABOUT THE PUBLISHER

The Sager Group was founded in 1984. In 2012 it was chartered as a multimedia content brand, with the intent of empowering those who create art—an umbrella beneath which makers can pursue, and profit from, their craft directly, without gatekeepers. TSG publishes books; ministers to artists and provides modest grants; and produces documentary, feature, and commercial films. By harnessing the means of production, The Sager Group helps artists help themselves. For more information, please see TheSagerGroup.net.

# MORE FROM THE SAGER GROUP

## The Stacks Reader Series

*The Cheerleaders: A True Story* by E. Jean Carroll
*An American Family: A True Story* by Daniel Voll
*Flesh and Blood: A True Story* by Peter Richmond
*An Accidental Martyr: A True Story* by Chip Brown
*Death of a Playmate: A True Story* by Teresa Carpenter
*The Detective: And Other True Stories* by Walt Harrington
*Soldiers in the Army of God: A True Story* by Daniel Voll
*Original Gangster: A True Story* by Paul Solotaroff
*The Dreamer Deceiver: A True Story* by Ivan Solotaroff
*Mary in the Lavender Pumps: A True Story* by Joyce Wadler

## General Interest

*The Stories We Tell: Classic True Tales by America's Greatest Women Journalists*
*New Stories We Tell: True Tales*
by *America's New Generation of Great Women Journalists*
*Newswomen: Twenty-five Years of Front-Page Journalism*
*The Someone You're Not: True Stories of Sports, Celebrity, Politics &*
*Pornography* by Mike Sager
*Lifeboat No. 8: Surviving the Titanic* by Elizabeth Kaye
*Stopping the Road: The Campaign Against a Trans-Sierra Highway*
by Jack Fisher
*Notes from the Road: A Filmmaker's Journey through American Music*
by Robert Mugge
*What Makes Sammy Jr. Run?: Classic Celebrity Journalism Volume 1,*
edited by Alex Belth
*Secrets of Ash: A Novel of War, Brotherhood, and Going Home Again*
by Josh Green
Please visit our website: TheSagerGroup.net

Artifex Te Adiuva

Made in the USA
Middletown, DE
27 October 2024

63372875R00151